Advance Praise

"There is no turning away from the past in *Dispatches from the Couch*; this beautiful, thoughtful memoir explores the legacies of trauma through the lens of a neuroscientist and her therapist. Tender, thought-provoking, and difficult, Hettes' story dances razor-thin territory of what we forget and what we remember, and who we become in the remaking of our stories. Brave, smart, and big-hearted."

— Tessa Fontaine, author of *The Electric Woman and The Red Grove*

"In *Dispatches from the Couch*, Dr. Stacey Hettes teaches us that living with trauma is an ongoing and difficult journey, but that healing is possible. By openly sharing her painful but moving personal journey, Dr. Hettes inspires others who are living with the effects of trauma, and she provides insight to those who wish to understand the therapeutic healing process. I thank her for writing it."

— Dr. R. Michael Furr, Professor of Psychology, Wake Forest Univ., editor of *Character: New Directions from Philosophy, Psychology, and Theology*, Oxford University Press

"This is such a personal and powerful account of how trauma exists in the aftermath of sexual violence. Dr. Hettes' vulnerability allows the reader to feel like they are on the couch with her in each therapy session, working through this absolutely daunting topic. This book shook me to my core, but I needed to experience it. Her story offers a rallying cry to break the silence around these issues. This book will speak to many families that are working through the trauma that sexual violence creates. I found hope through her resilience and feel empowered by her courage. *Dispatches from the Couch* has had such a profound impact on me."

— Dr. Matthew Hammett, Executive Director for the South Carolina Institute on the Prevention of Sexual Violence on College Campuses

"'The [psychologists] of that era held little awareness regarding how predictably a tiny girl's brain hardwires for self-loathing when a man reaches his body into hers.' Stacey Hettes, a neuroscientist and survivor of sexual violence, uses her scientific expertise and first-hand experience to map the inner workings of a traumatized brain. And like the brain searching for equilibrium, Hettes ricochets through time, tone, and narrative styles, trying to make sense of the senseless. 'As if flipping the channel on a television, my brain pops over to the adage 'no use crying over spilt milk,' along with an image of a milk jug shattering to the floor... Do I have it in me to gather the pieces and patch them together?' So often, we call books unflinching, but *Dispatches from the Couch* beautifully flinches. In her story, Hettes hesitates, she backslides, she panics and obscures. And of course she does! She is contending not just with traumatic memory, but with the culture of silence, religious conservatism, and patriarchal social structures that can keep victims of sexual abuse trapped in a cycle of re-traumatization. On her therapist's couch, the little-girl Stacey trapped in a cell, the gold-star good girl she convinced herself she had to become to make up for shattering her family's Leave it to Beaver idyll, and the passionate, curious scientist who sees problems and possibility in the mind-body connection meet and make amends. Like *Boy Erased* and *Somebody's Daughter*, *Dispatches from the Couch* shows us that people can hurt and people can heal. An invaluable book.

—Anna B. Sutton, LCMHCA, author of Savage Flower

"*Dispatches from the Couch* is the story of an arduous, complicated, and ultimately hopeful journey in the direction of healing. Dr. Stacey Hettes, a professor of neuroscience, plunges into a midlife unraveling when she chooses to say in public that she was a survivor of sexual abuse as a child. In the capable and loving hands of Piper, a therapist, Hettes confronts the snakes that have awakened in her brain and reveals herself to have a heart full of honor and integrity. As Piper says, 'There's a badass in there.' A powerful exploration of trauma, this is a book for everyone who toys with walling themselves off to live with loneliness."

— Betsy Teter, Founder, Hub City Writer's Project and Hub City Press

"The narrative that Dr. Stacey Hettes so expertly crafts in *Dispatches from the Couch* brings readers along her powerful, laborious and triumphant journey of self-discovery. Stacey's is a story of courage—the courage to say no to oppressors and abuse, the courage to say yes to herself, and the courage to show up, session after session, committing and recommitting 'as many more times as it takes' to cultivate and grow the person she is."

— Dr. Mara Welsh Mahmood, Executive Director, University-Community Links, UC Berkeley School of Education, co-editor of *University-Community Partnerships for Transformative Education: Sowing Seeds of Resistance and Renewal*, Palgrave Macmillan

"It's easy enough to label child sexual abuse as horrific, but the acts themselves are only part of the problem. Through detailed accounts of her therapy sessions, Dr. Stacey Hettes reveals the crushing, long-term consequences of sexual violation and our culture's collective failure to address it. You can't read this book without seeing how the "good-girl" complex sets up girls and women to be victimized. And you can't read this book without being enraged by men who—whether deliberately or ignorantly—manipulate women and then blame them for their pain or resentment. By sharing her journey toward healing, Dr. Hettes not only reveals her vulnerability but also showcases her immense power and strength."

— Sheri Reynolds, *New York Times* bestselling author of *The Rapture of Canaan* and *The Tender Grave*

DISPATCHES FROM THE COUCH

DISPATCHES FROM THE COUCH

A Neuroscientist and Her Therapist Conspire to Reboot Her Brain

Stacey Hettes

Apprentice House Press
Loyola University Maryland

Copyright © 2025 by Stacey Hettes

All rights reserved. No part of this book may be reproduced or transmitted in any form or by any means, electronic or mechanical, including photocopy, recording, or any information storage and retrieval system, without prior permission from the publisher (except by reviewers who may quote brief passages).

First Edition

Casebound ISBN: 978-1-62720-566-5
Paperback ISBN: 978-1-62720-567-2
Ebook ISBN: 978-1-62720-568-9

Internal Design by Apprentice House Press
Cover Design by Molly Gerard
Promotional Development by Aminah Murray
Editorial Development by Rebecca Cruciani

"On the Pulse of Morning" from ON THE PULSE OF MORNING by Maya Angelou, copyright © 1993 by Caged Bird Legacy, LLC. Used by permission of Random House, an imprint and division of Penguin Random House LLC. All rights reserved.

Content from LET YOUR LIFE SPEAK: LISTENING FOR THE VOICE OF VOCATION by Parker J. Palmer, Copyright © 2000 by Josey-Bass. Used by permission of John Wiley and Sons. All rights reserved.

Published by Apprentice House Press

Apprentice House Press
Loyola University Maryland

Loyola University Maryland
4501 N. Charles Street, Baltimore, MD 21210
410.617.5265
www.ApprenticeHouse.com
info@ApprenticeHouse.com

Disclaimer and Content Warning

I am not a healthcare provider. I am a healthcare recipient sharing my story. It contains accounts of childhood sexual abuse and related traumas, some graphic. Particularly intense scenes and flashbacks are italicized as an indicator of potentially troubling content. As I cannot anticipate all that might provoke or be upsetting to anyone individually, I urge everyone, especially abuse survivors and parents, to take steps to care for themselves and reach out for help if needed. The National Sexual Assault Hotline can be reached at 1-800-656-HOPE (4673). At the very least, you might want to wear a helmet.

Author's Note

The following contains authentic experiences, memories, emotions, and inner dialogue with names and relationships fictionalized enough to protect the innocent, which unfortunately also protects the guilty. Dialogues between Stacey and Piper are not transcriptions. I recalled them from memory as a way to further process and gain greater insights from the psychotherapy I undertake. While most of Piper's words stem from work with my current therapist, I sense the influence of prior therapists' advice and wisdom emerging at times as well.

To Mom, we win (also, sorry about all the cursing)

Practical medicine is and always has been an art, and the same is true of practical analysis. True art is creation, and creation is beyond all theories. Learn your theories as well as you can, but put them aside when you touch the miracle of the living soul.

—*Carl Jung, Contributions to Analytical Psychology, 1928*

Contents

Author's Note xi
Foreword xix
Prologue 1

PART ONE: Occupational Hazards
Chapter 1: Welcome Back 5
Chapter 2: A Brief History of Therapy 23
Chapter 3: Becoming Dr. Hettes 33
Chapter 4: *Spongia empathicus* 43
Chapter 5: An Empath at Work 51
Chapter 6: Learning from Dolphins 59
Chapter 7: Peonies, Lots and Lots of Peonies 67
Chapter 8: Body Memories 71
Chapter 9: A Kiss Is Never Just a Kiss 79
Chapter 10: Drowning in Puddles 89
Chapter 11: Dr. Hettes Opines on Panic Attacks 93

PART TWO: Memories, Motherf*$#ing Memories
Chapter 12: I Really Wanted a Turn with That Controller 101
Chapter 13: Sausage, Mushroom, and Artichoke 111
Chapter 14: Grieving What They Did Not Know 119
Chapter 15: Mom 129
Chapter 16: Asking for It 135
Chapter 17: How I Ruined Everything 141
Chapter 18: A Big Angry Secret 149
Chapter 19: There Is a Power in This Girl's Bones 161

PART THREE: Deprimere, Latin: "to press down"
Chapter 20: Base Camp 175
Chapter 21: When New Wounds Traverse Old Scars 181
Chapter 22: A Temporary Pardon 191
Chapter 23: Tracker Jackers 195
Chapter 24: Inflection Point 203
Chapter 25: Fool Me Twice, Shame on Me 217
Chapter 26: Like Mopping Up the Sea with a Sponge 225
Chapter 27: Real or Not Real 227
Chapter 28: Session 115: A Glimpse Into the Future 235
Chapter 29: Conundrums and Puzzles 239
Chapter 30: Forty-Two Reasons 247

PART FOUR: Better, Not All Better, But Better
Chapter 31: Be Like Iris Dement: Let the Mystery Be 253
Chapter 32: Now What? 259
Chapter 33: Back to Work 265
Chapter 34: Progress 271
Chapter 35: Checking in with Dr. Hettes 279
Chapter 36: Six Months Later... 289
Chapter 37: The First Circle of Hell Is Still Hell... 303
Chapter 38: Detached Retinas 313
Chapter 39: No Pieces Big Enough to Mend 319

Epilogue 327
Maybe the Final Chapter 327
Source Notes 335
Acknowledgments 337
About the Author 339

Foreword

Dispatches from the Couch, the moving memoir by Stacey Hettes, shows that a person can be going along, day to day, doing the best they can, and then have their lives thrown into chaos through no fault of their own. It shows those of us who have had something similar happen to us that we are not alone. And not only that: it tells us—it *shows* us—that we can find our way back out of the chaos again.

I met Stacey Hettes about twenty years ago when I joined the faculty at Wofford College. Stacey taught in the natural sciences, and I taught in the humanities. Even though our offices were across campus from each other, the campus is small, and we got to know each other through meetings and over meals. Soon, Stacey and I knew the names of each other's siblings, pets, and hobbies. Stacey was someone whose company I enjoyed, whose work I could trust, and whom I respected. She was someone I was eager to sit beside if there happened to be an open seat available next to her.

Our friendship reached a much deeper level when, several years later, we were two of the first three people to fill new administrative positions that had been created to help address the demands of a growing student population. Along with a third colleague, we were figuring out the contours of our parallel positions as we went along, all while realizing that the way we were building our roles was setting a precedent for anyone who might succeed us in these jobs, which were term-limited.

We were in hybrid administrative-teaching positions, which were exhausting but often exciting and fulfilling during the first few years. It seemed that we shared a vision for the future with many colleagues and had a sense of working together as a team for the continued flourishing of a college, profession, and body of students we cared about deeply. Our work grew increasingly difficult, however, toward the end of our second term, which coincided with the intersecting crises of the Covid-19 pandemic and the murder of George Floyd. This period of time, which was almost unspeakably difficult for so many, impacted college campuses in specific and complicated ways.

The early part of Stacey's book takes place during this time, when many of the tensions that continue to hold our country in their grip were starting to make themselves felt on our campus. The social fabric that had held us together for so long was beginning to fray; or, perhaps it is more accurate to say that the fabric was wearing thin in places where what had been covered up was beginning to show through. At any rate, in retrospect, I think a few things drew Stacey and me more closely together during this time than we had been before. First, we were two of the very few women in academic administrative positions. Second, we were also still teaching faculty, so we were in an odd position of both having colleagues and students confide in us about various problems in hopes that we could do something to help on an administrative level, *and* of trying to talk about these difficult things with people who held more power than we did, and often, not being entirely believed. Third, the two of us had similar skills. We were both good at reading rooms, setting others at ease, absorbing emotions, and mediating tense situations. These very skills were also, for both of us, things that eventually became detrimental to our well-being.

We all bring past injuries and traumas to whatever roles we play in the present, and we never know what influence our past might have on the way we walk in the present as colleagues, as friends, as siblings, or as parents. Stacey describes a day at work like any other day, where she went to a meeting, thinking that parts of her past were firmly behind her, paths grown over and no longer visible to anyone else. But instead, the meeting set off a psychic mudslide that wiped out all of that new growth along with, it seemed, any remaining paths to safety.

Reading this incredible book has been like a lifeline for me. For the years leading up to the meeting Stacey describes, the two of us, in our own ways, had been dealing with a slow drip of sexism, gaslighting, and power imbalances that was both so insidious and so profound that it began to make each of us question our grip on reality. Luckily, we had each other. But we were both confused by what was happening and a little shell-shocked. *Dispatches from the Couch* has allowed me to breathe more deeply than I have in several years. I've realized I had been holding my breath, still waiting for another shoe to drop. I'd grown habituated to assuming a crisis would occur. Then I would have to mitigate it, and then, once the dust had settled, I'd be told that the crisis hadn't actually happened and I shouldn't talk about it. I had been tamping things down and went into an existential deep freeze.

It is a terrible thing not to be believed. Reading Stacey's words reassures me that I'm not the only one who has felt this way. Nor is something wrong with me because I've felt this way and I've been angry about it. If you try to address uncomfortable truths for a long time and people don't want to hear them, after a while, you might just decide to stop talking. Or you might decide to stop feeling. But Stacey overcame those pulls toward silence and numbness and found her voice again. In reading her words, I'm reminded I'm not alone. And, like Stacey—in many ways, because of Stacey—I can hope again.

Stacey once told me that this book was "for women who feel like they have to apologize for being successful or smart or good at their job. Maybe not outright, but that they have to show it by being meek, compliant, or going the extra mile." I am grateful to Stacey for telling this story so well, for showing us how to break compliance when we can no longer breathe, and for showing us that hope is still possible.

Katherine (Trina) Janiec Jones, Ph.D.
Spartanburg, South Carolina

Prologue

"Okay, let's get started. We'll continue our tour of subcortical neuroanatomy today. Shout out areas of the brain's limbic system, which, I hope you remember from last time, plays a vital role in our instinctive behaviors and emotional responses." As students rummage and swipe through notebooks and tablets, my mind drifts to a time when we neuroscientists taught limbic system function by the "Four F's": fighting, fleeing, feeding, and fornicating.

We know better now. Our subconscious "fight-or-flight" responses demand a more complex consideration than that earlier alliterative quartet leads us to believe. Psychologists and neuroscientists currently include freezing, fawning, and sometimes flopping in a separate list of "F's" evoked by danger, both actual and perceived.

The class comes to life as amygdala, thalamus, hypothalamus, basal ganglia, and cingulate cortex echo around the room. "Good job, what are we missing? There's one more I want to focus on."

"Hippocampus?" arises from somewhere in the back.

"You got it."

"Dr. Hettes? I thought the hippocampus was responsible for learning and memory."

"It is, but that doesn't exclude it from the limbic system. Threatening, scary experiences often teach us a great deal. Why do you think I write such challenging tests?" No one laughs. "This is especially true early in childhood. The limbic system forms and develops more quickly than the cerebral cortices, our reasoning and thinking brain regions. They mature more slowly, well into adulthood in fact."

Another hand goes up. "Then how come people sometimes don't remember horrible things like bad car accidents or being attacked?"

"Good question. One neuroscience doesn't provide us with a complete answer for yet. Some experiences are so capital-T Traumatic that our brain circuits become disrupted somehow. Traumas like you described often fail to encode as fully accessible, long-term memories. Sometimes, we're left with a few snapshots rather than a full documentary."

PART ONE

Occupational Hazards

You, created only a little lower than
The angels, have crouched too long in
The bruising darkness

— *Maya Angelou*

CHAPTER 1

Welcome Back

A wet snoot reverse boops my forehead. Please let it be four, not seven. Good, a quick trip outside and the big Milk Bones will buy me a few more hours in the embrace of these thread-worn sheets. As I nestle back into my pillow, Chili and Pepper crunch their pre-breakfast. My mind navigates our early morning ritual without waking up to the events of yesterday afternoon.

***

Chili startles from the tangle of my feet as my body bolts upright. My mind tunes in to the slitherings of serpentine memories as they emerge from hibernation. Some slink toward my brain's limbic system while others traverse the nerves that innervate the atria and ventricles of my heart. Snakes regularly crawled through my nightmares as a kid. Mr. Jay, a church deacon and close family friend, gifted me these parasitic mementos with each invasion of my little-girl body.

"Do not call her. You cannot call her." Pepper stares intently, questioning whether this unfamiliar command is meant for him. He stations himself at my shoulder as his hypervigilant alarm system syncs with mine. His sibling wonders when actual breakfast will be served.

Every muscle remains constricted as I will myself to inhale. "Do not, do not... do *not* call her." After an hours-long paralysis, I have no other option. She picks up on the second ring.

"Hi Stace, have the Chili Peppers taken you for a Saturday walk yet?"

Her jubilant question is met with the all-too-familiar quavering sound of her eleven-year-old. "Mom..."

"What happened?" The force of her transition from mother of adult daughters to triage nurse surges through the phone line.

In the safety of her voice, knowing she's plotting the fastest route from Pennsylvania to South Carolina, my last barricade disintegrates. "I am right back where I started. I am right back where I started... I am right back where I started." It is all I can say, but it is all she needs to hear.

Session 1

How is it all therapists' offices smell the same? A sommelier might say this clinical aroma holds a penetrating nose with notes of mint, ink, and warm paper. That is, all of them except my grad-school therapist, Indira's. Her home office smelled delicious—like cumin and cardamom. It was downwind of her kitchen. Meeting with her there felt more like visiting a friend than paying someone to analyze my damaged brain.

This practice seems small. Perhaps they see a low volume of clients. Maybe I won't bump into a former student. As a professor for one of the best pre-med programs in the state, I hesitate when entering doctors' offices. I may remember their faces, but rarely guess whether Dr. Ashley Jones-Pinckney is the same Ashley Jones who still holds a grudge over her cell biology lab report. As this is a therapist's office, it's more likely I'll run into a current student. Thankfully, their world holds less stigma around therapy than mine did at that age. Still, such an encounter might distress them more than me. Better rehearse some greetings to set them at ease. I try not to worry. Dr. Hettes will know what to do.

"Stacey? Hi, I'm Piper Manna. Would you like to come back?"

No. No, not really. Thanks. I know what's coming. I've walked similar halls before. Many times. Each signified the slow death of the so-called recovered survivor, who believed she was done with this shit. If dogs carry memories from one life to the next, I bet strays feel the same way that I do right now when they head to the euthanasia chamber the second, third, or fourth time. At least for the poor pupper, the walk is short. I must endure the one thousand paper cuts to my ego, doled out fifty minutes at a time, until the serpents Mr. Jay left behind make their way back into hibernation.

"Stacey?"

"Sorry, yes, do you need a minute? I noticed your previous client just left." Shaking her head, no, she waves me in. Here goes nothing... or everything. I cannot fucking believe I am here again.

***

For twenty-plus years, I've clung to the belief that no more therapy would be necessary. In my mind, the long-ago road trip to my new career, navigated by the queen of cross-country adventures, my older sister, Carrie, put 2,296 miles between me and any memory of the wounds of my childhood.

Yet, if looks and accomplishments are all one has to go on, I am fine. Better than fine, if you consider that, within the world of higher education, physical appearance and fashion sense rarely factor in. I earned all the degrees there were to earn. Landed a tenure-track position at a close approximation of my dream college—and out of my first pile of applications, to boot. I even managed to land in a location south of my hometown's latitude, where snow blankets the roads from November to March. Growing up, these tiny crystal formations were one of the many reasons Mom kept us from leaving the house. By the time I had my driver's license, she understood danger lurked everywhere—even in the church family, which instructed her to trust Christian men with blind faith.

Within a few weeks of arriving in South Carolina, I discovered a professor's work meant I need not make any plans, no matter the forecast. Academia requires a great deal of time, energy, and emotional labor of its adherents. It also permits those wishing to avoid anything smacking of a well-rounded life the cover to skip right over the messy parts.

***

At first glance, Piper's office is inviting, awash with colorful paintings. A framed photo of her in an English riding outfit jumping a chestnut-colored horse over a triple-barred fence hangs beside her diplomas. Still, the space unsettles me. There is nowhere to hide. Her desk abuts the wall. The over-engineered office chair faces away from it. There is no coffee table. No throw pillows to anchor you to the couch, a white couch, which looks to be my only option. *Be careful not to get it dirty.* A short-pile area rug grounds the hardwood floor. Is this four-by-six foot rectangle up to serving as a no man's land between the couch and her chair? It will have to do. I tell myself not to worry; the rug is lava. She would not dare cross it.

"How do you say your last name?"

"HETT-iss, like lettuce."

"Ah, thanks. Did you bring your intake form? It will take most of our time today." My face mirrors the "fine by me" that my lips hold back as my backside registers the softness of the cushions. They suck you in a bit. It will be difficult to bolt if necessary.

As I hand her the paperwork, I strategize an escape route. The less bringing my little-girl self back to therapy requires my Dr. Hettes-self to expose her own vulnerabilities, the better. After all those rounds of therapy, I know I shouldn't be pissed at my "inner child" for what happened back then. I full-on loathe her. Thinking that term in my head unleashes a tiny convulsion in my throat. If this new therapist insists on calling it molestation, our escapade will end before it begins. Why can't there be a surgical option to cut any remnants of that chubby little misfit out of my adult self?

Piper eyes the intake form as I speculate on the irony of a therapy client who appears steadfastly opposed to speaking. "Oh, you typed it. It looks so neat." Less than two minutes in, I earn my first gold star. Is she insightful enough to already sense that performance-based compliments readily bypass my defenses? Each gold star, A+, professional accolade, or compliment on a new blouse equates to six minutes of relief from the incessant self-criticism, which overflows the shores of my brain. You think I'm joking? I timed it. More accurately, on average I get six minutes plus or minus twelve seconds. One's brain never fully recovers from a science education.

"My handwriting is atrocious," I say. "My students often need me to decipher the feedback I provide on their tests."

"What do you teach?"

"Biology, more specifically cell biology and neuroscience."

"Wow, which is your favorite?"

"My PhD is in neuroscience, which is how I found my way to the Upstate. I was looking for East Coast liberal arts colleges offering a neuroscience curriculum. Actually, though, I only get to teach one class each semester during my term as assistant dean." I relax a little as the familiarity of my professional life dials back the adrenaline.

"Your form indicates you've been to therapy before. Can you tell me more?"

"Uh-huh, I went quite a bit. It's been a long time though."

Practically a lifetime. "My parents and I went together after I told them about the abuse."

It is going to take a while before I can say the word sexual aloud here. I barely managed to type it on the form. "I went on my own in high school, college, and, for the last time, in graduate school."

I headed West for grad school and to escape the ugly bits of childhood. Fleeing California, I abandoned the mess I became after Bobby, the one man I believed might spend his life with me. A physically unavailable, closeted man and an emotionally and physically stunted abuse survivor seemed like the perfect match. Sadly (for me) around the time my career as a professional student wrapped up, more and more gay men were finally free to shed their beards, no longer needing a girlfriend to hide their sexuality. Good for them, for him especially, but not so much for a woman like me whose singular strategy for intimacy was duck and cover.

"And it started, when?"

"We saw the first one, Dr. Tracy, when I was in fifth grade." Remembering ages is tough. I mark time by school years.

"I'm sorry. I was not clear. When did the abuse start?" My face heats from the friction of my teeth grinding together. I thought Indira and I buried those memories for good when we wrapped up our therapy in 1999. *Pull it together Hettes, she's gonna think you're pathetic.*

"I don't know for sure. Before I knew how to tie my shoes. My best guess is the summer before kindergarten." It is astonishing how quickly stress wraps a blood pressure cuff around your trachea, inflating it till your air cuts off.

"Yuck, I am really sorry to hear that." I take note that her 'yuck' sounds both spontaneous and genuine. She continues to document my answers, then pauses to make eye contact. She has that therapist's gaze. The one for which they were trained to peer past the thin skin on the bridge of your nose directly into the deepest portions of your brain. I manage to look up for three-quarters of a second. The kindness in her eyes does its level best to convey that I am safe as she searches for the least triggering question that can move the conversation forward. "How long did it last?"

"I was eight or nine when I finally told him no. School was out. It's hard to remember. For sure, once I stood up to him, that was the end of it."

***

Mentioning my last run-in with Mr. Jay catapults me back to the sleepover at his house during that early 1980s summer. Carrie, his son, his daughter, and I slept downstairs in their rec room. As with many memories, my mind offers up fragmented splices—as grainy and out of focus as ancient 8mm home movies.

Despite my short pajamas and light sleeping bag, it's already too hot. Even the basement where we kids slept never cooled off from the scorcher the day before. I hope we'll go swimming again today, I think, as I lay awake staring at the brightness of a tiny basement slot window. Be quiet or Carrie and his son will get mad. Unlike mine, their preteen bodies have annoyingly transitioned to sleeping-in mode. His daughter could sleep through an avalanche. As always, my bladder wakes me before anyone else. How long can I hold it before I won't make it up the stairs?

Turns out, not long enough.

As I exit the bathroom, he's holding a tasseled throw pillow from their TV room couch. Waiting. His balding head and gingery blond mustache are framed by a halo of sunlight streaming through the patio door at the low angle of morning. It's super bright in the way that forecasts an extra hot day. Does he know I always wake up first? Were any of the other times he cornered me in the morning? Now, it's clear that pillow hid his excitement. "Come watch TV with me."

"No." A force stronger than the mind of a little girl who took to heart the lyrics of church songs like "Trust and Obey" released a 100 percent prohibited word when it came to grown-ups. That same force pivoted my whole body into an about-face march back to the basement. A whimpering "Why not?" reaches my ears. Without turning around, I sense he's transitioned to his soft-furred puppy state. One who had his enthusiastic attempt to jump into my lap rejected by a swift arm block. This time. I hurl another magical, forbidden, "NO," through my teeth.

Somehow, I know. He will never touch me again.

***

Piper cuts into my flashback, saying, "You were brave to stand up to him. I am glad you did." The composite of fright and relief reawakened by this memory combine to leave me mute. She understands that sometimes a therapist's best intervention is to provide the silent safety in which clients can slowly dredge up memories. If our recollections surface too swiftly, they hold the potential to swamp us. "Normally, it does not get this intense so quickly," she adds. "How are you?" The past, which I'd pay the entire contents of my 401K to evaporate, surges through the floodgates of my brain.

A stark reality becomes clearer by the minute. Whether I like it or not, cleaning up this mess again will take time. I spent from Saturday—which in my mind has already earned the moniker Breakdown Saturday—until today in an attempt to convince my Dr. Hettes-self that all my little-girl self needs is a quick tune-up.

I respond with a simple, "I'm fine," and a well-rehearsed smile as Dr. Hettes comes back online. "You can keep going." Patients who do not prove themselves during the initial intake hold no shot at becoming their therapist's star pupil. My bluntness on the form likely gave no indication of the depth-charge level triggers words like the m-word set off. As you might guess, the m-word stands for molestation. For me, it is the holy grail of triggers. Even typing it generates an uneasy tickle at the base of my tongue.

"How old were you when you disclosed?" Damn it. There's another one, "disclosed." So tidy, so clinical, so capable of propelling my stomach to my ankles. Oh, you mean how old was I when I crawled into bed with my mother and dropped a bomb of tears and snot, of wailing and confusion, all over her book, pillow, and bedspread?

"Fifth grade, ten or eleven?"

"Right, you said that, sorry. Can you remember what prompted you to disclose?" Transferring the form's information to a new file distracts her. She handwrites her notes—impressive. Research suggests it is more effective for retaining information than typing... or so I tell my students.

The night of my confession, Dad and my sister Carrie were out. He probably took her to youth group or a softball game. Maybe I said I was too sick to go? I draw a blank as I try to remember. I waited until my baby sister, Sam, was asleep. The time is empty between lying in bed urging myself to stay there and whatever force walked me to my parents' bedroom. The rich warmth of its paneling combined with the milky, pressed-glass lampshade offers a golden aura to my memory. I loved rubbing my fingers over the perfectly spaced little bumps protruding from the shade's surface. *Is this what braille feels like?*

"I thought you went to bed, Stace."

"*I have to tell you something.*" My voice breaks as air squeezes out the narrowing aperture of my throat.

"What happened?" She must have been accustomed to these moments when all I could do was weep. I imagine they were more *frequent than she wished, but more regular than she knew. Mostly, I used our only bathroom to release the pressure valve. It was the one room in the house with a lock. For what felt like hours, I watched tears roll to my chin, then drop to the sink. The hair of the girl reflected in that bathroom mirror is a mess, the way girls who play outside a lot get sweaty and disheveled. Any return to an elementary school causes the intertwined scent of schoolchildren to hit my nostrils in a way that puts me right back into that unkempt body.*

"Mr. Jay kissed me," I manage to respond.

"Well, that's okay, people kiss each other."

"No, not like normal." She sits upright, training on my face. "He told me to stand on a chair. His tongue pushed my mouth open and he made me keep my eyes closed."

Before I can say more, Mom's emergency voice interjects, "Stacey, did he ever make you touch his pee pee?" What? No. I remember thinking, what did going to the bathroom have to do with kissing?

I did manage to tell her, "he made me do other stuff too." Then, the eruption of a secret I'd held for half of a little girl's lifetime washed the room with an intensity I still hold no words to define.

***

I cannot face any more memories yet—how this moment feels like the instant I unleashed a pack of hellhounds into our happy home. If I could time travel, my first voyage would aim for these exact coordinates. I'd stand in the hallway to block my little self from entering their room, crawling under their covers, and birthing a new era for our family which I've spent every moment since attempting to compensate for. As I will myself back to the present I say, "I'm sorry Piper, can you repeat your question?"

"Sure, do you remember what prompted you to tell your parents?"

"A lady came to our school. I suppose it upset me enough that I told my mother about it." The lady's poodle-tight curls skimmed the collar of her navy suit jacket. I sat in the farthest row to the left, the third desk back. My mind replays the question that my hand never raised to ask: *Are you talking about the stuff that happened with Mr. Jay?* The lady's visit predated sex ed by over a year. I didn't even know my body came equipped with a vagina. I'd concluded at some point that he must like reaching inside my intestines. Back then, my mind shielded me from any memory of his private parts.

Unlike me, Piper does not mask her emotions with a flat face. The conversation continues, but her face tells me she is thinking, sick fucking bastard. I will soon find out that she does not shy away from the occasional issuance of a well-placed f-bomb. Every other person my parents or I discussed this with remained neutral, almost blasé. Maybe they were. The details of our story are far from the worst such professionals have to endure. Moreover, those who face the reality of our nation's pandemic of child sexual abuse head-on likely encountered my exact story, or much, much worse, ten other times that same week. Mr. Jay was a family friend, not a blood relative. There was no rape. Most memories are hazy, but he never ruptured my hymen. There was a time it hurt to pee afterward. Anyway, after rehashing this sludge with a social worker, a lawyer, half a dozen therapists, and two gynecologists, Piper is the first whose reaction does not fall under the responses I cynically label, "What else is new?"

A pro tip for therapists: You may not be shocked anymore, but if we find our way to your office, it is the worst thing that happened to us. We do not know you. Your professionalism comes off as unfazed at best, patronizing and unsupportive at worst. Manufacturing a little emotion, as Piper did, will not blow your cover. It will go far in gaining our trust and doing so quickly.

I don't know what I expected her to say, but what she offers next provides a remarkable comfort. "I am so sorry." Giant pause. "Also, I'm sorry the explanation from the woman at your school was so confusing." I initiate eye contact to decipher the genuineness of her words. The warm wash of compassion that I find there causes me to stiffen. My body instinctively remembers that kindness and attention can be double-yoked Trojan horses that hide others' true intentions.

"Thank you for saying that."

"On your form, you also checked the box for seeking therapy for work-related reasons. Would you like to tell me about that?" Good. Knowing she will not push for further details, I forcefully relax my shoulders.

"A few weeks ago, faculty and staff were invited to a forum on sexual violence. Some faculty members asked for a discussion with the administration to review the college's sexual harassment and assault policies. It's likely the #MeToo stories unfolding everywhere at the time inspired their request. Such meetings are tricky for me to navigate, no matter the topic. Though I am not fully an administrator, some of my fellow faculty members perceive me as no longer really one of them. Long story short, about halfway through the meeting, an older male colleague with a lot of social and political influence, let's call him Vic, appeared to lose his temper over the sympathy and concern our discussion held for survivors of sexual harassment and sexual violence. Like many, he began with what came across as a disingenuous statement in support of victims, before stating that it would piss off our conservative, wealthy, and most importantly generous alumni if we stood up publicly for believing women."

"Really? Are they that afraid of their alums?"

"Sadly, yes, some are. But, colleges depend on their support in the same way corporations depend on their stockholders. It's understandable to some degree."

"I guess that makes sense."

"Anyway, Vic, as the defender of maligned Fox News enthusiasts everywhere, continued with what amounted to a victim-blaming tirade for a good ten minutes or so. Our campus lives with a long history of southern gentility. Our culture places a particular premium on civility and decorum. He pretty much left the hundred-plus attendees speechless. A few people, all women, hurried out, fighting back tears. I have a feeling their memories were ordering them to flee. Mine told me it was time to fight."

My legs begin to squirm. Divulging these details, even to a therapist, feels like betraying a family secret. She does not fill the void my discomfort creates. "Vic acted as if he was talking about abstractions," I say imploringly, "as if none of us might be survivors, or that women's experiences even matter."

"That must have been wildly uncomfortable for you."

"Uh-huh. With that much cortisol pumping through my veins, I can't remember every detail. The tipping point for me was the 'let she who is without sin cast the first stone' undercurrent of his diatribe." To explain my actions, I add, "From the size of the gathering alone, I'd guess the room included dozens of sexual violence survivors, both women and men." My shoulders tense as I straighten up, recalling how my amygdala's fight-or-flight instincts rallied to defend us. "Once Vic finally shut up, we continued with a fumbling conversation about the original policy issues and possible resolutions. It was halting... stunted. It was a mess." I expect her to follow with a question. She stays quiet, motioning her head to continue.

"We were stuck, speechless. I raised my hand. And why, I do not know, said, 'As a survivor of sexual violence, I appreciate that we are having a discussion. I think it is important.' Naming that truth was a pivotal moment. Somebody finally stood up. And not just to Vic, but to the way our culture silences victims. Then, since these meetings do follow particular protocols, I made a formal response."

"Good for you, what did you say?"

"Well, that's also tricky. One of the reasons I was tapped to serve as an assistant dean is that I work hard to be diplomatic. For better or worse, after speaking out and breaking Vic's hold over the gathering, I offered a compromise to resolve the immediate conflict over changing our policies. I expect that was the right thing to do. I expect that my resolution was met with relief by most people in the room, including Vic himself by then. Here's the thing. Did I betray myself and all victims by walking us back from the whole mess in a way that allowed Vic, and anyone who tacitly agreed with him, to save face?"

I tell Piper all this as a complete unfragmented story. Compared to our earlier halting conversation about my childhood, she realizes these facts are nowhere near the most pressing issue. Much like the spark that sets off a wildfire might flame out unnoticed at another time or in another situation.

"What made you decide to say out loud that you are a survivor of sexual molestation?" Ugh, there it is. It's like she shoved an ice-cold Q-tip in my ear.

"I don't... I didn't... I didn't have time to think... to give myself credibility?"

"How do you feel about your disclosure now?"

After a deep sigh I say, "Well, it's complicated. Despite my attempt to smooth things over, a rift opened between a group of faculty members and some of the administration. Also, between members of the faculty who want to let sleeping dogs lie and the ones pushing for change."

"What happens when such rifts occur?"

"Since the faculty have no real power over such things, we usually give up and move on." Even as I answer, the gaslighting all women experience colors my thoughts. Why am I here, wasting her time? My harshest inner critics lob grenades from one side of my brain to the other. "Suck it up, snowflake" alternates with "Don't be such a crybaby."

Piper does not chime in. "For me, things came to a head last Friday. A senior administrator, Dean Grant, tasked with smoothing things over and quieting the faculty, dropped by my office in the late afternoon. Knowing diplomacy is not his strong suit and it is mine, he laid the whole thing in my lap to fix. I have amnesia for much of the conversation, but it was clear to me his objective was to manipulate me into taking this task off his plate. He definitely said these words: '*You* are the one with the authentic voice.' My rational frontal lobe had two seconds to process his statement before my limbic system's instinctive survival mode took over. I remember thinking there is no threshold of discomfort for a woman that a man will not cross for his own convenience.

"He went on to flatteringly suggest that my authentic voice gave me the power to convince the group of faculty members seeking change to back off. Maybe it did. Maybe it does. But, the way he went about this flipped the switch. I can put up with a lot. But, to me, his attempt—whether malicious or self-protective—was to use what I revealed during the forum about my past to wriggle himself out of an unpleasant job. To place me, still raw from outing myself, between him and this hornet's nest. My brain went into a tailspin in a way it hasn't in decades." My amygdala tried its best to flee even though my body could not.

"Ugh, that must have been awful. How did the day end?"

"Another colleague was hosting a little happy hour. I had to attend, but sat there, my frontal lobe MIA, while everyone around me chatted and laughed."

After I fill her in about Breakdown Saturday, which returns us to the earlier disjointed delivery pattern, I say, "On Sunday, I emailed your associate, who I know socially, for a referral. I'm grateful you could see me this quickly." I almost slip up and say us instead of me, meaning adult-me and my little-girl self.

Piper absorbs the jet stream of words I blew across the space between us. "First, thank you for trusting me enough to share your experiences." She adds, "Can you tell me how you are feeling?"

"Ridiculous."

"In what way?"

"I mean what the hell? Why am I unraveling? I've outed my past loads of times without falling apart. It's like my brain is ten years old all over again."

"That sounds pretty overwhelming. You have every right to feel frustrated and confused, but I also think that what you experienced at work goes way beyond normal triggers." Her words soften my shoulders. "Who do you reach out to when you are overwhelmed?"

"Um, I know a lot of people. The assistant deans I work most closely with are terrific. My little sister, Sam, lives about an hour away. She is our family's court jester. She knows how to distract me from the messes I make."

"I hate to have to stop, but our time is almost up. It is okay if you can't answer this yet: What do you hope to accomplish as we work together?" I think for a bit about what it might be safe to say.

"I'd like to avoid having my work affected. I have a pretty successful work life, even as a female administrator in a male-dominated culture. Even more, I adore my students. I need to regain my footing. I want to be there for them. I've lived for a long time without feeling as though what happened when I was a kid could hijack me again. I'm back to where it is all-consuming. It's impossible to function when the word victim is scrawled across my forehead."

"Okay then, we've found our starting place. I'd like you to bring a picture or two of yourself as a little girl for next session. Can we plan for this appointment time again next week?"

"This time works, thanks." I hope this time, meaning this dive back into therapy, works as well. I am getting too old for this shit.

CHAPTER 2

A Brief History of Therapy

The all-too-familiar feeling I get meeting a new therapist, namely that I've been hit by an emotional wrecking ball, makes way for its aftermath—insomnia, hypervigilance, plus a replay of the worst moments of my childhood on a perpetual loop. Thus, the ire aimed at my little-girl self for arriving on my doorstep with her bags full of memories does not subside. Instead, I'm flooded with even more of her recollections than before Breakdown Saturday. This is how therapy works. It gets worse before it gets better.

It's difficult to remember that the total sum of hours I spent alone with Mr. Jay adds up to a fraction of 1 percent of my childhood. Is that because I don't remember a time before he and his family regularly joined ours for picnics, holidays, or to offer both his opinions and prayers over everything? His wife and my mom grew up together. His son was one of my sister Carrie's favorite playmates. Their closeness left me to either fend for myself or stuck with his daughter, who seemed much younger than me.

I need to get ready to share some more general aspects of the last forty-six years of my life. While Mr. Jay's face is plastered on the inside of my eyelids every time I blink, it's hard to remember my childhood earned our family the nickname "The Cleavers," thanks to the *Leave it to Beaver* reruns that played constantly on cable TV back then. Carrie's junior high school friends chidingly labeled us as such, and they were not wrong. We had it pretty good.

My mom loved being a mom, especially to little kids. She turned most summer days and every snow day home from school into something fun.

The way she relished taking care of babies made my sister Sam's arrival when I was eight-and-a-half years old a cause for jealousy on my part. By that age, I was well established in the role of the younger sibling. The difficult transition to middle child status was compounded by the escalation of Mr. Jay's abuse in the year or two leading up to my shift in rank.

We were a decidedly middle-class, college-educated family—Mom a nurse and Dad an engineer. Both my parents were likely the smartest among their siblings and well-matched in ambition and values. I'd guess integrity and security rank highest on both their core values lists. Their commitments to our actual family and to their extended sense of a church family, especially on my mother's side, were thoroughly integrated. My great-grandpa Van Sickle was a founding member of the small Pentecostal church we attended twice on Sundays and every Wednesday night for Bible study and children's programs. All this added up to a great deal of pressure for us to present as perfect, especially for my mother.

Within the walls of our house, the overarching sense that we were a healthy, stable family dissolved overnight when fifth-grade Stacey opened her goddamned mouth. For months after her original confession about what happened with Mr. Jay, each time his name came up, it was like mustard gas replaced all the air in our once happy home. I concluded that our exposure to this poison was all my fault. I know now that my parents' reactions stemmed from guilt, anger toward Mr. Jay, their own confusion, and mountains of grief. Mom tried so hard to protect me from any further damage that she never admitted how upset she was, but we all knew. When she'd fly off the handle at Carrie and Sam's prankster antics, I believed it was my fault.

The worst was the first six months or so when we went to counseling. Once a month, Mom and Dad took me out of school early to drive ninety minutes to see a fundamentalist Christian counselor named Dr. Tracy. I later understood how our church's teachings to be suspect of anyone who was not explicitly fundamentalist complicated things. Since Pentecostals identify with the broader category of Evangelicals, we were further caught up in the Reagan-era tribalism of the "moral majority."

I don't know who chose Dr. Tracy, but there was a definite sense that he should be trusted because he was "one of us." Mr. Jay was seeing him too—on different days than we did, thankfully. Mr. Jay and his family had moved to a new town and a different Pentecostal church by then. Did someone from there recommend him? Dr. Tracy's office was not far from Mr. Jay's new house. As far as I could tell, no one in our congregation ever found out what happened. At that point, I had not even considered whether Mr. Jay might have hurt other kids too.

Each trip to Dr. Tracy required confusing lies and cover-ups in order to leave school early. His waiting room smelled like magazines and cheap coffee, but his office smelled like the dentist. He talked with me alone, to Mom and Dad, then all of us together. No more than halfway through our first meeting, I learned not to trust him when he asked, "I like your shirt. Is that pattern called buffalo plaid?"

"I don't know. My mom bought it for me on sale," I replied with all the preteen disdain I could muster toward an adult's inane comment. This was the only part of our conversation he kept to himself. Focusing on my shirt was his segue to ask whether Mr. Jay touched my breasts. *Dumbass, I was in elementary school. There were no breasts to touch. The bastard had the audacity to ask if I liked it. What in the actual fuck?*

Worse, he parroted everything back to my parents. For instance, he told them that I felt invisible because they were busy with Carrie's sports and three-year-old Sam. Of course, all that did was make my mother feel worse. Before he'd release us, he'd pray. It wasn't safe enough to close my eyes.

I tried not to tell him anything. Which was fine, I guess, because I had no idea what any of this meant, let alone what mattered. There was only one question I wanted him to answer: Why are we driving all this way to make the Styrofoam coffee cup in my mom's hand shake?

For both the week before and after a Dr. Tracy trip, there was no telling what might set Mom off. Whether fury or tears followed, it didn't matter. Both flooded my insides. Both confirmed for my little-girl mind what Mr. Jay's actions taught my body. I was bad. Everything was my fault. As a further complication, Mr. Jay had ordered me to secrecy and this little girl did. what. she. was. told. By confessing, I became something even badder. The storms blowing through our house back then were all the confirmation I needed of how bad I was.

My dad's quicker-than-usual temper, irregular speedy exits to the garage, and hours chopping firewood as if prepping for an Alaskan winter rather than a Pennsylvania one, reinforced my sense of responsibility. Dad was the most even-keeled person I knew. Not anymore.

If my Dr. Hettes-self were around at the time, she'd have found a way to teach preadolescent Stacey about the importance science places on the distinction between correlation and causation. Just because my parents' behavior changed after I told them what happened, it did not mean I was the cause. But Dr. Hettes wasn't there. Neither was the burgeoning field of therapy for post-traumatic stress disorder (PTSD). The Dr. Tracys of that era held little awareness regarding how predictably a tiny girl's brain hardwires for self-loathing when a man reaches his body into hers. Psychology and neuroscience know better now. Current events suggest many churches, schools, and courtrooms still do not.

Mom and Dad decided to stop seeing Dr. Tracy but insisted we could find someone else whenever I wanted. My parents did get one useful tidbit from him, which they only shared with me once I began writing this book. Dr. Tracy divulged how he struggled to convince Mr. Jay of the severity of the damage he'd done or the further trouble it would likely cause me down the road. For that, I need to be grateful. It's likely what made Mom and Dad offer to help me find therapists (and pay for them) each and every time I was willing to admit that I needed help moving forward.

This brings us to Therapist #2, Dr. Mary Anne. She came several years later, after Mom found my journal, bursting with teen angst. I did a few stints with her through my high school and college years. Out of the six therapists I've worked with, she is the one I have the most love-hate feelings toward. She was right about a lot of things, but I usually wasn't ready to hear it.

She once asked me what I pictured when I thought of myself as a little girl. "When I was small, we toured an old jail on a trip to Connecticut to visit my parents' college friends. It had dirt floors and brick walls—they'd been painted at one point. All that most of the cells had for a bed was a slab of rough boards." My throat seized, but I eventually untangled my vocal cords. "She's in there." After a bit I added, "One cell had a straw mattress and quilt plus a little table and candlestick. The guide explained that debtors stayed there, not criminals. Sometimes I let her go there instead."

"Why not let her out of prison?"

"Why would I?" A dull gray smokiness clouded my response.

In an attempt to clear the air, I said, "Sometimes when my mind checks in on her, she's not there. It's one way to know things are getting better after a rough patch. Other times, I drag her down the steps and hold open the cell door." I don't remember what Dr. Mary Anne offered in terms of a response to this revelation. She mostly stuck to a script that suggested nothing I could say would surprise her. Ultimately, she was helpful, but I imagine Piper and I will need to unpack some of the baggage she left my young adult self with.

The stints with Dr. Mary Anne overlapped with Therapist #3, Dr. Fedora, who worked in my college's wellness center. He was the first one I really connected with. I found my way to him during my first year thanks to dissolving into a puddle of tears during Professor Grassley's office hours. He'd given me a B on an English 101 essay. Freshman composition was not going to keep me out of medical school. I was pre-med at the time—like half of my first-year class. Professor Grassley more or less implied I was doing as well as I was capable of. To explain my meltdown, I pulled my copy of Ellen Bass and Laura Davis' *The Courage to Heal*, a staple of early '90s trauma work, out of my backpack. "This is what I am dealing with." With a silent acquiescence, which suggested he'd carried out a similar routine before, too many times, he dialed the switchboard to connect with Ms. Pam, the counseling office receptionist.

Our college employed two counselors, both men, but I came to like Dr. Fedora. Then, my sophomore year he returned from summer break with a mustache. Somewhere in my psyche, his sporting one similar to Mr. Jay's signaled betrayal. Luckily, I saw him from across campus before our first meet-up. The trigger hit me so fast, I lost track of where I was. It took a few weeks to book an appointment, by which time I was beyond desperate. When I showed up, I couldn't look at him; I couldn't talk. As he worked every angle to break down this inexplicable new barrier, I admitted from behind a throw pillow, "It's your mustache."

"He had one?"

"Uh-huh." After six beats of silence, I pulled the pillow away. He was sitting there with his index finger covering his upper lip. We laughed and laughed and laughed. Does therapy school require an improvisational theater class? If it doesn't, it should.

I told Dr. Fedora more about what happened to me than anyone else up until then. He not only heard me speak the murkiest details into existence but also my dankest fear: that sexual violation is akin to a vampire's bite. Was I destined for monsterhood too? He excised these internalized myths with surgical precision. He belongs in the box labeled, "The People Who Deserve Credit for My Survival." I still have the pair of faux Ray-Ban sunglasses he gave me when I was accepted into graduate school in California. The note he wrote said, "If you are heading to the Golden State, you are going to need these."

The first five years of graduate school did not require a therapist. The breakup with Bobby sent me back for more. I began with a few sessions at the university counseling center with a graduate student on clinical rotation. He was sweet, but no match for the years of buried emotions and self-hate I'd stockpiled by then. He bridged the gap until I found Indira, and yet, he was so inconsequential, I don't even remember his name. Indira was the game changer. I mentioned her in the acknowledgments of my doctoral dissertation.

Thinking back to one of the turning points that made working with Indira fruitful forces me to contemplate one of the more complicated consequences that early childhood sexual abuse leaves behind. The paradox of how, without fail, the abuse brands us not only as bad but as 100 percent unlovable. Indira employed an unorthodox strategy to confront my misconception.

During one session, without explanation, she handed me her preschooler's videotape of a Winnie the Pooh cartoon. I can't remember for sure, but based on a little Googling, it was likely the 1997 film *Pooh's Grand Adventure*. In this tale, Pooh, Tigger, and the gang go exploring a cave at the edge of the Hundred Acre Wood. Unsurprisingly, poor Pooh Bear is overcome with fright by the monsterly shadows projected on the cave walls by their headlamps. Once they made their way out, daylight revealed that what appeared life-threatening wasn't anything at all.

My response to her sending me off to watch some kids' show with no explanation went something like, *What the fuck? What am I missing? If she is trying to tell me Mr. Jay is not the monster I know him to be, she can shove this video back into the cave where she found it.* On the other hand, my heart knew exactly how Pooh felt: his wobbly footsteps spinning him this way and that, attempting to dodge the dangers all around him.

Indira intended to reconcile the battle between my analytical mind and my emotional heart. She was among the first who guided me toward acceptance that my fears, along with all the other feelings I forbade myself to acknowledge, were not ogres but well-intentioned security guards. By my twenties, I had a wine cellar's worth of bottled-up rage, disgust, and other sinful thoughts good girls should never admit to. The deepest, most secret thoughts of all were the anger and disappointment toward my parents. Those feelings were dangerous. When Indira merely suggested they might exist, I spit words back at her like some reptiles spray venom in defense. "*MY* mother did *nothing* wrong."

My still-maturing mind clung to this truth. I could not entertain the possibility that my parents could have stopped Mr. Jay somehow but didn't. Worse, Mr. Jay's actions sowed the seeds of another, equally invalid, explanation. Those seeds grew into the belief that I was not worthy of protection. In the same way that my mind tried to black out the memories of what happened to my body, it wiped away any notion that what Mr. Jay did happened to me, not because of me. I was twenty-seven years old before Indira guided my first steps toward naming these misconceptions—giving those weeds season after season to propagate throughout every acre of my being.

Most of these long past therapy sessions blur together into general themes and memories of physical and emotional discomfort. Not the one that followed Indira's Pooh Bear homework. Her home office renovation coincided with our work through this. She'd rented space in a co-op office suite and was agitated when I arrived that day, as we were stuck with a tiny, windowless room. In hindsight, the den-like nature of what may once have been a supply closet allowed me to feel safe—kind of how Chili prefers to sleep in the nook under my desk when I work from home. Even the confines of that little room were too much. Mostly, I scrunched my eyes shut as Indira prodded and pried and wiggled the feelings loose. Once they gave way, I spewed them out as one might the poison sucked from a snakebite. "*If my mother doesn't even love me, how can anyone else?*"

Even thinking those words again, more than twenty years later, reconstructs the tightness of my jaw as I battled birthing their existence as actual sound waves. The "anyone" that most concerned me was the Boogie Monster "Gotcha" God our church schooled us in every Sunday of my childhood. Not one sin, not even stealing a fresh-baked cookie from the counter, slipped past this thunder wielder who documented our every move in the Lamb's Book of Life, the record by which every second of our lives would be held to account when we died.

The effort it took to confess my belief that my mother couldn't possibly love me would have hurled me to the floor had I not been white-knuckling the chair's armrests. At one point, when Indira asked me how I felt, I told her I might throw up. "Right now?" she asked as she grabbed the trashcan. After the tsunami of my deepest fear crested, I opened my eyes. Indira's face beamed. "You did it. You've drawn enough light into this cave to see it for what it is. For you, the worst thing is the idea that what Mr. Jay did made you permanently unlovable—even to your parents. This will be scary to face, but we'll find a way through it." It took many more months and some excruciating work, but we made a lot of headway back then. It was, by far, my most challenging journey to that point. After twenty-five years and the revictimization I feel thanks to Dean Grant and the faculty forum, I don't know if I have the stamina to make my way through all this again.

CHAPTER 3

Becoming Dr. Hettes

Wrapping up with Indira as I finished my dissertation, I sought a blank page to begin the story of Dr. Hettes. If the philosopher John Locke had it right when he proclaimed each soul is issued a single tabula rasa,[1] the only way to commence with a clean sheet is to erase what came before. Unfortunately, the imprints of earlier scribblings endure. They compress the fibers of the page, even if we expunge every speck of graphite from the paper, saddling us with a bumpy surface on which to begin subsequent searches for identity. Perhaps our pasts are not words on a page, but rather tattoos on our minds and hearts. Thus, we are marked—as abused, as violated, as victimized—with ink that permeates every tissue layer.

The reset button that naturally presented itself in completing this phase of academic life was the perfect opportunity to reinvent myself as a shiny new persona: Dr. Hettes. Though the signatures were still wet on my diploma, I began the road trip to South Carolina ready to become an entirely new self. The unfamiliar mix of confidence and euphoria bolstered by my family's pride in finally "having a doctor in the family" got me off to a good start.

Amid this dizzied transition, it appeared I indeed found a place for my best work and my best self. I settled in quickly as the students and I passed ideas and energy back and forth. After a few

---

1 Peter A. Schouls, *Reasoned Freedom: John Locke and Enlightenment*, (Ithaca, NY: Cornell University Press, 2018), pp. 19-20, https://doi.org/10.7591/9781501718342.

years, alums reported that they were well prepared for whatever came next. In reinventing myself, I found the clothes and countenance of Dr. Hettes a perfect fit. They covered every scar, every remnant of the ugly awkward girl concealing her from my new colleagues as well as from myself.

Of course, this is not to say everything was perfect. The past two decades held major hiccups. I weathered too many relationships with friends and colleagues with less-than-ideal grace or diplomacy. It would have helped to have someone to hold up a mirror revealing how old wounds projected onto new people. I could've used a guide to coax me to confront the workaholism and avoidance of intimacy that has left little time for friendships and zero chance of dating. anyone. ever.

***

About midway between my first and second therapy appointments, no students show up for office hours. I remember Piper's request for old pictures. I have no interest in the exercise I expect is coming—a prompt to examine them, seeing oneself as childlike and innocent. Been there, done that. From my current vantage point, this will do nothing but reap more loathing. Plus, all my family photos are in the attic, and I am now way over the weight limit to trust its flimsy drop-down ladder. Arriving empty-handed is in no way gold-star behavior. I consider a compromise. Could I bring some of the notes I've received from students over the years? Though a poor substitute for pictures, they might win me points for creativity.

A hefty box of notecards sits on my bookshelf under a one-sixteenth-inch layer of dust. As I read names and recall faces, dozens of students, especially women, emerge from their places in my heart. Among the stationery with calligraphed initials, a scrap from

Tori Trent tumbles to my lap. The frayed edges of the spiral-bound notebook page fold every which way. "Dr. Hettes, sorry I missed seeing you. The other professors said you are teaching lab. I've finished my first semester of physical therapy school! I was the only one in my neurophysiology class who knew all the cranial nerves and how to test for damage thanks to your neuro course. Thanks for making me look so good! Love, Tori."

This box holds the best gold stars—not even gold stars—the best actual stars. Yet, even thinking about sharing these notes with Piper makes me uneasy. It feels like bragging.

Good Christian girls are humble. They do not draw attention to themselves or their accomplishments. Who cares about kind words from your students? So what that you love teaching; that it's your dream job? Nobody wants to hear some woman tell you how fabulous her life is.

These messages, which permeated our church's admonishments of young women, are complicated by my particular experiences. I land somewhere midway along the continuum of sexually violated women. I am neither the most wretchedly abused victim, consigned to coping via a life of drug addiction or prostitution, nor the most compelling survivor turned superstar victim advocate. I do not bust my hump to triumph against pedophiles in court or organize gala fundraisers for women's shelters. I own my successes, but through the lens of my middle-class upbringing and high family expectations, my life has played out exactly as expected—no more, no less. And yet, when I have the privilege to listen to any other person share their survival story, I find them admirable—their triumphs, great or small, inspiring.

It is easy to tell Piper—to tell myself—everything was... is... fine. Except, of course, for this little bout of indigestion brought on by Vic's dyspeptic rant and Dean Grant's bullshit attempt to push the cleanup of Vic's vomit off on me. Yes, teaching is great. My students mean as much to me as I imagine having my own children might. Unfortunately, it's the other work—working with certain colleagues, speaking up, navigating lunch in the faculty/staff dining room—where I now struggle to find a comfortable fit in Dr. Hettes' wardrobe.

Despite making my way through more of my childhood crap in grad school, I found the work of a professional student exciting and rewarding. Thanks to a great dissertation adviser, I navigated those years blind to academia's misogyny and sexism. Even as I fell into predictable patterns myself, I failed to recognize the ways women are expected to take on more of the unrewarded tasks, laboratory "housework," and emotional labor.

In response to my earliest hints of burnout, all my new male colleagues offered as advice was: "No one is going to tell you to stop." My apprehension over being sized up by a yardstick designed to measure males was lost on them. Other women were too busy mopping the sweat from their own brows to notice my shirt, too, was soaked from exertion.

The job I waited my whole life for began to feel like a performance of someone else's script, where I, as the actor, held little leeway to improvise my lines:

Act I, Scene I: Dr. Hettes loves teaching her first courses and finds great fulfillment in working directly with students.

Act I, Scene II: The only other woman in the department volun-tells an exhausted Dr. Hettes to host an end-of-semester social event at her new house. Likely, she was relieved to finally have someone else to share this task. I don't think I even had wine glasses at the time.

Act I, Scene III: The faculty elects Dr. Hettes to the committee with the heaviest responsibilities, both a sign of respect and a heavy burden that adds to her workload with no guidance as to what other tasks she might set aside.

Act II, Scene I: A newly promoted dean, one who preceded Dean Grant, tasks Dr. Hettes with the first overhaul of faculty governance structures in decades. This largely thankless assignment comes with no guidelines and plenty of landmines.

Act II, Scene II: After her success, that same dean "strongly encourages" Dr. Hettes to accept an appointment as assistant dean, moving her out of the classroom and into meetings and desk work for the majority of the week.

I had no time to consider how long I might sustain such a role or how often the directors would rewrite my lines. I imagine many women could roll with these relatively minor punches without comment or incident. Not me.

Act III begins with a move from the science hall to the administrative building. I became the lowest-ranked administrator in a space that held the college president, several vice presidents, and a few others. I was one of two women at my rank, again. He never came right out with it, but I suspect Dean Grant was the one who pushed for this. After a frustrating first year with us, maybe he thought it would help to have someone beneath him nearby. From my original office across the quad, he seemed to manage well. Up close, I discovered his impatience mixed with our traditional culture about as well as a lump of sugar in cold iced tea. Down here, you learn to add the sugar while it brews. Successful transplants change their pace to deal with how things evolve in academia, especially below the Mason-Dixon line. It was not long before the role of "woman behind the man" emerged as Dean Grant's and my subplot to this third act.

The geography of my new office—adjacent to the stairs, which lead to the upper admin offices—positioned my space as both a staging area as well as a recovery room for many administrative skirmishes. I became a de facto strategist as well as the field medic as my colleagues prepared for and recovered from the inevitable clashes between faculty members and administrators. As one of two women in the vicinity, it was a given that much of this emotional labor would fall to me.

Supporting such battles felt normal after holding the weight of responsibility for telling my parents about Mr. Jay. Past attempts to absorb every drop of my parents' suffering have translated into a lifetime of mopping up any messes that cause others distress. Administrative work requires a good communicator, skilled in diplomacy, with firm boundaries. I had the heart for the job but underdeveloped tools. I struggle with whether I was enlisted into this duty or if it comes so naturally that I just fall into it. Are my experiences typical of the way gender norms play out unless actively disrupted? Regardless, I felt and feel obliged to offer a comfortable chair and an attentive ear, which few turn down.

What if I'd questioned, or even understood, more about leadership and gender roles? If I understood more about the triggers—beyond the overtly physical—likely to reawaken the serpents Mr. Jay left behind? Who might Dean Grant have found across the desk that Friday afternoon? As it happened, my past collided violently with his conscription of my "authentic voice." His attempt to draft the vulnerability I mustered during the faculty forum left me in a puddle. Not a puddle of tears, but a puddle of defeat. Whether he knew it or not, whether he meant to or not, Dean Grant siphoned my last drop of emotional energy.

Session 2

I like Piper. Though she's a lot younger than me, there's something about her that says she's lived as many years as I have, maybe more. I get a sense that she will take no shit from me, but in the gentle way an artful preschool teacher redirects a three-year-old who cannot keep their fingers out of the jar of paste.

As the week passes by, I stop holding my breath for no apparent reason. This will have to count as progress. We ended last time with a discussion of the Friday afternoon Dean Grant meeting—and the forum that prompted it. That was good. It left me hopeful. Can talking through work stuff for a few weeks do the trick? Perhaps I won't need Piper to become the new Indira.

***

"How are your coworkers at respecting your boundaries?" I laugh for the first time in her presence.

"Well, not great. To be fair, I'm not great at suggesting which boundaries to set. When things got bad recently, I kind of instituted one by closing the blinds on my office door. I think they got the hint."

"If the blinds are open, do they walk in at any time?"

"Uh-huh, we have scheduled meetings of course, but they stop in unannounced. I mean, they ask if I'm busy, but I never feel like it is okay to say I am." Women academics, like women everywhere, earn gold stars by making time for everyone else. It is not fair, however, to paint all my colleagues with the same brush. "There are a few people who gladly listen to me vent when I let them."

"Why are you so uncomfortable with sharing your frustrations? That's how we all survive them."

"I used to be able to. Now, I imagine every person I speak with is picturing the moment that I announced my victimhood during the sexual violence forum. What happened with Mr. Jay was the darkest kind of secret. My mother would have lost it if anyone found out." Can Piper sense my body heating up from across the rug?

"Is it possible your mother was trying to protect you?" *Um, excuse me? Why are you taking her side?*

"Maybe... probably. I struggled a lot in college. That translated into fear that Mr. Jay was at it again. I wanted to out him to protect other kids. When I told her, Mom got what I read as a panicked look on her face. She convinced me that he would not have the opportunity to hurt anyone else. From their agreement with his wife, Mom was certain Mrs. Jay was taking measures to ensure he didn't have access to kids. There are things that happened back then, agreements and conditions for not pressing charges, that they never let me know about."

"Did you ever ask them about those details as an adult?"

"No." Such a small word. If deployed with the right tone, it's more effective than following it with a thousand more.

"How well did you know Mr. Jay's wife?"

"My mom knew her since they were kids. Her family were also members of our church."

"Sorry to interrupt."

"No problem. Anyway, my mom told me his wife drove their daughter to school and stuff."

"He molested his daughter?" Bile collects in the back of my throat. Molest: I fucking hate the sound of it. The onomatopoeia of the word mimics his chubby chest and arms enveloping me from behind as he sat me in his lap, his lips mauling my neck.[2]

"Yes, he abused his daughter. My dad once told me they found out Mr. Jay did it to her a lot. They adopted her. I think when she was four." My mind flashes to a memory of Mrs. Jay complaining about how, unlike their son, she was impossible to motivate in the

---

2 *In case you need a quick English class refresher, onomatopoeia refers to words that imitate the sound of what they represent. Think words like buzz, or sizzle. For me, molest sounds like the moans and body sounds of sexual activity.*

morning, *she just sits there staring at her shoes and socks.*

"How did your dad come to know this about their daughter?"

I need a deep inhale. "My parents left us with my grandparents one Saturday. They told us they were going to have lunch with some friends. Instead, they went to Mr. Jay's house and confronted them."

"Was it upsetting when your parents did not tell you what they were doing?"

"I don't know. I was a kid, and it's not like they asked my opinion on serious stuff like this."

"Do you remember how you felt when they told you?"

"Confused. I wanted it all to disappear."

"Did you tell your parents that?"

"No," flies at her a second time.

"Did you ever see Mr. Jay again?"

"No, they'd moved. We saw them a lot less, especially once Sam was born and Carrie was busy with sports. I never told my mom, but he called our house one time not long after I blew everything up. She must have been working outside while I kept an eye on Sam. He asked me how I was and I said okay. He mumbled something about this being a hard thing to talk about and I said 'Yeah.' I don't think he said he was sorry. I would remember if he apologized. He did write me a letter. He put rainbow 'Jesus Loves You' stickers on the outside. I looked at the letter, but I don't think I read it. If I did, I don't remember what he wrote, but I remember his handwriting looked pretty—not like my dad's. I tried to forget about all of them. I felt bad for his wife and kids, you know, since I ruined their lives too."

"What do you mean, 'too'? Ruined their lives along with your family?" Piper sounds a little frustrated by this.

"Yes. I'm sorry my talking is so choppy. I haven't talked about this in... a long time."

"That is trauma. And not the way that word gets tossed around to describe Starbucks running out of the latest Frappuccino, actual Trauma with a capital T. We do not remember it as a story in our mind the way we remember other things. But, I want you to look at me when I tell you this." Raising my head half an inch to meet her gaze feels like lifting a boulder. "You say you ruined lives by disclosing. I want us to acknowledge the real possibility you saved their daughter's life, possibly even your own."

"Thank you for saying that."

"Will you tell me how you are feeling?"

"You are making this as painless as possible. But Christ, how many hits are we supposed to take? I'm already exhausted and we haven't addressed anything that matters."

"I know it feels like that with a new therapist."

"I am so fucking tired of this story. Especially at times when it becomes my entire story. I managed to live my life just fine for a long time."

"Tell me what tired feels like." I must pry my teeth open to let my response escape.

"I'm... I'm pissed."

CHAPTER 4
Spongia empathicus

As I wait for my turn, I cannot help but wonder what Piper thinks. The voice of my friend and fellow assistant dean, Trisha, comes out of the blue: "You absorb other people's emotions like a sponge." It was not a compliment—more a diagnosis for the struggles she observed. She was one of the few people offered a peek behind the curtain of Dr. Hettes and one of even fewer who was privy to the aftermath unfolding in my mind and body from the Friday Dean Grant meeting.

This spongy fundamental of my nature has resulted in both compliments and criticisms my whole life:

"You know how Stacey *is*..." as if it was such a malady, one should not even name it.

"You are unbelievably sensitive."

"You are a good listener."

"We could not even look at you when you were little or you'd burst into tears."

"You were so sensitive, you cried if you had to send someone back to home base while playing Sorry!."

"You always know just what to say."

"He could not have picked a worse victim to do this to."

"You are wonderfully and beautifully sensitive." I'll wait forty-five years for someone to suggest this one. Piper will say it sometime in the coming weeks, after witnessing one session at a time, the toll words like the ones above exact. It is ironic. My sensitivity, which draws the most disparagement, and my empathy, which earns the most gratitude? They come from the same place.

In the aftermath of disclosing, my preteen self concluded her sensitivities were the problem, not the abuse itself. Lest I inflict more damage, I fortified my outward appearance against the hurricane blowing through my insides. I repeatedly, even angrily, insisted I was fine. I was just afraid I was in trouble that night when I told my mom about Mr. Jay—what happened was over and done with. My father retorted that we would keep seeing Dr. Tracy. Dad "wasn't going to let what happened be a problem on my wedding night." I had no idea what he was talking about. No understanding that what Mr. Jay did was any more related to weddings or honeymoons than what our pediatrician, Dr. Rose, did when he lifted my shirt and felt my belly. My skin reflexively shivered at both.

Whatever my dad was trying to say, it made me all the more determined to find a way to make this whole situation disappear. I had not and did not always succeed. My mom, God bless her, often asked with desperation in her voice—before she found out about Mr. Jay—"*What is wrong?*" My memories around her inflection are hazy. There were certainly times I mistook her desperate concern for intense aggravation.

How could I explain what was wrong? Mr. Jay forbade me to tell. Plus, I had no words for what he was doing. The only part that made any sense to my little-girl self was the kissing. This child concluded the truth must be that she was what was wrong. From my insides to my outsides, I was the problem. The anguish my porous body absorbed, but also generated, fermented a despair that surely would contaminate anyone it touched. As a sponge, my gift to the world is a determination never to wring myself out. To hold in every drop of the sludge, which collects wherever despair lingers.

The nail in the coffin of my self-esteem came a few years later. I do not remember the entire context, but an air of strained conversation between a teenage daughter and her father filled our Subaru as my dad drove us to a long-since-forgotten destination. Eighteen words lodged themselves into the gully between the two halves of my brain: "Your mother was never the same after she found out about what happened to you as a kid."

I, adult Stacey, with credentials, paychecks, and a mortgage, acknowledge that the statement my father made intended to emphasize the words, what happened. I, adolescent Stacey, with glasses, braces, and a poodle perm intended to make me feel pretty through my awkward phase, zeroed in on the words, found out. Here is the rub. From age eleven or twelve until this very morning, my brain has tormented me with the notion that Mr. Jay's actions were not the problem. He amounts to a few dozen horrible hours in an otherwise typical childhood. Better than typical—idyllic. The real fucking problem was my inability to keep it to myself—to deal with it myself. I crawled into Mom's bed as the storm inside me spilled over the sea walls, flooding our lives with confusion, rage, and despair.

I did that.

To us.

Even for a girl made of sponge, it was an awful mess to clean up.

Session 3

"Hi there, come on back."

"Hi," I say, "Do you need a minute?"

"No, but thanks." As I sink into the couch she asks, "How have you been this week?"

"Okay, busy, it's easier to keep my mind off things."

"Is this a typical way for you to deal with stress? Distraction?"

"Yeah, if I can stay busy, I don't have to deal with it," I say with a hint of pride. This strategy is one of the secrets to my professional success.

"Do you enjoy your work?"

"I love teaching. They wouldn't even have to pay me to teach. It's the most content and fulfilled I've ever felt."

"Do you teach as an assistant dean?"

"Only one course, but at least teaching gives me something to look forward to."

"I want to go back to something we were discussing last time. Actually, I want to say something else first. I recognize we brought up a lot over the past two weeks. I appreciate what you shared and your trusting me with it. I sense you find it hard to trust many people."

"Uh-huh." It's good to hear her say this.

"We need time to develop trust. However, I want you to know: I do not lie. I will never lie to you."

"I trust you as a professional. It's clear I can say things here that I wouldn't otherwise."

"Okay, good, when we were talking about work, it seemed like you felt the need to defend your choice to speak up to Vic. Am I accurate?"

"Yes. But only because I always overreact to what happened to me as a kid."

"Who's told you that you overreact?"

"Men who found out what happened to me and told me to get over it. 'It was just a little diddling.' One time, a grad-school friend launched into a full-on treatise on the expansive definition of the word 'molest' after he jokingly referred to someone as a 'Chester the Molester,' and I physically shivered."

"I am sorry anyone ever said that to you."

"Thank you for saying that."

"You also mentioned, if you were not so sensitive, you could live a normal life. What about your life isn't normal?"

"All right, I should say I could live the life I want to. A life where I feel satisfied with who I am. A life that is not a constant battle to compensate for how horrible I am."

"What makes you horrible?"

"Look at me," I say as my hands sweep through the air from my shoulders to my knees. "Isn't it obvious?"

"No. Honestly, it isn't. Although we are still getting to know each other, I see an intelligent, caring person. Do you know what you do each time we meet? Something I do not think any other client has ever done?" Her question surprises me, but also draws me fully back from the triggering memory of my friend's asshole maneuver.

"I am not sure what you're referring to."

"When I walk my previous client out, even though I am running late, you ask me if I need a minute before we start. No one does that."

"Well, you might need a bathroom break or a few minutes to yourself."

"Exactly, you, a person who is struggling, still thinks about others' needs. Even the needs of the one here to help you, which is rare. I want you to know that."

"Thanks. I do care. It's my reason for coming here. I don't want to isolate, but I can't help it. These walls are keeping everyone out, not only the people I need to protect myself from."

"Caring enough to take risks even while you feel this vulnerable is a good quality. It makes me wonder, then, why you think you are horrible."

"I just am. I do kind things, work hard, act as a good mentor to my students. I want to do these things—be this person. It also compensates for how bad I am."

"Tell me what makes you bad."

"I wasn't strong enough to deal with things on my own. I told my parents, and it ruined my mother's life." Piper does not respond with words right away, only the kindest facial expression one could imagine. She has all the proper degrees and training, but her best tools are her eyes—her whole demeanor. It fills the room with empathy, which, like an invisible mist, brings the ambient temperature into perfect alignment. As supportive as Indira was, it was never like this. Indira prided herself on not being a "feel good" therapist. With Piper, I feel cared for in a way the walls I've built around myself rarely allow for.

"Believing that you ruined your mother's life is an awfully heavy burden to carry, Stacey."

"Uh-huh." Despite her saying my name, I cannot look up. The tears are hot and unimpeded. I used to watch these same tears in the mirror alone in the bathroom. Writers use the term welling up, which is exactly right. It is different from crying. Crying includes your torso, your lungs, your diaphragm, and intercostals—the muscles between your ribs. There are ways these body parts can disrupt crying. These welling-up tears originate from a place so deep it might be below our feet.

"I wish I could know who I would be if this had never happened."

"In what way do you want to be different than you are?" For me, there are a thousand answers. I shrug my shoulders and stare at the carpet. "Tell me the first thing you thought of."

"I'd like to believe victim is not my primary identity. I'd like to know if I could have been more trusting. I'd like to know if I could have liked myself, even a little. Is there any scenario where I could have accepted myself enough to become close to another—other—people?" I correct myself.

"Are those qualities we can work on?"

"There have been periods in my life when it wasn't this intense." After a pause, I add, "I wish you knew me before."

"I like who I am getting to know. I want to help you figure out what contributes to these feelings. That way, you can see yourself how I see you—how I bet your students and family see you as well."

"Thank you for saying that." Despite Piper's smarts and insight, does she get what I mean by adding "for saying that" to my thank yous? It's one of my most subtle power grabs. It shuts down whatever someone's trying to convince me of while I remain the good girl who does not argue. Adding "for saying that" is a way to acknowledge someone's kindness or effort to help without acquiescing to the idea that their view of reality, in which I am a person worthy of their compliment, is more accurate than mine.

"You're welcome. Can you tell me how you are feeling?"

"I feel like a sponge full of mud. Sludge covers everything around me. I need to clean it all up before it contaminates anyone else. At the same time, I don't know how I can absorb more without leaking out the mess I already hold."

"Sponges are important. They also work better with buckets, mops, and a little soap. I want you to try to notice when you attempt to do everything yourself. One time, ask for help with something, even if it is minor."

"I don't know why anyone would want to help a dirty old sponge."

"I do. But I want to reiterate. I highly doubt there is anyone else who ever thought of you that way."

Oh Piper, then why do the Dean Grants of the world treat women as nothing more than tools to clean up their messes?

CHAPTER 5

An Empath at Work

We're meeting early today since I have a committee meeting this afternoon. I must be her first appointment, because I don't think she's here yet. If I had to guess, I'd wager there is never enough time in Piper's morning. That everyone needs her to do something. That's what happens when a daughter arrives a decade after two sons. The same way my sister, Sam, did.

From a few glimpses into her home life, I get a sense that her preschooler already insists on matching her hair "jewelry" to her outfit, needs *Mommy* to sing the toothbrushing song, and six times out of ten dribbles toothpaste on her shirt. Piper is a problem solver. I bet the linchpin to making it out the door on time most days was their transition to brushing at the kitchen sink where Piper sings "Brush side to side, brush up and down..." while she packs lunches for all five of them.

Session 4

"How is work going?"

"Pretty well. My class is starting to gel."

"What do you like about teaching?" My head lifts and my shoulders widen.

"My students. With eager pre-med majors, the grind many teachers experience with unmotivated students is not such a part of my day. The challenges I face are more about creating space for creative thinking and problem solving beyond their compulsion to gobble up facts preparing for the GRE or MCAT graduate school or medical school entrance exams. I relish challenging them within the safety of trusting that I will not grade them harshly for taking chances. For this to work, I have to model it, as well as the vulnerability it requires. My classroom is the place where I—and I hope therefore they—stretch toward farfetched, sometimes even ridiculous, ideas."

"What do you do that's ridiculous?"

"Hmm, seniors present us with superlative awards around graduation. A few years ago, mine was, 'Dr. Hettes, the only professor convinced that *this* is a miracle.'" Pointing my index finger upward, I bend it back and forth at the middle knuckle. "In neurobiology, I teach the intricacies of this relatively simple example of muscle control to drive it home as the complex marvel it is. If *this* takes the coordination of that much muscle and brain mass, the fact that a person can write a poem or score a point at beer pong is beyond comprehension. Teaching the functional beauty of the human mind and body fills me with such awe. Sometimes it spills out as tears. Another year, my award was something like, 'Dr. Hettes, the professor most likely to cry over the beauty of mitochondria.'"

With a spark of recognition, she says, "That's the 'powerhouse of the cell' right? Tell me what it's like to teach about mitochondria."

"Those powerhouses are actually little sacs, like tiny cellular organs, where the Krebs cycle takes place. In fact, there's evidence they were once separate smaller cells who found safety by residing inside bigger ones in exchange for sharing the energy they produce. It's puzzling to me that the Krebs cycle has become such a punching bag among tech sector neo-elites who harp on learning knowledge as a waste of time. I kinda get it. Memorizing a sheet of eight chemical reactions and their regulatory enzymes in a four-hundred-student lecture hall is a hard way to make connections. For me, this cycle is one of the best chances I have to share with my twenty or so students per course the wonder we gain through deep understanding of extremely complicated things. As we methodically work through each step, we discuss what it must have been like to puzzle out how the biochemicals inside these tiny sacs interact with each other to perpetually transform energy. How Hans Krebs realized it's a cycle because the product of each reaction becomes the driver for the next. How from mystery we can extract profound awareness. At the core of us—of all living things—we find a cooperative enterprise of interdependence. Our cells are just the most beautiful things." Her face suggests she sees me, not my pain, for the first time. "What's even more beautiful is the opportunity to look each student in the eye as they connect to the fact that they are all absolute miracles of biology, chemistry, and physics."

"I don't think I've ever heard a biologist speak like this about cells before," she says as I blush and look away, feeling the discomfort of receiving the recognition and acceptance I crave, but hate myself for wanting. I want to matter. This comes from a more genuine place than earning gold stars. What we are discussing feels more like an acknowledgment of the person I could have become if Mr. Jay had not done what he did.

"My students motivate me," is all I can say.

"It sounds like you motivate them too."

"Thank you for saying that." I wish I could stay in this reverie of the Krebs cycle a little longer. As a kid, any compliment was accompanied by a put-down. Some came from others—sisters, cousins, classmates, adults—but most came from me. There were never enough chances to be happy—not happy exactly—maybe content. It was as if it was the worst possible thing for this ugly, awkward girl to think she was not broken, even for a minute.

Dr. Fedora helped me a great deal with this. He acknowledged that people may have ridiculed me. He asked why I chose to record these messages to play back on a perpetual loop. I never made him understand. I felt no more empowered to adjust the volume on these insults than a prisoner being tortured with bright lights could put in a work order to have a dimmer switch installed on their cell wall.

My number one personal put-down, for sure, is the fact that I fell for Mr. Jay's advances. What an idiot. A close second is that I let him ruin me. My coping mechanism was, and is, food—fat girls cannot be pretty. No one wants to be around ugly girls. If this were not true, Mom and Dad would not have tried so hard to convince me a haircut and poodle perm would somehow make things better. Also, my dad, the most frugal man I know, would not have quietly offered me one dollar a pound to lose weight. I've found safety in the androgyny of a midcareer teaching professor's life. I don't think my students even see me as a person—more like one of the less horrible hurdles on the way to their diploma.

Piper continues, "It is interesting that twice now you gave the students all the credit. It is also interesting that your admiration for the human mind and body, down to the mitochondrial level, does not extend to your own."

My neck stiffens.

***

My mind flashes to my sister Carrie during our post-graduation road trip to South Carolina. Reality was setting in. It must have shown on my face as we filled up on the free hotel breakfast somewhere in Kansas.

"I thought I'd wait until you looked like you needed a pick-me-up

to give you your graduation present." She hands over a crumpled package, which traveled through four states scrunched in her duffle bag. It was a t-shirt that read "The Truly Educated Never Graduate." Her sense of humor and mine don't always see eye-to-eye. She explained, "Just because you'll be the teacher, doesn't mean you have to change who you are. You'll be good at this job because you will learn whatever you need to be good at it."

***

Piper regains my attention. "Can you acknowledge that to get here, you had to achieve a great deal?"

"Well, yes. But I had more time to put toward it since I am such a miserable failure at everything else."

"Like what? When have you failed?" It is as if a perfume bottle sitting above my diaphragm releases a mist: *Eau de Shame*. As it ascends to the back of my throat, it tastes like actual perfume when you accidentally breathe in as you pump the spritzer.

"I always knew I would never find a husband or have children, or even be much of a friend. I needed an all-consuming career. It's hard when you spend your twenties buried in a windowless laboratory. I have colleagues who, once their kids are grown, I plan to reach out to more." I note that this excuse wears thin more than a decade later. "I was more social when I first moved here. I was a lot more social in graduate school. I was happiest then. I loved California. Plus, there was the year Bobby and I were together." I don't want to tell her how isolated I feel.

"What's changed to make you isolate more?" Damn, she is wearing her mind-reader goggles today.

"I'm tired, I guess."

"What makes you tired?"

"Well, I am older now. My sister, Sam, says I am too young to use that as an excuse. She is good at getting me to have some fun on the weekend." It's not safe enough with Piper yet to admit that, in the aftermath of Breakdown Saturday, I am emotionally and spiritually tapped out in a way I don't think I'll bounce back from. I don't want to admit that I let Vic, but even more so Dean Grant beat me down this much. "Teaching is tiring, but it's the good kind of tired. It's everything else…"

"Why not step down as assistant dean and go back to teaching full time?"

"I couldn't fail like that." Quitting was not allowed in our house. "It's hard enough to admit what's happening as it is."

"I need more. Tell me one frustrating thing about your work."

"I don't like how hard I have to fight when we appear to be headed in the wrong direction or as though women's voices are ignored. I wish I didn't care. Something compels me to take a stand. The sexual violence forum wasn't the first time I stuck my neck out, just the time with the worst consequences. There was a blurb on Instagram that speaks to this more succinctly."

"Can you find it?" Yes. Yes, I can. I bet I can even drag this out until this never-ending session is over. Praise the sweet baby Jesus we've only got twelve minutes left. I scroll to it and then read:

> *When you debate a person about something that affects them more than it affects you, remember that it will take a much greater emotional toll on them than on you. For you, it may feel like an academic exercise. For them, it feels like revealing their pain only to have you dismiss their experience and sometimes their humanity. The fact that you might remain calmer under these circumstances is a consequence of your privilege, not increased objectivity on your part. Stay Humble. -Sarah Maddux, @happyvulcan*

"There is a lot to unpack there, huh?"

"Yep."

"Which words stand out to you?"

"Emotional toll."

"Why do you think that is?"

"It's my job to make everyone happy. Others get to feed off conflict."

"Can you tell me more?"

"I can't bounce back from Dean Grant's deployment of 'you have the authentic voice.' His sentence sliced open my past. It's still hemorrhaging."

"It's helpful to hear you describe what happened. We need to stop the bleeding before we clean out the infection. I don't know if you are ready to hear this, but I think the underlying infection has festered for a long time."

She's right. I don't want to accept these words. I begin a response but she interjects. "Let me say one more thing. There is nothing you've told me that suggests failure. At most, it sounds like you are, at least once in a while, trying to establish healthier boundaries."

"I hear what you are saying."

"Good, that's a start. What do you think it will take for you to believe what I am saying?"

"I do whatever it takes to earn an A, an A+ even. Taking care of myself feels like a distraction, feels selfish."

"Will you consider whether you want to continue to let someone like Dean Grant dictate what 'earning an A' looks like? Because I have to say, theirs are not behaviors I would want to emulate or teachers I would want to take a class from."

"Thank you for saying that."

"I have to let you go. It's good you pinpointed and acknowledged the complexity of what we need to work on."

"I am sorry it took so long to finally say it."

"Okay professor, we need to adjust expectations here. Reaching this point four sessions in feels like warp speed to me."

"This isn't my first course on this subject."

"True, which brings me to my next point. I'd like to give you some homework if you are up for it." Is this her subtle way of reminding me no pictures of my little-girl self have surfaced?

"Okay."

"Will you write me a letter about the quote you read? Tell me why it hits so close to home."

"I can do that."

CHAPTER 6

Learning from Dolphins

When you debate a person about something that affects them more than it affects you, remember that it will take a much greater emotional toll on them than on you. For you, it may feel like an academic exercise. For them, it feels like revealing their pain only to have you dismiss their experience and sometimes their humanity. The fact that you might remain calmer under these circumstances is a consequence of your privilege, not increased objectivity on your part. Stay Humble. -Sarah Maddux, @happyvulcan

Dear Piper,

You asked me to write a letter about the meme I read. I copied it above in case you don't remember. It struck a chord because my brain is wired for affect. I feel deeply the good—that I wish you were able to see more often in our sessions—the bad, and the ugly. I am the highly sensitive being for which I am criticized. People tell me to brush things off, ignore it, be happy. It makes no sense. It is as if we are different species. I'd never tell Chili and Pepper to ignore whatever magical smells draw them to the spot in the grass that, to me, looks like every other damn spot. We're working with different equipment.

Imagine you met a talking fish underwater. The fish notices your distress and asks, "What's the matter?" If you respond that you are *running out of oxygen, the fish might say, "What do you mean? Why can't you pump more water over your gills?"* I have lungs, not gills. I have a brain wired to feel... to feel intensely. I do not have a brain that will agree to "just not think about it." I experience emotional responses to the events of my day even when the people around me do not. They may wish to control me. They may wish to contain me, as many do who train their dogs to march in a straight line limited to a six-foot lead. Not us. Chili and Pepper get all the leash I can safely allow them. We zigzag through the woods or around the park to their ginormous olfactory bulbs' delights.

To parse the quote's first sentence, rarely do I meet someone or find myself in a situation that affects the other person more than it affects me. On some level, I must acknowledge this is a choice. Especially because I've lived my life in the land of education. Early on, I was encouraged to reach for the stars. Later, just when I thought I could reach them, the rules changed. When considering success in higher education, particularly in the sciences, the rules are all about debating—no, more competing—from an unfeeling place.

Please do not mistake this for a call to throw scientific objectivity out the window. In fact, we'll be more objective if we stop pretending to have no feelings. Hmm, that's got me thinking. Perhaps I am not so differently wired. Perhaps I cannot (will not?) hide the fruits of my limbic system's emotional, fight-or-flight, reactions.

I watch what happens to men when they reveal something, which exacts an emotional toll. Here's an expression they use: it got the better of them. They train us to do the same. Whatever the "it" was, we must apologize when we dare to feel at a time or place where feeling is verboten. Funny, anger, which the Vics of the world are free to usher forth, is also a feeling.

For me, the idea of someone demanding I not feel is akin to saying I should not allow myself to breathe air. Just don't let the need *for oxygen get to you. Surely, you can conquer this defect. Is it? Or was fear the original advantage?* Fear manifests from the survival instincts that allowed our primordial ancestors to escape the ravages of a Cambrian ocean, crawling to sanctuary on land.

I am tired of their accusations. Tired, as a lunged being, attempting to live in a world best suited for gills. To continue the analogy, let's learn from our marine sisters. Orcas, penguins, turtles, and the like—they found a way to live amongst those gilled fishes with their less than perfectly suited lungs. Their ancestors crawled out of those ancient oceans in search of a better life. At some point, their cousins glided back in. Marine birds and mammals do not hold the privileges of gill holders. Yet, they manage to get by, even thrive, in a world that partially suits their bodies. I cannot imagine a scenario where a dolphin looked upon a fish with envy or made apologies for her need to surface. It is time I take a page out of the dolphins' playbook.

Boy o' boy, Piper, is this what you had in mind by suggesting I write you a letter? I hope this makes even the least bit of sense, but it is coming together for me. Is that the point? Did you intend for me to dive into my own thoughts? Maybe I'll walk the pups, then give this another try tomorrow…

***

Okay, I think I get it. I live in a world where my intense emotions are not welcome. Where they lead to pats on the head or my dad saying things like, "That's just because you're so sensitive" in a loving but babyish voice. Moreover, male colleagues declare our emotions unprofessional when I wonder if what they really mean is uncomfortable. Further, the alpha males meet our emotional expressions with hostility and ridicule.

We think of environments as the part of ecology to which animals and plants must adapt. In Biology 101, we rarely discuss how *humans have, for most of our history, not only adapted to new ecosystems but also changed the nature of the environment itself to make it more hospitable. We clear entire forests to raise food, reroute rivers to transform energy, and turn the earth itself into bricks and cinder blocks to do with as we please. As these considerations fall into the realm of anthropology, my thoughts get limited by disciplinary dividing lines. We are not speaking often enough with our colleagues in the social sciences. They are the ones who understand dominant and minority cultures; they are the ones who can help us adapt our institutional environments to allow empaths to live more harmoniously.*

The key is respect. Much like we need to respect the Earth to stop misusing it, we need to respect the empaths, the emotional ones, for what we bring to the table. Instead, they treat our gifts as hindrances, or worse, burdens. As we consider ways to inhabit the arid landscape of Mars, are the fish and lobsters going to show us the way? No, not even a little bit. The desert fox, the cactus finch, the tortoise, and the Gila monster—these are some of the diversities of creatures whose approach to a waterless climate might guide us.

This applies directly to my life and my little part of the world. I, an empath of extraordinary degree, have attempted to fit into work and social structures that treat feelings, especially tears, as something to avoid, something shameful. That is about as effective a strategy for someone like me as telling my dogs to relieve themselves where I want them to rather than on the proverbial fire hydrant.

I am what I am. Pretending to be something else... no, more than pretending... having the expectation that I become someone else is bogus and dangerous. I, as both a thinking and feeling human, have something to add to this competitive land—red in tooth and claw, as Lord Tennyson would describe it. I no longer can or want to pretend otherwise, or worse, beat myself up because I happen to have lungs, which power grief as well as joy.

Thanks for suggesting this...

Session 5

"I emailed you my homework, but not until yesterday." The line exits my mouth the same way my students ask whether I've graded their tests yet as they walk through the classroom door the day after the exam.

"I saw it in my inbox. I've been swamped. How about you read it?" This is the first of what becomes a regular practice. My nerves go jiggly, but I'm accustomed to an audience.

***

Before I can look up after reading the final sentence I hear, "Who is this person?!" The temperature of my skin rises ten degrees as red patches surface on my neck.

"That was cathartic."

"I bet. I need a minute to absorb it. In fact, I want to reread it." My whole face is the shade of a farmers' market tomato. "Stacey, there is a badass in there somewhere."

"Sometimes it takes a while to get my thoughts together. My speaking brain and thinking brain don't always sync up. I censor myself less when I write."

"How long did that take you?"

"Um, not long. I do some of my best writing by dictating into my phone when I walk the pups." A memory pops into my head and then spills out of my mouth without my permission. "One time, a yellow jacket landed on my arm. I recorded my entire conversation, convincing it not to sting me, 'Oh my god, oh my god, go away. I'm not... I'm not flower... not a flower and you need to get off me.' We were so discombobulated I nearly tripped over Chili." Piper laughs harder than I have seen anyone laugh in a long time. It feels good. It feels good to let her know more about me—in ways the topics that brought me here haven't allowed.

"If writing helps you process, keep going."

"Okay, I am not a daily journal writer. It feels more like something I should want to do than I actually want to do. Writing to explain myself to you helped, but expecting you to read things feels like asking too much."

"I don't mind, but as a therapeutic practice, it's better if we listen to clients read aloud. In fact, I'd love it if you wrote about teaching, or about Chili and Pepper. What kind of dogs are they?"

"C.L.W.D.s, Cute Little White Dogs—technically medium sized. They are brother and sister. Pepper has some black spots sprinkled across his back. Chili has a brown patch above her right eye and one brown ear."

"They sound adorable."

"They had a rough start, but we make a good team. I do have a short piece on teaching I wrote for a resiliency workshop. I'll bring it next time."

"What would it be like for you to read this letter to coworkers?" *Geezus, we were having such a good time. Why did she have to bring them up?*

"I don't think I'd have a problem sharing it with other women—I'm pretty sure they could relate. I cannot picture a scenario where I'd be willing to with most male colleagues, maybe a few."

"I hear you, but I'd like you to tell me why."

"One-on-one, it wouldn't bother me. Academia is still a patriarchy even if my male colleagues themselves are, by and large, pretty great people and our faculty is approaching gender parity. That legacy is by no means in our rearview mirror. After all, my career overlapped with the first female professor at my college. It is better than it was, but it certainly has the potential to become better than it is."

"Do you ever talk with female colleagues?"

"Sometimes. Early on, I was more interested in adapting to and fitting into our culture as it was than considering whether I could work to change it."

"Do you think stating you are a survivor of sexual violence had an impact?" My shoulders shrug.

"If I asked your coworkers, what would they say?" Ick, I am not ready to head in this direction. I have no interest in going back to being outspoken. All I want to do is lick my wounds. I want to focus on myself, not put what is happening at my college ahead of my needs. It feels selfish... but healthy at the same time.

"They might say it was memorable." My eyes creep up to catch a glimpse of her face. Compared to what her other clients are going through, I must sound like some privileged drama queen. I shouldn't be wasting her time.

"Do you suspect there were other victims attending the forum?"

"It was a big group. Some wrote to me after." The last part comes out as a whisper.

"What did they say?"

"Thank you—called me brave. Others wrote, but not as victims. Some felt bad for me."

"Yeah, you were brave. There is so much courage in this letter. I wanted to cheer as you read it." I transition from a sun-ripened tomato to a Thai red pepper. "Stacey, look at me. What is embarrassing about hearing me call you brave?"

"Good girls do not rock the boat. Sometimes I can't help myself."

"Tell me the names of some women you admire." Dr. Hettes lights up and chimes in.

"Dr. Lynn Margulis is the scientist I admire most. Her insights were staggering. She transformed the way we think about evolution at the cellular level. She made us see the benefit of cooperation, in addition to competition. Remember the mitochondria we were talking about last time? She's the one who uncovered their story of evolutionary cooperation. Doing so required her to stand at podiums and speak the truth of the evidence she collected, often in rooms filled only with men.[3] Men who had no interest in hearing what she had to say because they interpreted it as a contradiction."

"Interpreted or felt?"

"Good question. The truth is, she presented evidence that adds to their assumptions, rather than undermines them. But you may be right. Maybe they felt too threatened to see that. As women make more headway in science, cooperation as a biological driving force is finally getting some wind in its sails. Dr. Margulis deserved a Nobel Prize. Yet, she is better known for being Carl Sagan's ex-wife." I add an eye roll for emphasis. "Beyond science, I admire Anita Hill, Abigail Adams, Eleanor Roosevelt, the poet Nikky Finney, Sister Joan Chittister, Krista Tippett, Marian Wright Edelman, Michelle Obama, my great-aunt Ellen who divorced her husband to become a minister."

"Sounds like a bunch of boat rockers to me."

"Uh-huh," I say, managing a smile.

---

3 "Margulis-Dawkins Debate," VOX-Voices from Oxford, last modified December 3, 2012, http://www.voicesfromoxford.org/margulis-dawkins-debate/.

CHAPTER 7

Peonies, Lots and Lots of Peonies

As I search my files for the piece about teaching, my mind returns to a call with my mom shortly after I became Dr. Hettes. We talked about how I love this job—no, this vocation. It allows me to embrace my inner science dork in all her glory. I have not revisited those early days in quite a while. That was a time when a precocious, smart girl blossomed into a woman capable of knowing difficult things and committed to pushing her students toward forming new synapses. My mentors, the women whom I emulate, taught me that making connections with my students, rather than for them, matters most.

As I locate the file from the workshop, my thoughts turn to the particular student whom I wrote about. This young woman is a standout in a sea of beautiful souls. Reading the lines, where I simply refer to her as she, it dawns on me. I've held the honor of reliving such experiences with similar students hundreds and hundreds of times. I indulge myself a moment to linger over this time unfragmented by intrusive images of Mr. Jay. A time when my singular intent was to become for these students everything my mentors are for me.

It's restorative to delight in what I love most about being Dr. Hettes. To embrace the gift that writing gives us—whether we do it well or poorly, whether we expect others' eyes will ever fall upon the marks we generate upon a page.

She was awkwardly ahead of her time arriving at morning classes in full makeup and hot-rollered hair. The harder she tried, the worse it went. She was an eager, talented pupil who deserved better-matched peers. The choice of a scholarship close to home, where unbridled curiosity was regularly absent, was a gamble for her type.

Add to that the residual patriarchy of the college's history of female exclusion, and this peony budding at the edge of a battlefield was in danger of being trampled.

She had two choices: me, the jovial neophyte, blissfully ignorant of the surrounding psychological landmines, or my senior by a decade, whose default expression was a walking homage to "never let 'em see you sweat." She chose me. Then, finally, quaveringly, she composed the question, "Can I be a physician and still have a family?" Serendipity shined on us both. Without missing a beat, my empowered ignorance issued the declaration "Of course!" Her sigh of relief suggested she had granted a reprieve to the plan that she jettison her dreams.

After which, we kept growing. Side-stepping the landmines and celebrating the victories, even as our rose-colored safety goggles, cracked and pitted with debris, were no longer protective. One March day, at that school year's requisite gathering to honor the history of women in this land of men, she found a platform to speak our truths. Though a student, she was the braver and more battle-weary of the two of us, for she sprinted while I paced myself for the marathons to come. The roar of her testimonial missile left us gasping.

"A male professor told me there was no way I could be a physician and have a family."

The shrapnel of her explosive confession landed adjacent to my jugular vein. She had never shared the reason behind the doubt that brought us together. Ever the embodiment of diplomacy and poise, she granted him the camouflage of anonymity. Nonetheless, her retaliatory strike ricocheted, landing square on my sternum. I realized then: these trainees needed better air cover. We mentors needed to dispel the notion that we had made it through the battles of earlier wars unscathed. After all, we were upright and still crawling.

I wish it had been a quick metamorphosis. It was not. I wish it had been a glorious triumph. It is an incremental advance as we weave imperceptible wins into titanium chainmail. Her battle, in this theater, concluded with an impact that was subtle but oh-so profound. She may yet be unaware of it; perhaps I should write her.

At commencement, after the obligatory hugs and beaming smiles, her mother and I found just seconds to unite in that electrical way where eyes and emotions lock. In barely a whisper, a mother's lips, tongue, and jaw transformed a lecturer of science into a cultivator of women, offering a simple, "thank you for her." The connection broke as our eyes, welling with the moment, fixed on our shared purpose.

The thing about peonies—once they blossom, their fullness is something to behold.

CHAPTER 8

Body Memories

Last session was the first that helped—the confidence boost I desperately needed. My current administrative task is to lead the first formal review of our tenure and promotion policies since the 1970s. We've been using the same policies for evaluation and promotion since Nixon was in office. I know. I know. How lucky am I? Fifteen months of committee meetings and shuttle diplomacy culminated in a meeting with my boss that lasted over two hours but felt more like two days.

Three years of law school—not the seven I spent in a neuroscience lab—would have helped. I will leave it at this—one sentence, out of the 133 in the policy, uses the word, "or," instead of the word "and." That's the power of language. One little "or" made sure our policy read exactly as the committee of faculty members agreed it should.

I enjoyed six minutes of private euphoria for carrying this work across the finish line before the full weight of the effort it required landed hard. This morning, the dashboard gauge for my emotional labor tank dropped to "E." It's gonna be tough for Dr. Hettes to keep little Stacey in check today.

Session 6

As we settle in, my eyes search for the Kleenex box, a hint that the despondent groundwater is working its way to the surface. I'm too exhausted for the small talk that gradually forms a foundation of trust between Piper and me. I do not want to rehash my work week. It'd seem like whining to talk about how hard it was to get this win on the tenure policy.

"You look kind of down. What's going on?"

"Work's been a lot, but nothing to do with the victim-blaming mess."

"What about more personal things?" This is how it works. After an uplifting session or two, therapists push a little harder for some truth-telling. Piper has earned enough trust to unzip one of the duffels I carry.

"There's a recurring picture in my head of a dirty-faced girl—second or third grade. She sits on a cot in a grimy jail cell. I do feel bad for her, but I put her there." I pause, hesitant to dig through this baggage. Even without the chit-chat, there is a need to stretch a bit—to warm up these emotional muscles. My mind offers up a less troublesome thought. I use it to pivot. "One day in elementary school, Mrs. Miller, the kindergarten helper, was on playground duty. In my memory, there are no other kids nearby, which, of course, cannot be true. It's just me on the slide, joylessly climbing the ladder over and over. When I climb to her eye level, Mrs. Miller says, 'You look like you lost your best friend.' She says other words too. In my head, a response comes out of my little-girl mouth but the words sound like mumbles. Whatever I said, it was a lie. Like when I told my mother—like I still tell my mother—I'm just tired."

"It is interesting. You feel bad for these images of a little girl, and yet, you make no room for sympathy toward your adult self. Do you ever cut yourself some slack?" I give her a blank stare. "Processing memories and grieving is hard work. It is okay to be tired—not sad, or drained, but physically tired." More blank stares as my brain and body resist this compassion. "I want to go back to the playground; how old do you think you were?"

"It'd been a long time since I'd seen Mrs. Miller. Second grade? I don't think it was third grade; my body seems smaller than a third-grade body. The hood on my coat is up, but there's no snow. The horizon blends into the grass."

"Do you have memories with Mr. Jay where your body feels the same size? If that is too much, it is okay."

"Yes, we were all at my grandmother's house for Sunday dinner. It was a gray winter day that time too. Our play clothes felt icy. We left them in the car during church. Carrie would never have tolerated playing in a church dress when Mr. Jay's son was around. I guess Mr. Jay got sick, but I did not know he was resting in the spare room. Gramma kept the toys in that closet. His back is to the door." My eyes squeeze tight.

"It is okay. Try to stay with it." I lean into this overwhelming sense of disgust as long as I can. After a bit, little Stacey retreats.

"It's crazy how muscles contracting in particular patterns for the first time in decades recreate a sensation. These memories stem from a time when those muscles were literally made of different cells. What we experience is actually a perception—a pattern of neuronal activity across several brain areas. But damn it, it's like you are the size, height, and proportion to the world that you were when it happened."

"That is interesting, professor," she says, letting a glimpse of a smile slip across her face. "I'm learning to recognize what you attempt to do. I will not let you distract me with a fascinating biology lesson. I want to talk about what it was like to stand in that doorway."

My eyes close as I attempt to rekindle the belief that shutting them is all it'd take to escape this moment. My mom loves to remind me that I used to close my eyes as I reached on tiptoe for a fresh-baked cookie from the cooling rack. When she would call me out, I would say, "You can't see me; my eyes are closed."

***

Back in Piper's office, I respond, "My stomach hurts." Freeing these words plunges me into a body memory that overwhelms Dr. Hettes in an instant. Too fast to recall how to breathe, how to stay present in the way Indira taught me for times like this.

"Does anywhere else hurt?"

"My neck..." I drop to silence for what seems like twenty minutes. My hands conceal my face as a last line of defense against the sight of both her office and Gramma's spare room. My palms push tight against my lips in an attempt to keep them from admitting anything else. The hormones in my saliva taste metallic as my body mounts a full-throttle defense against the words I am about to betray my whole self with, "and down there."

My ego wants to leap from this body and flee. If there were a blanket, I would hide my whole self under it. My breathing becomes shallow. I clench my neck muscles to push the words back toward the blackness from which they spill. "I feel him inside me." *My back arches to assist my pelvis as it tries to eject this fictive memory.* "It hurts. It hurts really bad."

His hand split me open as it rubbed against the dryness of my little-girl insides. Where is it going? Is he stretching where my pee comes out? Remembering these questions causes the seeping groundwater to erupt into a geyser of guttural cries and hyperventilation. There is nothing to do but ride it out. To scream the cries of terror my little-girl body dared not.

Piper inches closer, leaning as far as she dares into the no man's land of her area rug. She knows full well that we mistakenly interpret those who are here to help us as threats when we are in a panic. Somehow, she manages to waft invisible waves of sympathy and protection toward the couch. Even though we have never touched each other, not even a handshake, she creates a physical comfort, the kind I barely accept from anyone. Not since the night my mother held on to me with a love that drew me back from the riptide that threatened to carry me out of reach as the confession of what Mr. Jay did poured out of me.

***

Once this storm surge subsides, my lungs scrub the oxygen from each breath. Adrenaline drains every muscle's efficacy. I want to fold myself into the enveloping comfort of her couch. The weight of this memory-soaked brain could snap my cervical column. After a while, Piper lifts the blanket of silence.

"How are you?"

"I'll be okay. I can take care of myself when this happens."

"I'm sorry this is hard." She pauses. "It is also terribly important. The body memories need to find their way to the surface. You must allow your body to reconnect the sensations and emotions you had to suppress then."

"It's not my first time dealing with what just happened."

"I know."

"I hoped it wouldn't come to this."

"I am guessing that you understand it's what we are here to do." My stare—feebly blank—does its best to agree. "As hard as it is, it's a good sign we are making some progress."

"Thanks for not telling me to calm down." My elbows shift to my knees as my head drops to my chest.

"You never have to calm down for me. Stacey, will you look at me, even for a second? I want you to see my face, to know you are safe to say and feel whatever you need to as many times as it takes to find your way through this."

"I think my body recognizes that. My mind's still working on it."

"Which is fine. There is no script, no schedule. I'd hazard a guess that there are likely more body memories on the way. If you are up to it, I'll give you an exercise. It can help if more show up this week."

"Sure."

"I will say it once all the way through. If you want, you can copy it down:

This body memory is not comfortable, but it will not kill me.
I can sit with these sensations.
I notice the sensation of _____.
All sensations come and go.
This feeling will not last forever.
There will be another one behind this one."

"That's simple enough, thanks," I say as I pull a notepad out of my bag.

"You're welcome. You can substitute emotion for sensation when it fits better."

"Makes sense. Thanks. Do you think something happened before I talked to Mrs. Miller on the playground?"

"Most likely, but it is not all that important a question to answer. Sexual abuse is not stored on a timeline. Whenever you and Mr. Jay were alone in the spare room, your body recognized the threat. More importantly, it was discovering ways to protect itself. Do you remember anything after you froze in the doorway?"

"I left. I made sure I didn't go anywhere near that room again. I am almost sure he didn't get to touch me that day."

"Good! Can we give little Stacey some credit? She protected herself."

"This feels like it happened before I told him no, but after I knew how bad it could get."

"Okay." She seems a bit puzzled by that but is willing to let it be. Which is good, because it's all I have the strength to say. My body is wrecked.

***

Piper's mention of protection reminds me of how many times I failed at that—even beyond Mr. Jay. Especially how my teenage self let hormones and her boy-crazy friends convince her to let her guard down. But no boys came calling. Unfortunately, once again, a man did. A coach fooled me into believing he was safe. Beyond safe. I thought he wanted me. Cared about me. Piper, as yet, has no idea about him.

Admitting what happened with him is too much. In some ways, my coach did more damage than Mr. Jay. Besides, we've got to be out of time. With high school Stacey, there's even less sympathy for her than little Stacey. From behind my barricades, adult Stacey sits in furious judgment. I should have fucking known better by high school.

I'm guessing we'll have to cross this bridge at some point. I doubt I can anytime soon. My coach—and the issues he left me with—buried themselves deep. I didn't even mention him on the intake form. Again, I am left to wonder how long I will need therapy. I also make a note to check my insurance coverage. If we wade into this quagmire and I no longer have someone to guide me, I might be lost forever.

***

Now that I've caught my breath, my brain wishes we could

keep going. Processing all this in a tired, middle-aged body, but with a sharper, more perceptive mind, is harder. I hate to admit it, but a retreat to therapy might've been inevitable at this stage of my life regardless of the catalysts that landed me here.

CHAPTER 9

A Kiss Is Never Just a Kiss

My phone dings with a meeting reminder as I head to the parking lot. Break's over, Dr. Hettes. I should keep a little oxygen tank like high-altitude climbers use in my trunk for post-therapy therapy. Experiencing my little-girl self's memories in this adult body prompts a nurturing attitude toward her. My Honda swings through Sonic for a strawberry lemonade slush. Little Stacey learned early on to accept sugar in lieu of love. I consider getting her some candy mixed in, or one of the technicolor varieties. The truth is, I like real lemons. Plus, Dr. Hettes pretends the teaspoon of fruit compensates for the heaping scoop of disaccharides.

Over the years, survivors come to recognize the subtle differences between cathartic memory extractions and ones that manifest like seizures. The first leaves you with a sense of triumph. The second: like a pile of dirty rags. This one was cathartic but brutal. If I had time, I'd go for a swim. Submerging in the YMCA's heated pool is the closest thing my body accepts to the pressure of human touch. The seizure-like memories require a different strategy. Straight home—push my way through a minimized routine for the Chili Peppers—then straight to bed. There is something peculiarly wonderful about the gentleness of pajamas when you put them on before dark. Even blankets become more soothing, like how they felt on sick days home from school.

When I do eventually sink into bed early that evening, its safety encourages my thoughts to wander. Though my body is wrecked, that scoopful of sugar has yet to cause a crash. Consequently, today's session volleys around my mind like a tennis ball. What were the first years of my life like? What was it like to live in innocence—not knowing the fear of unexpectedly finding myself alone with Mr. Jay? I search for a single good memory to hold. None materializes.

Body memories that recreate the abuse are unlike anything else. Worse, they come in waves and dislodge all sorts of visual aftershocks. I'd like to bring my neuroscience colleague, Kate, to Piper's office to measure my brain waves during a body memory to see what we can learn from them. One consolation of this ordeal is that, on the whole, the attention these memories require overrides the din of perpetual naysaying for a while. There is that.

Embracing the comfort of my bed feels reminiscent of my mother's care. In response to physical symptoms, this variety of her attention, which usually was reserved for others, transformed her into the nurse for us. I connect to an ancient memory of my security blanket, Softee, whose soothing power leveled up each time Mom warmed him in the dryer. The drill sergeant of a mother, charged with training up her children "in the way they should go," took a break on such days. In our church, "the way" was all about rigidly adhering to the Bible's literal do's and don'ts, enforced by constant admonitions against "being left behind" when The Rapture fell upon us.

No matter the ailment—a skinned knee or upset stomach—we were sure we were the luckiest kids alive to have a nurse right there to fix it. How much harder these expectations must have made the ones she placed upon herself. My mother was not only educated as a nurse. Those instincts are encoded in her DNA in the same way teaching is steeped into mine. Once, with nothing but popsicles, she managed to stop the bleeding from a toddling little Samantha's tongue after a headlong tumble into the coffee table nearly chomped it in two. We were far from the nearest hospital. Serious injuries required ninja-level first aid. That this woman, whose very existence orients toward triage and recovery, held no knowledge of my insides' secret lacerations? Reconciling this aspect of my early years required hours of long-ago therapy. Piper and I have barely broached the subject.

I hope we won't need to start from scratch. Re-excavating each layer of my past is turning out to be as bad as it was in college, maybe worse. This time, realizing that Mr. Jay was a master manipulator, but also cautious in his own right, will play a more prominent role in my sessions. Perhaps because Dean Grant's actions, which felt so fucking manipulative, caught me so off guard. I'd stood firmly in his corner before all this. Dean Grant, like Mr. Jay, plays the nice guy until his authority is challenged. I remember a time when Mr. Jay offered to watch the kids: "You ladies can go shopping and out to lunch." In the safety of my sheets, hearing his voice in my head cues up the first aftershock from today's session.

***

The steps from the house into the garage were unfinished with no railing. I knew how to grab onto the doorframe so I didn't fall. Lifting my red Zips, with the rubber that coated the toes, across the doorway required a big step over and down. These were the shoes I later learned to tie all by myself.

Their garage smells different from ours. Ours smells like oil and grease. Maybe because they have a cat. Her name starts with an 'S'—Shadow? Maybe Spooky? and her tail is crooked. Mr. Jay's son slammed the door on it by accident.

"That chair looks like the ones at church," I say.

"Oh yeah? Here, come stand on it." It does not even cross my mind

to wonder why as he unfolds the seat and steadies it as I climb. A shirt with some little pattern covers his great big belly. I'm close enough to see it but I can't name it—diamonds or little flowers? Not polka dots. I know polka dots.

Straight ahead, I see where his hairs stick out the top of his shirt. My daddy doesn't have hairs there. Tilting my eyes upward, all I see is his face—each whisker of his mustache distinct, like the hairs of a monster in a horror movie.

"Close your eyes."

Do I get a surprise?... Wait, how did he make my mouth open up?... Is that his tongue? It's touching mine. That's weird. This all felt a lot like jumping in an icy swimming pool—a little jarring, but not at all scary. As safe as wearing my orange life jacket that buckled around the middle and tied under my chin. "What does that feel like?" he asks.

"Your mustache tickles."

He smiles super wide but with his mouth shut. His eyelids lower as his mouth comes for more. His eyelid skin is darker and shinier than the rest of his face. When they open, little flecks of blues, yellows, and browns make up the green of his eyes. My eyes are blue. So are my mommy's. I don't think I ever saw someone be this kind of happy before. "You're supposed to keep your eyes closed," he says in the gentlest, most loving man voice I ever heard.

"Oh."

More kissing. Where are his hands? I don't think they're resting on the back of the chair. Its cold metal reaches through my thin summer shirt. Maybe they fit on either side of me. My tummy only fills the middle of the seat back. The rest of my body is missing. There is nothing beyond my tongue, my lips, and my tummy.

"We better get you back in the house with the other kids."

"How come you did that?"

"It's special kissing. Do you like it?" My shoulders do that *exaggerated shrug kids use when they don't know the right answer.* "It is sooo nice once you get the hang of it."

"Oh," I say again, not knowing what is supposed to feel good or bad. One thing's true. Mr. Jay sure likes it.

It's funny, TV shows make the bad guys out to be sinister, rough, violent. That day, Mr. Jay was anything but. He saved his scariness for when he was yelling at his kids or his wife. Those green eyes came alive with anger in a way my daddy's never did.

"But it has to be a secret. Something special for you and me. You can't tell anybody, okay? I wasn't supposed to show you. It's the way grown-ups kiss each other."

There is no better card in a pedophile's hand than a shared secret.

***

My body jumps to recalling the texture of Indira's throw pillow against my cheek as I folded my head into my lap—along with the lingerings of her sandalwood incense. Teeth clenched, I strangle each word as it exits my mouth, "because I did like it." The shame, the disgust, the self-loathing those five words contain was, is, impossible to circumnavigate. I felt all those things. I feel all those things. Mr. Jay fucking played me better than a card shark winning a hand with a pair of deuces.

His kisses tingled the skin on my neck and tummy. They were warm and soft and safe. What do you imagine when you envision child sexual abuse? When I imagine another's defilement, it's violent, thrusting, terrifying. The soundtrack that my mind underlays adds additional wickedness.

That's not how he initiated it. He fit the Greek origins of the word, pedophile, to a T—*pedo/ child; phile/ lover*. Did he think of himself that way? That what he did was loving?

Mr. Jay made those moments he stole special and covert. The

only other secret I'd held before that was the time my dad gave me a peek at the surprise firecrackers he'd bought for Carrie. She was all about loud noises and danger. I was afraid of mostly everything but tried hard not to act like it. Why was I not at all afraid of Mr. Jay that day? That stupid little shit should have known better.

***

I can't believe I've spoiled the comfort of this pre-sunset snuggle by releasing these memories into being again. The weight of Chili's body pressed against my back and her gentle snuffling snores connect me back to my adult body. Standing on Mr. Jay's chair wasn't anything like the things that happened later or how his early sweetness later soured beneath my skin.

The tickles of his mustache, which made me a little uneasy then, haunt me now. Its soft shafts and prickly ends press into my nose and face to this day whenever I see facial hair. I once kissed a college hookup with a '90s-era goatee. My mind went into a tailspin. Luckily, our campus culture promotes preppy, coastal vibes— no full-bearded hipsters for us.

This liminal time of feeling special, even a little excited, by Mr. Jay's attention left me with mountains of self-revulsion, hatred, and shame. I still chastise myself when a longing for any kind of attention arises. Feeling left out, like a third wheel, made that gullible little shit in her goddamned red shoes culpable from the get-go. The bile making its way from my gall bladder to flush out these greasy recollections fills me with loathing all over again.

As far as I can decipher, the chair in his garage was the first time he got me alone. Piper will re-teach me the term grooming. The subtly progressive way abusers prepare us for a childhood of... of what? I have no words. After I confessed to Indira what I understood to be my culpability, no, even worse, the responsibility

I felt for climbing up that chair, she told me about a child she once treated. It sounded as though, after a while, this little girl would attempt to initiate intercourse with her abuser, sometimes in front of other people. He would simply shrug her off and say we can't do that now. My heart floods with anguish for this unknown, unnamed innocent. I want to axe murder that fucker. Indira's attempt to draw a parallel to my own innocence? Nope, never found a chink in my armor.

For me, there is no room for discussion on this topic, yet. There is no space to entertain the notion that a society, whose silence tacitly condones this type of child abuse, at least has the obligation to adequately warn us that it happens. My mother remains flabbergasted that it was never mentioned in nursing school. I made it to fifth grade, age eleven before the topic was ever broached. Was the class presentation that day mandatory? Was Mrs. Delano a lone heroic teacher bucking the system that silences us? Regardless, I want to remember her as the hero she is. What about children who are homeschooled? Who teaches them how to deal with Grandpa, Aunt Lucy, or what the seemingly nice neighbor down the block might instruct them to do while standing on a chair? Stranger Danger stories did not exist in 1970s rural America. Are there adequate warnings today? As we know, even churches were too busy protecting the abusers and their political empires to devote any effort to protecting us. Here again, four decades later, churches, along with other entities, still end up in the news for enacting similar choices.

These choices get backed by a legal system that rarely provides victims much more than a shrug of the shoulders plus a "boys will be boys" in exchange for the bucketloads of courage they need to come forward.

It makes me want to scream! Keep your tongues in your

mouths, your hands to yourselves, and your goddamn dicks in your fucking pants.

It eludes me.

Some men—thank every form of god, not all men—instinctively step into a primal crouch on behalf of their gender in the face of terrible truths—even when they observe it with their own eyes. During the discovery of the unforgivable actions of Jerry Sandusky, journalists reported on another member of the Penn State football coaching staff who walked into the locker room as Sandusky penetrated a little boy.[4] This other coach walked away from this child in the grip of a demon from the depths of hell. Can there be a situation where a victim could feel more alone? His hope for liberation dashed against the back of the man who walked out as evil macerated his insides. I pray for the man that little boy became every time I think of him. I don't know how his soul survives it, but I hope he does. So many do not.

I have little first-hand experience with abusers gaining cover and fortification from their families and institutions. I am confident my parents, grandparents, and other important adults—for example, people in our church—had no idea what Mr. Jay was doing. Except for his wife.

When I told my parents, their reactions made it crystal clear. They had no idea such things were even possible. My mother was protective to a fault. Hardly anyone except my grandmothers even babysat for us. Once, when visiting my parents' college friends in Connecticut, they arranged for Carrie, their two girls, and me to stay with a teenage babysitter. I was puzzled, but curious. This was something people did?

---

4 "*Jerry Sandusky Witness Tells of Staring at Coach in the Showers With a Boy*," ABC News, last modified June 11, 2012, https://abcnews.go.com/US/jerry-sandusky-trial-hears-key-witness-mike-mcqueary/story?id=16545142.

***

When I wake the next morning, the cocktail of cortisol and adrenaline working its way through my liver keeps my brain in a fog until teaching class dissipates it. I revisit Piper's words regarding the difference between thinking and feeling. It's clear that hundreds more bits of memories and emotions are on their way to challenge my endurance. I doubt I am ready to share even a fraction with Piper. Some may never make their way to my vocal cords. Although it's something Indira and I worked through, I dread telling Piper about the kissing.

I make a note to share one thing with her. Something I was not mature enough to consider with my previous therapists. I want to acknowledge that theirs must be some of the hardest, most soul-crushing work on the planet. To sit with us day after day, eyewitnesses to our agony. To assure us they will firmly anchor our lifeline as the abyss wraps its murky tendrils around our ankles.

Piper reminds me repeatedly that sexual abuse is less about the details or the acts themselves and more about what the experience does to our minds and bodies, a topic that receives far too little attention. Our lack of consideration as a society when confronted with the depths of victims' stories is fed by the sound-bite culture of sensationalist headline-grabbing that in many quarters has supplanted journalistic integrity. They feed us trauma porn and we lap it up, ultimately deadening our ability to detect and respond appropriately to such awful, awful stuff. We placate our minds with words like, "She is probably too young to remember," "It was not that bad," or "She did not know what was happening was sexual." She was not. It was. Her body did.

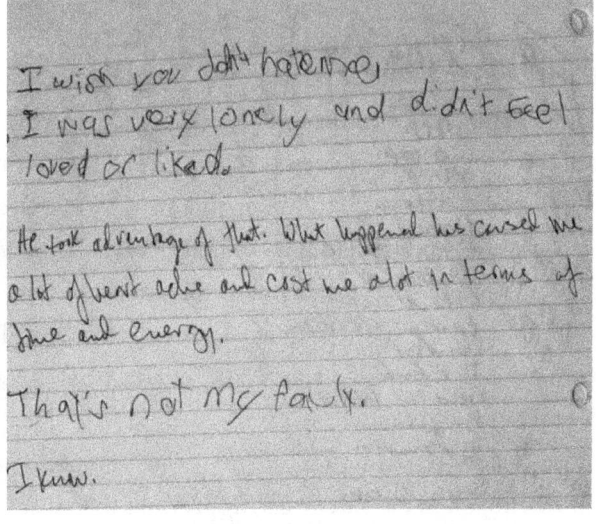

None of the other memories that dredge up feel safe enough to swim toward without Piper standing guard. Instead, over lunch I try to write some thoughts about loneliness like she asked me to. It's not easy. Dr. Hettes built her story around absolutely loving life alone. I consider an exercise from the *Courage to Heal* that I used in college—writing with both hands. The idea is to write a conversation between your adult self by using your dominant hand and your younger self by using your non-dominant hand. I have not studied the psycho-physiological reasoning behind it, but for me, it forces a slowdown and some truth-telling.

Non-dominant hand: I wish you didn't hate me. I was very lonely and didn't feel loved or liked.

Dominant hand: He took advantage of that. What happened caused me a lot of heartache and cost me a lot in terms of time and energy.

Non-dominant: That's not my fault.

Dominant hand: I know.

Look at that, even my dominant hand is willing to lie—to pretend that I do not blame that little girl. She knows better.

CHAPTER 10

Drowning in Puddles

Session 9

Forty minutes in, my mind refuses to relinquish its survivalist crouch, tossing what it thinks are useless bits of conversation asunder. I failed to warn Piper that my brain's control dial spun to "crisis" sometime earlier this week. I've navigated work wearing a disguise of professionalism much like movie stars don bucket hats and sunglasses. Home meant nosedives into the couch as *The West Wing* played on perpetual loop. Aaron Sorkin's dialogue conjures the presence of other people without—you know—the actual people. I do think the President's Press Secretary, CJ Cregg, and I would be good friends.

The compassionate reprieve my little-girl self earned via those body memories last week proved short-lived. Their aftershock recollections prompted a retreat behind this fortification that I've built between the world and me. To give Piper credit, she propels the session along, hacking away at my barricades. Her efforts must feel like ripping open sandbags with a butter knife.

With ten minutes to go, the tears flow unabashedly—more grief—desperate, destabilizing. The kind that convinces us not even one minute of our lives has been worthwhile.

Piper breathes waves of kindness across the divide. Some part of me responds, assuming it's safe to make eye contact, just as she glances at the clock. As I spy the slightest glimpse of alarm, she grabs her phone and says, "Let me text my next client." It does not register at first what's happening. She frets a bit before saying, "Let me just check if she's still here," as she exits the room.

Tensing upright, the tears retreat as quickly as they arrived. "Oh, my god, it is twenty-five past the hour," my mouth proclaims to no one, milliseconds before my hyoid muscles clench around my trachea. The back of one hand swabs away tears as the other gathers my things. Before my body manages to stand, Piper returns, seeming nonplussed.

"She's not out there. She must have left," she says as pure nitrogen replaces the ordinary office air and I begin to suffocate.

"I'm sorry, I'm sorry, I'm sorry."

"Sorry for what? Stacey, it is my job to keep track of the time, not yours."

"I took her time, I took her time. What if she's in crisis? What if she needs you? I need to go. I need to go. I'm sorry. I'm sorry," vibrates across my tongue as I suck in this useless nitrogen.

"Stacey, it is okay. Things happen all the time to disrupt my schedule. You didn't do anything wrong. I made the choice to keep going."

"I try to keep track... It's hard... you hide the clock... I can't know," comes out staccato, as air attempts to resuscitate my body and escape over my vocal cords at the same time.

"That is by design. Watching the time is my responsibility." She hands over the tissue box. "I want you to take a slow deep breath... good... and another. This time, breathe out a little harder. That's better. Try to notice something in the room. Can you name something you see?"

Direct orders must be followed. Accordingly, my cerebral cortex comes back online but my amygdala still runs the show. "The painting."

"Good, tell me something you hear."

"The space heater's fan."

"Good, take another breath. Push out long and slow. This one might not be possible. Can you tell me something you smell?" The glaze coating my bronchioles thins, allowing a few molecules of oxygen to find their way through the epithelial cells that line my lungs.

"I smell the tissue." There's just enough dopamine left in my prefrontal cortex for me to wonder whether she saw the snot dripping from my nose all the way over there. Crumpled in my palm—wet with face drippings—it offers wood pulp and comfort. Also, a whiff of supermarket.

***

After another few minutes, my diaphragm contracts normally again. My head angles itself to maximize the distance between my eyes and Piper's. As the panic subsides, gobs of shame roll in to replace it, right on cue.

"You recovered quicker than I expected. What is it like when that happens alone?" My ears pick up that she uses neither the word panic nor attack.

"I fight it until I get by myself. I am lucky to have my own office." Internal gratitude is a good antidote for shame. Admonishments to be grateful are not. "I slipped into a pool when I was a little kid and the lifeguard had to fish me out. This feels like that. Afterward, your brain needs to be... flat. Your lungs forgot how to fulfill their purpose. Each breath becomes an effort to relearn what it means to breathe."

"We do need to wrap things up, but I am curious, what was so triggering about what just happened?"

"I don't like to hurt anyone. Taking her time was selfish. These sessions have become essential. That I kept someone else from their time with you..."

"Thank you for telling me that. I appreciate how important it feels to you to stay on schedule. You know it is not something I tightly adhere to, but that's because it is sometimes in a client's best interest not to. I will try to keep better track of the time. However, it is important that you practice relinquishing control over when our sessions end. It is on me to judge whether we should stop or not." She manages to say all this without sounding as though she is scolding an unruly child. More like formulating an agreement between adults in equal partnership.

"I'll try." Even as the words make their way out of my mouth, the frontal lobe of my brain plots how to keep better track of the time moving forward. Over the coming weeks, I work in statements like, "I am not sure how much time we have left." I try to hold off until I estimate we are midway through our sessions. Piper appears to notice these little intrusions but ignores them.

"Will you let me see your eyes so I can know you are okay?" My neck angles up as my lips try their damnedest to smile. If she had asked me what age I feel, I would answer nine, which intrigues me. Nine happens to be an age that I can pinpoint as falling between the summertime morning that I said no to Mr. Jay and the night a few years later that I walked into my parents' room and told Mom the things he'd done. What was life like for my third-grade self? How did she cope with the fact that nine-year-olds, especially nine-year-old girls, hold little control over themselves, or their bodies?

"How does it work when you need to bill for a double session? Do I write you a check?" Piper smiles as we both stand.

"It is okay, let's call it a freebie."

CHAPTER 11

Dr. Hettes Opines on Panic Attacks

My closest biology department friend, Tammie, texted later that evening—just checking in. I must have told her that Piper and I meet on Thursdays. Tammie has no trouble telling anyone that she is in therapy or regaling us with stories of what her time on the couch revealed. To ease my lingering mortification for dissolving this afternoon, I tell her about what happened in the most sarcastic texts imaginable. She replies with her own recounts of similar meltdowns.

It's marvelous how a few autocorrected words and an emoji or two between friends can lighten the load.

***

Panic attacks are tricky—eliciting buckets of shame, which summon memories of retorts from family and schoolmates. "Quit overreacting; don't be so sensitive; I knew you'd make a big deal about this." That last one was a favorite of more than one boyfriend and my sister, Carrie. I imagine panic attacks create no joy from the bystander's perspective. If your limbic system has never hijacked you this way, watching a panic attack might be akin to observing someone insist they are drowning as they stand in a puddle. Whatever the internal danger, by outward appearances, it must seem trivial. To our psyches—reduced to the helpless mental state of a preverbal toddler—this tiny wet patch is as dangerous as the open ocean.

***

My maternal family history overflows with low-grade psychological struggle. For the most part, we focus the stories around Great-Grandpa Van Sickle's nervous breakdown, which led to my grandmother leaving school in eighth grade to help keep the farm afloat. After all, it was more important for her brothers to finish high school. This family history of struggles with mental health, the underlying genetics which tilt me toward anxiety, along with what Mr. Jay did, combine like phosphorus, potassium, and nitrogen fertilizing the soil in which panic grows best. The costs in emotional energy make a measurable contribution to the entropy of the universe. Add to that the expense of maintaining the appearance that all is well.

Within the circles that middle-class Gen Xers navigate, anything that threatens this veneer of control is an absolute nonstarter. We will be damned to let it all come crashing down. In my campus's culture of civility and decorum, most colleagues, even those cognizant of my facade, would never betray their awareness that things may not be as they appear, perhaps for fear I might return the favor.

Normalizing self-empathy and mental wellness both on campus and more broadly, along with establishing expectations at a level somewhere below perfection and continual sacrifice would help. Sadly, the internalized capitalism we accept as the bargain for the American dream demands a stronger remedy than the impromptu manicure or medium-priced bottle of wine that passes for self-care.

My earliest panic recollection elucidates how, also why, panic attacks reduce me to an infantile state. Unbeknownst to me, my parents and grandparents planned to meet at the mall and get pizza. I was accustomed to Grampa's Sunday clothes. I shrieked, grasping for my mother, when a stranger in blue worker's pants and a driver's cap walked straight at me, gathering me up in the middle of JC Penney.

***

Did someone turn off the store music? My ears hear bumble bees. How come the makeup ladies' perfumes all smell so strong? Who is this man? My legs gotta get away. My mouth only knows how to scream, but the voice inside me is yelling, Mommy! Mommy! There she is—my eyes see Mommy and Daddy. Why are you laughing?! Help me. HELP ME! Don't let him take me.

***

I have no idea if Grampa tried to explain that it was him as he gripped my flailing body tighter, preventing me from dropping to the buffed and polished floor. My twenty-something parents stood motionless in the hilarity of my mismatched reaction to this man whom, in reality, I adore. My tiny, flooded cerebrum could not process this betrayal. Mom and Dad chuckled their way through the event my three-ish-year-old self feared most: a kidnapping in broad daylight.

No further memories made their way from my hippocampus to the storage bins of my cerebrum that night. I guess we went for pizza as planned. Surely, Gramma spoke soothing words of reassurance. I wager she even snuck me an extra peppermint patty from her faux leather handbag with the gold clasp. The hypervigilant alarm system I inherited from her, as she had from her father, made her acutely aware of how one's amygdala hijacks one's entire body.

As an adult, panic attacks recreate similar perceptions of disembodiment, terror, and confusion. In an instant, we reduce to a toddler's comprehension of the world. On top of that, a culture that prides itself in holding power over ourselves and others teaches us there's shame in displaying such exaggerated losses of control. Each episode adds to the pile of evidence that testifies to our lack of fortitude and reserve.

When anxious and maybe ancient Van Sickle genes married into the Hettes family of stoics, this proved especially true. With no such experiences to draw from, those on the stoic side are left annoyed, baffled, or sometimes entertained, in a schadenfreude way. Their exasperated retorts co-opt our names as weapons. "Staaay Ceee, stop being such a crybaby. Calm down. You are such a freaking worrywart." I promise to be the first in line if you stoics ever cease the ridicule long enough to bottle whatever elixir keeps you firing on all cylinders at moments like these.

Piper was among the first outside of my family to bear witness to my dissolutions. It takes great skill to sit with this type of psychic pain while hovering around neutral. Hovering is the key. Remaining in neutral, unwilling to vacillate from empathy to firmness, does not help. She deftly projects that she is here in my reality with me. At the same time, she pushes back against the notion that the drowning sensations my limbic system manufactures are real. When we believe we are drowning, it helps for someone to remind us that our head is above water. That our lungs will not be flooded if we open our mouths.

***

The summer after this session, my family picked a central meeting point in the Virginia mountains to celebrate my parents' fiftieth anniversary. We toured some nearby caverns, something I had not done since a trip with Carrie to New Mexico in my early twenties. It did not dawn on me that I had since developed a progressing case of claustrophobia. About midway through the tour, the guide announced that we were standing under several thousand feet of solid rock. Despite the enormity of the space, my brain hinted that there was not enough air for everyone.

I managed to hold it together until we made it to the surface. Once I saw daylight, my brain understood it was safe to release its fear. Carrie, whose claustrophobic husband was self-aware enough to skip the cave altogether, talked me through it. My sister, who as a kid complained that I ran, biked, and drove go-carts far too slowly, supplied all the time in the world to sit there and breathe our way out of this pseudo-danger. I appreciated her so much in this embarrassing moment of public display. As my shame triggered the guilt of becoming the party pooper yet again, Carrie was the non-judgmental caretaker I could not be for myself.

As awful as the cave experience was, it served as an important reminder that as adults, my sisters and I have long since outgrown childhood rivalries and ridicule—that the messages my brain tries to convince me of—especially since Breakdown Saturday—are not real today. Despite the possessed old jukebox that replays the cruel, taunting words Carrie and Mr. Jay's son hurled at me back then. Taunts I later turned into weapons of self-destruction.

PART TWO

Memories, Motherf*$#ing Memories

History, despite its wrenching pain,
Cannot be unlived but, if faced
With courage, need not be lived again.

— *Maya Angelou*

CHAPTER 12

I Really Wanted a Turn with That Controller

Session 16

There will be no gold star for Dr. Hettes today. I pray to the vending machine version of God for a forcefield to keep the other therapist I know in her office. Occasionally, we cross paths and I try to chit-chat as we might at a cocktail party. Did those guttural wails a few sessions back pass through the wall that her office shares with Piper's? Mercifully, I am left to stare at my phone.

When Piper appears, she waves me in silently as she studies whatever body language betrays me. My legs move as if sloshing through ankle-deep water. After class this morning, I sat at my paper strewn-desk, willing myself upright. I hope my wrist flicked my mouse around its pad enough to convince anyone walking by that it was a normal day—that I was a normal person. I feel anything but. This torment of cortisol, on the rampage each time a memory pulses across the outer six layers of my cerebrum, will undo me.

Positioned on her couch, my face depicts both defeat and fright. The two have begun the seventh round of the cage match taking place in my brainstem. I consider a request for fifty minutes of silent safety for a nap. Would Piper stand watch, like my sweet Pepper does from the vertical window beside our front door?

"Wanna tell me what's going on?" The sound of her voice jumpstarts the waterworks. The tears are on their own today. My torso is incapable of the rhythmic contractions required for sobs.

"I'm tired."

"Anything in particular that might account for that?" I shake my head, barely enough to register as I remove my glasses to press my hand over my eyes. Thumb over the right, index finger on the left, my palm presses against the right side of my nose as my pinky anchors in my left cheek. If only my hand could shield me from the images in my head. I take in a huge breath, slowly releasing it between pursed lips.

"I cannot stop seeing his face."

"What else do you see?"

"His shirt, the wall behind him."

"Tell me about his shirt."

"His wife sewed him a rust-colored shirt with a collar and V-neck. He wore it all the time. Their bedroom was wallpapered."

"You are in his bedroom?"

"Yeah, it's just after Christmas."

"Do you remember how he got you there?"

"I really wanted a turn with the controller."

"What?"

"Santa brought his son a racetrack. He got all the boys' toys Carrie wanted."

Of the two, red was obviously the better controller than yellow, but it didn't matter. There were three of us. It was never going to be my turn. Did I ask for a turn? It depends. If I was five or six, probably not. I hadn't found my voice yet. If I was seven or eight? You betcha.

Those were the years that my most powerful weapon was "It's not fair." But such words landed with a lifeless thump on the threshold of Carrie's ears when Mr. Jay's son was around. He was closer in age to

Carrie and her number one favorite playmate. I was tossed aside like a boring old toy replaced by shiny new ones on Christmas morning whenever he was around.

Had my declarations of unfairness drawn Mr. Jay to the little platform hallway where we played? Had he been listening for them? The hallway was the perfect spot. The two steps down to their sunken living room worked great for kneeling beside the track. Mr. Jay's bedroom, with its own bathroom, was right there too. Whenever—however—he joined our threesome, Mr. Jay managed to slide me in the bucket seat of his crisscrossed legs. He would make sure I got to play. That's how he did it, taking my side against the injustice of being the youngest.

He waited until he could see I was nearly broken by the bias his son held for Carrie's tomboy-ness. Of course, his son wanted to race his red car against my sister's yellow one; she was cool and capable. "Okay, guys, it's time to let Stacey have a turn. You two go play downstairs. I'll race Stacey." He gave me the red one. He gave them what they wanted more than the racetrack—freedom from the tag-along.

I don't think my car made it one whole loop around before his lips were on my neck. Was I wearing my hair in pigtails? Or did he brush the shimmery strands aside? Was this after my Dorothy Hamill haircut? Whatever my hair looked like, this time: I knew this was not good. My body did not like this. Instead of constricting with tension, it flopped into his massiveness.

Fight-or-flight? Out of the question. Freeze or fawn? My amygdala chose fawn, chose compliance. Freeze might alert him to my distaste, and that's not fair. After all, he let me have the red controller.

My pants were purple. My underwear had little flowers and sat above my belly button.

Whether I could get my pants on and off all by myself, I don't remember. It didn't matter. After lifting me onto the satiny peach bedspread, he took delight in undressing my bottom. We'd left our snow boots in the garage—no pesky shoes to hinder his access. Did he leave my socks on? He didn't take off my shirt, no need—nothing to see there. Besides, he wouldn't want me to get cold.

"Lay down." My head didn't reach the pillow. He sat sideways, his legs hanging off the edge. His hands were the size of baseball mitts. I bet he could hold me in the air by one ankle if he wanted to. I didn't bend my knees or tilt my pelvis, as one might learn from a partner at a time—in a bed—where things like this were supposed to happen. The bed smelled like their laundry soap. Will his wife sense what happened on this comforter today? There won't be physical evidence. My little-girl glands had no idea lubrication could come in handy. Will she strip the bedding? Add a capful of bleach to sanitize our sins?

***

What is going on? Why are his hands pulling my legs apart?
What just happened!?
What is he doing down there?
Why is he pinching my pee pee?
Wait a second... is his hand... inside me? What?... where?... is he reaching into where my poop comes out?

Ouch... ouch that hurts. Please. Please don't push so hard. Stop wiggling your fingers. That hurts worse.

I scrunch my eyes against the sight of the room. "Stacey, open your eyes." They dutifully open to a full view of the wallpaper. It felt fuzzy, like stiff velvet. The pattern looked fancy.

If his wife caught us near it, we got yelled at: "Don't touch that, you'll get it dirty."

I wasn't supposed to close my eyes, but it was okay to stare at the wallpaper. A gentle "Hey," draws my attention back to his face. It grinned like that awful cat in Alice in Wonderland whose teeth *appear out of the darkness. "Does that feel good?" He looked so happy. More than happy, but the only word my little-girl mind knew for what I saw on his face was happy. I knew what the answer was supposed to be. And I said it.*

You lied, Stacey! You better remember to ask Jesus to wash the black out of your heart when you say your prayers tonight.

***

My mind squelches, as fast as it can, a flash of me under my own covers sometime shortly after. My little-girl fingers recreated what he did to me on my doll with the pink cloth body. Santa brought me that doll for Christmas.

Back with Piper, my eyes open as my hand lowers. I do not see her office. Only white, as if it's an overcast day and the sky fills my visual field. "Mr. Jay set this up," I blurt out as the realization slaps me right across the cheekbone. "He knew we were coming to visit."

It takes what feels like twenty-five minutes for me to summon the courage to speak again.

"He hunted me. He knew he'd catch me if he set a trap." One hand clenches my middle as the fingers of the other squeeze tight over my mouth. Acidic thoughts spill from my mind, melting my insides. I've had it all wrong. Flash after flash reveals I am a detective in a low-budget cop show who's finally uncovering a long-buried crime. The real killer planted evidence to frame someone else. Someone the detective convinced themself was guilty.

"I think you are right. And, as horrible as that is, it makes sense. He orchestrated opportunities to isolate you." My lips clench as my shoulders fold my head into my lap. "I know this is hard, Stacey, but try to stay with it. I want you to tell me more." She pauses before adding, "You won't hurt me."

"It's not that this time." I swallow hard attempting to keep the liquefied contents of my stomach from making their way to my throat. "I've been mad at my sister and his son…" This confession slides out of my trembling lips before the muscles around my mouth clamp my jaw so tight my chin dimples.

"Stacey, it is okay to be angry. They did leave you behind. Mr. Jay set it up—expertly—so that they would. Can you finish what you were saying?"

"They never wanted to play with me." My voice sounds like little Stacey proclaiming something wasn't fair. "Especially, his son. He constantly tried to get away from me." I notice the heaviness taking over my body, registering the weight of each vertebrae stacked on the one below it. "My mom loved to laugh about a story of babysitting their son. He played with one arm while pushing me away with the other saying, 'no no Tay-see, no no Tay-see,' over and over. It was one of those 'remember when' stories for her, but every time she told it, I felt horrible. I was too little to remember it myself—probably one going on two."

I take a few breaths and push on. "Another time, we were in the car. My mom told us about a plan for his son to come to our house while I went to their house with his daughter. I begged—I mean begged—not to have this happen, but nothing worked. I threw his daughter so far under the bus she skidded out the other side."

"So, you went alone to his house?"

"Of course. It was a done deal before I ever knew about it. I was horrible to her. They had Atari and we didn't. My hand glued itself to that joystick as the crocodiles ate Frogger every single time."

"Why the Atari?"

"The TV room was next to the kitchen. I could usually see his wife." My eyes fixate on the far corner of the room. I gotta numb out.

***

"Can you tell me what you are thinking?" Geezus, why not ask me to dig to China through the floorboards?

"Such a sucker. How could I be so fucking stupid?"

"Stacey." She lets the smallest drop of frustration mix into her voice. "You were a little, little girl. So little, he put you in his lap as he sat cross-legged..."

I interject like a child who can't wait to tell you what they know and you don't. "And he put my pants back on. Not me. Like when you are really little and still need help getting dressed." Saying this one detail out loud leaves me somewhere between levitating above my body and praying the couch will swallow me up. Piper knows my mind just relived what happened before that.

She does not push, adding, "... and he was an adult. An adult who managed to fool and manipulate many adults. He would have continued to if you hadn't stopped him." She pauses as if she is deciding what to say next. "I haven't focused on this, because you might not be ready to hear me say it, but *you* stopped him. Look at me. Do you realize how little nine-year-olds are? We need to find a way for you to accept what a fucking badass that makes you."

"Thank you for saying that." This response, which has become a touchstone between us, brings me fully back to the room. "There was a time—after I had done a lot of work in college—that I could accept what you just said a little bit. I switched from saying I was a victim to calling myself a survivor."

"Good! That also gives us the chance to consider something else. These memories and flashbacks are playing out in your brain as if you are back in those rooms with Mr. Jay. However, your thoughts and the considerations that follow them are an adult-level analysis. They cause you to treat the little girl you were in those memories as the adult you are now. That leads you to hold her to a level of accountability that's entirely unfair. Those experiences happened to a very different, entirely innocent little girl."

"That's a good insight and worth considering further." It might be why I still don't want to look for pictures of her. "Still, it boggles my mind that I could live my life for so long... I mean from graduate school until Breakdown Saturday, I honestly believed I'd done what's necessary to live my life free from all this. Here I am, back at square one."

"It's not fair, but capital-T Trauma does that to us."

"I guess, too, my therapists mostly focused on the abuse itself. Right now, what he did once he put me on the bed? It seems less relevant than what he did to get me there."

"We don't always know what is more or less relevant, especially in response to different triggers or at different times. That your previous work focused more on the abuse may be one reason we can consider more subtle things. Processing the past is not linear. When we need to revisit this, we will." Gawd, I hope we don't have to any time soon. "Before you go, let's talk about ways to take care of yourself when intense memories surface."

"The Chili Peppers take care good care of me." I manage the smallest fraction of a smile. When the notion of relying on others comes up, my frame tightens. I don the mask of self-reliance employed by women everywhere. I swear to god, they must have handed them out in the girl's locker room in junior high. "Chili is a super good snuggle-pup." (As I write this, she's repositioned her head under my desk so that it's lying on my foot. Surely, she can sense the tension coursing through my body and wants to make it go away. We don't deserve dogs.)

"Can we name some people to reach out to?"

"My sister, Sam. I told her what's going on."

"Good. I care about you too, Stacey, please know you can text me."

"Thank you… I know that… I do. I want to respect you as a professional. That makes me more rigid about boundaries." Even before I finish saying it, I wonder if she buys that. Probably not. She knows people like me would rather drown in our own tears than inconvenience someone by asking for a tissue.

CHAPTER 13

Sausage, Mushroom, and Artichoke

On Fridays, I deliver one pepperoni and onion with extra sauce plus one sausage, mushroom, and artichoke to Sam's house. Her husband takes his slices of pepperoni to his mancave while Sam and I hunker down in the living room. If we can't find a new show to binge, we spend the evening with the characters Sam refers to as "the girls," reminiscing about early aughts fashion via old *Sex and the City* episodes. Sam has played the role of "Carrie Bradshaw" in every friend group. It's a good way to spend time together when our middle-aged bodies are too tired for much else.

Sam never fails to ask how my week was as we surf streaming services. She accepts whatever I offer up, whether it's a rant or a humorous update on the latest way I tormented students with an education that refuses to succumb to the "memorize and regurgitate" paradigm. Sometimes it's tears or—like tonight—complete silence accompanied by a defeated look that says, don't push for details.

"Do you want another slice of pizza, sister?" I cannot recall when we began calling each other sister. Her tone has a hint of concern, but she holds back from probing. She offers me the same patience she shows her geriatric physical therapy clients. As with them, she celebrates the inch or two of progress I make as though it deserves a victory lap. My sister is human champagne.

"No thanks, sister, I ate lunch late."

"Oh, hey, I found some pictures from up at the lake the other night." Sam has such a knack for knowing how to distract us from the scary stuff, like the serpents slithering their way through my memory banks. She hands over a pile of snapshots. The date stamped on their backs reads July '86 in indelible dot matrix type. They are from one of a hundred camping trips on my dad's uncle's property. We had no idea how lucky we were. Their lake would make the perfect spot for a Darius Rucker video about diving off the dock with your boots still on.

Sam wants me to feel better. I want to oblige. "Oh my god, look at you—so stinky cute!

Your hair! It's so blond it's white."

"Yeah, even camping, Mom insisted on putting it in pigtails," she says with an eye roll.

"She had to. It would have morphed into dreadlocks by day two if she hadn't."

"I would have loved that."

"Remember how you used to beg her for a Mohawk?"

"Not just any Mohawk, a green Mohawk. Get your facts straight, sister." As I flip through the pile, I find one of me waterskiing. I wasn't much for photos. Every time the camera pointed at me, I absorbed my parents' disappointment in the body it would document.

"Can I take this one?"

"Sure."

Session 22

Why didn't I think this through? Is the first photo I ever show her going to be one of me in a bathing suit? Blech, look at the way my suit cuts my saddle bags and thighs into distinctly disgusting mounds of flesh. Still, I've been trying to find a way to repay Piper for the panic attack, the awkward silences, and the unending river of tears. As much as I feel like a schmuck for losing control, Piper's kindness and capability have brought us a huge leap forward in how I trust her.

Here goes nothing. "My sister, Sam, found some old pictures and I brought one." She studies it for a minute and flips it over to the back.

"How old were you in 1986?"

"Twelve, summer after sixth grade."

"It looks like you were having fun." She doesn't seem to care at all about what my thighs look like.

"It was. My dad's side of the family loves to water ski. Staying upright for an entire trip around his uncle's lake is their equivalent of a bat mitzvah."

"That sounds like as good a rite of passage as any. You made it the whole way? How big is the lake?"

"Not huge, I'd guess about 100 acres. This was our vacation spot. We camped two or three times each summer. There were usually half a dozen cousins to swim with. My mom mostly relaxed her vigilance, knowing we were surrounded by family."

"Your voice sounds different from other times we've talked about your past."

"I loved it there. The rules were pretty much suspended. My dad was with his best buds; there were plenty of kids. I wasn't a third wheel. All the activity was centered around water. We didn't have room to take our bikes with us. We never had to hike up some massive hill. Sometimes we even took a 'swim bath' while Mom cooked eggs and bacon on the camp stove and Dad made toast out of last night's hot dog buns on the fire." The smell of Ivory, "the only soap that floats," wafts through my olfactory cortex.

"It's nice to hear this," she says with an approving smile. Tell me about another time you were happy as a kid."

"I loved art class. Our teacher was named Mr. Bardo. I loved clay day. One year—I suspect third grade—I was sick that day. Every week after that I asked him if we could have another clay day. For our last art class, Mr. Bardo let us work with whatever supplies we wanted because, 'If Hettes didn't get a chance to work with clay, she might not come back to school next year.' Everyone erupted in cheers."

"What feelings do these memories bring up?"

"I liked that I instigated something which turned out to be good for everyone. I also liked the raccoon I made. His body was blue modeling clay. For the black around his eyes and tail, I used pipe cleaners." Piper smiles, contentedly this time. How rare is it for her clients' sessions to focus on happy memories? I go on to say, "When I interviewed for my job, I learned that we could propose classes outside our discipline for our short winter term. Nearly everyone I spoke with brought up how great Winter Term was. At the final dinner, someone asked what I would propose for a class. The first thing that popped in my head came out of my mouth, 'I've always wanted to learn to use a pottery wheel.'"

"How'd they take someone interviewing for a science position offering that answer?"

"The table lit up. They talked about how few studio art offerings we had. One professor, who was on the board of the community science center, said there was a pottery studio in the adjacent art school that we might rent. I responded that my college sculpture course was essential to my education—that it taught me there are different ways of knowing. Also, that it was okay to struggle and grow via subjects that don't come easy."

"What a terrific answer."

"I suspect it's why I got the job. I also think the conversation showed me that this faculty was the real deal in terms of a liberal arts ethos and growth mindset." Pausing lets this appreciation sink deeper. "I'm glad we are talking about this."

"Me too. Thanks for bringing the picture."

"Sorry it took me so long."

"That's okay. Remember, my homework is not the same as what you give your students. Some assignments will be more effective if you wait until you are ready. What do you think your art teacher would say if he knew you teach a pottery class?"

"I found Mr. Bardo on Facebook a while back and sent him a picture of one of my vases."

"Did he write back?"

"Yeah, I think it made him happy. Retired elementary art teachers probably don't hear from many students. It was fun to see the comments from his friends, other teachers, and a former student whose kids recently found a coil pot she made in his class when she was their age."

"Aww, that's awesome. I want to see it." Remembering this leaves me curious too. I scroll through my feed to find it.

"Should I read you what I wrote first?" Had I remembered what I said, I would not have suggested this.

"Sure, go for it."

> *Mr. Bardo, You were my art teacher in elementary and middle school. One year, second or third grade, I was sick on clay day. I was devastated! It was my favorite art day. I asked you (probably) every class after that if we could work with clay that day. At the end of the year, you told us we could all choose what we wanted to do because if you didn't let Stacey work with clay at some point she might not come back to school next year. Fast forward too many years to count. I teach biology and neuroscience at*

a small liberal arts college. We have a winter term where professors are encouraged to offer experiential classes outside their discipline. This finally gave me the privilege to devote time to learning to wheel-throw by working with a local artist to offer a pottery course! When I tell the students the story of my interest in clay, I start with missing clay day in your class. I had a hand in establishing our first on-campus ceramics studio shared by our new Studio Art program, Winter Term courses, and a student pottery club. Art has enriched my life in immeasurable ways! Thanks for helping me discover my passion for clay. Here is my best piece from my summer studio-cation. You can see some photos of other pieces on my page.

I stop abruptly before I get to the part about establishing our campus studio. As I finish, I note the date on the post. This was eleven months before the Friday meeting with Dean Grant. It feels like I am reading something from before. Before my life fell apart.

"Where did you go?"

"Just realizing how much things have changed."

"Say more."

"You know how people talk about pre-September 11th, 2001, and post-September 11th?"

"Yeah."

"Dr. Hettes used to know how to be grateful for gifts and opportunities—like the privilege to learn alongside her students—but also, how to acknowledge when and where she had a hand in making a difference."

"And," Piper interjects, "hearing about what happened in art class, little Stacey did, too. What's it like to think about making a difference now?"

"That's a lot harder."

"Uh-huh, standing up to Vic left you feeling like you got your ass kicked. Dean Grant kicked you even harder when you were down. But I am glad you said it's harder—not impossible. It tells me there is optimism in there somewhere. You are beginning to realize you will find your feet again." The mashup of happiness, sadness, gratitude, and hope leaves me voiceless. Piper knows to give this unexpected lesson some time to seep its way through my defenses.

After a minute I say, "Shall I read you his response?" She smiles hesitantly. I think she'd rather stick with this turn in our conversation. I also think she realizes today's session needs to be more about giving me some breathing room than gaining three more yards of progress.

> *Thank you for the kind words and I feel proud to have been a positive influence on your life. Art, in its many forms, can reveal the power that we can acquire through the engagement and understanding of the stories behind art. And I'm grateful and humbled to have been a part of yours. The power comes from you taking the risk to create the art that inspires you and makes you feel GOOD. I hope this makes sense and you continue to throw on the wheel! BTW that's a sweet pot you created! Warm Regards.*

My voice cracks as I read *"The power comes from you taking a risk."* My eyes cannot look up.

"What's happening?"

"We've got a lot more risks to take, don't we?"

"Uh-huh, but that's okay. I am here. I won't let you take any risks I don't think you are ready for."

"What about the ones I don't think I'm ready for?" Piper smiles wide and blushes a little at my calling her bluff.

"Yeah, maybe, every once in a while, I'll nudge you toward them. It's almost time to go."

"Today was helpful." It is good to remember how many good things there were... there are in my life, like the texture of cool, slippery clay as it becomes something useful. "I want to say something else."

"Go ahead."

"I feel safe with you."

CHAPTER 14

Grieving What They Did Not Know

Session 28

The empty waiting room relieves me. There is no energy for holding myself together in the presence of another client. No energy to send soothing vibes across the waiting room saying, I see your pain, or whatever brought you here. Do not worry, I will not remember your face. You and your secrets are safe. My brain is woeful. Reliving memories over the last few weeks has made way for mourning.

I sit, enveloped in this inky scent as it gradually associates itself with a weekly dose of attention. Piper has extracted enough bricks from my barricades to allow her care to find its way in. Her hands must be calloused from chipping away at them. I should buy her some hand cream. I do wish to release myself from this fortress, but not enough to risk discovering that the world outside remains unsafe. In an instant, Dean Grant's razor-sharp sentence—evoking my "authentic voice"—gutted my entire sense of security. That Friday afternoon meeting seems like a lifetime ago and yesterday all at the same time.

As if flipping the channel on a television, my brain pops over to the adage "no use crying over spilt milk," along with an image of a milk jug shattering to the floor. It's the perfect visual for life since Breakdown Saturday. This fragile, brittle being fell hard, fracturing into a sticky pile of person shards. Do I have it in me to gather the pieces and patch them together? Not yet—maybe one day. Right now, I'm spilt milk. Just a person puddle soaking into the floorboards.

As I stand, I consider what I would say if Piper asked me what I was thinking. How would I explain that mental image?

"How are you?" she asks.

"Pretty low... sorry to show up with this mess again today." I have no energy to beat around the bush making small talk.

"Stacey, it's not your job to entertain me or to make this enjoyable."

My mind, which overflowed with words a minute ago, has tapped out. Piper invites my sorrow into the room. It rolls out like a low fog over the throw rug as my brain conjures a vision of exhausted soldiers in foxholes.

Piper does not push the sorrow back. Instead, she eases her way into its heaviness. "It makes sense to feel sad. We've been processing a lot of hard stuff."

"It's more like grief than regular sadness."

"Hmm, we grieve what we've lost. Tell me what you've lost."

"I think I lost myself." She takes this in and holds it for a beat.

"Tell me more." Tears once again spill over my lids and down my cheeks. Will this well ever level off?

"When I was working with my college counselor, Dr. Fedora, I had a hard time facing the fact that I will never know how I could have turned out if Mr. Jay had never happened. College is a space where many of us are privileged to figure out who we will become. Lots of the possible paths were washed out by the deluge of sludge that Mr. Jay rained down upon my life." My eyes look to her for help.

"You can do this, keep going."

"Whether or not I manage to accept things as they are, now even Dr. Hettes gets included in this narrative of myself as victimized... re-victimized." Words this heavy take time to make their way out of your mouth. This conversation feels like it is happening underwater. "I have almost no memories of who I was before Mr. Jay started doing what he did."

"Can you tell me your earliest memory?"

After a minute, I offer, "I have two. I don't know which came first."

"Let's hear them both."

"I'm in my pajamas standing on the toilet lid's fuzzy purple cover, which I did to reach the sink. Daddy's fashioning a coat hanger into a long wire as Carrie watches beside him. He fishes the hooked end through the drain and pulls out toothbrush after toothbrush. One was bright pink. One was light blue."

Piper does a spit-take. "What? How did that happen?"

"I think I dropped them down there."

"Are you serious? Why?" I can tell, as a parent, her loyalties have shifted to my dad.

"Maybe I was curious about where the water went, how deep the hole in the sink was?"

"That is hilarious!" she says, which opens a space for me to grab a tissue. "So even then, you were developing your experimental skills. How old do you think you were?"

"I'm not sure, but I couldn't see above the counter if I didn't stand on the toilet lid. In the other memory, I am in the same bathroom. I have on big girl panties. I must have had an accident. Mom and Carrie are scolding me. One of them mockingly says to the other, 'Uh-oh, looks like we're going to have to get the diapers back out.' With all the righteous indignation of a toddler, I tell them to stop it! I don't need diapers. I'm not a bayyy beee."

"Wow, most people do not have memories of toilet training." I try to continue but hesitate.

"It is okay, Stacey. It's okay to say what you're thinking."

"I feel like... like if I had been older when things started with Mr. Jay... if I had been older, at least, I might know who I genuinely am. I do not mean to downplay how hard anyone else has it. I don't mean to act like I had it worse than others. Lots of people have been through ten times worse. I can only imagine how hard it is for abused men, trans, and nonbinary people."

"I'm going to interrupt you for a second, but I want you to stay with this. I do not want my lack of response to become a validation of what you said. Yes, everyone's experience is different. That does not mean yours, including the age you were, was not horrible."

"Thank you for saying that."

"I want to be sure you know I mean it." She stops short of asking me to look up. There is no lever steady enough to balance the current weight of my head.

"What do you think I could be if I weren't damaged goods?" I've asked this question many times in many contexts. No one ever offers an answer. Which is good, I guess. Most of the time, I can't find the courage to entertain the possibilities myself. I might have made time for more art classes. Any classes where an 'A' was not a foregone conclusion. Other times, I suspect I might have tried harder to put myself back out there after Bobby inadvertently broke my heart in order to finally honor his own.

"Stacey, you may have trouble accepting this answer, but I have to say this first. I wish you could see yourself as I see you. Even if you could see one small piece of all that you are, I wish you could see your courage. Second, I do not in any way see you as damaged goods. What matters more though is how you see yourself. Tell me what about you feels damaged."

"So much. I am so broken." The clutches of serpents that hatched in the crevices of my soul with each invasion of my little-girl body rejoice in my suffering. "I'll never know if I might have been happy...

if it might have felt safe to get close to people...

if I would not have to expend this much energy protecting myself...

if I could just not loathe myself." Self-protective mode takes over. My neural circuits are close to shorting out. This surge of despair holds the potential to fry my motherboard. To add insult to injury, my brain takes me back to the afternoon when Mr. Jay took me down by the pond behind Gramma and Grampa's house. I can sense how loudly the decision-making part of my frontal lobe was screaming at the survival mode regions of my limbic system that day—willing it to fight. At the very least, I should take flight. My tiny, overwhelmed amygdala, like my tiny overwhelmed body, was stuck somewhere between freeze and fawn.

***

Mr. Jay's voice comes from behind my ear. *"I wish those fishermen would go away." His aftershave smells fresh. Was this after church? His mustache tickles the back of my neck as a hand the anglers cannot see roams over the softness of my little-girl skin. At least he can't reach down there. His hand can't fit down the front of my shorts with me in the bucket of his crisscrossed legs. My mind sends waves of determination over the water, willing the fishermen to stay right where they are.*

I have no memory of how it ended this time, how we even got here, how we rejoined the picnic. How the hell does he do this? Where is everyone? Is this the same weekend as the car trip when I picked the flowers or a different one? Was this caressing a kind of foreplay for what he hoped would follow or afterglow from getting off already? God dammit! How the fuck was it that no one put two and two together? Both Stacey and Mr. Jay are missing from whatever is happening! Maybe he asked me if I wanted to go skip rocks. No one would have suspected anything if they heard him ask me that. What a caring, Christian mentor.

***

Back in Piper's office, slow tears transform into quiet sobs. Without words, Piper somehow encourages them to come. "Can you tell me where you went?" I don't like it that Piper's progressed to asking this after I sit through a flashback. Isn't it enough that I remember it? Why should I have to say it out loud? It's doubtful the room holds enough oxygen to fuel my jaw muscles' recount of this memory.

When I get to the part about wondering where everyone is, whatever levee retains this reservoir of grief gives way, like when a terrified baby finally spots her momma and wails.

The force rising inside me could shatter glass. As with an inconsolable infant, Piper has no recourse but to let this work its way out. Most everyone would have told me to stop, to calm down, don't cry. Piper says none of that. She knows there is no stopping the mourning of the loss of yourself when it breaks through the last of your defenses.

"Why didn't someone help me? Why didn't anyone ask where I was? No one was taking care of me." Piper appears to scan her memory banks for resources. As this wave of grief crests, I breathe again. My body is a wrung-out dishrag.

"Stacey, I do not have an answer. I wish I did. For some clients, their stories let me respond, yes, the adults in your life were not present; they were irresponsible; they were not caring enough to protect you. I wanted you to hear me say that first. What I plan to say next is in no way meant to invalidate that you felt so unprotected. Because you were not being protected from Mr. Jay. But Stacey, everything you've told me suggests that your parents had no idea what was happening. Their reaction, once you disclosed, shows they would have done anything to stop it."

I sit with these words, knowing similar ones have come from my own mouth many times. My adult brain and adult heart know them to be true. They are the reason I never risked having a child. Even when I was open to relationships, I made it clear I did not want kids. I could not take responsibility for bringing life into a world where this could happen to my child.

"I want to believe you. These questions never go away."

"They are valid questions. What we can consider is the evidence that we have now. While the abuse was happening, you did not have the knowledge of how your parents might react if they knew. We need to reconcile an understanding of their actions back then with the way they behaved after you disclosed."

"Okay. It's hard. That time by Gramma's pond is such an awful, awful memory. So is what happened after I told my parents. Both confused me. I completely misread their attempts to help as blaming me and shaming me for fucking everything up."

"Stacey, you just said a really important word. Do you know what it was?" There is no bandwidth available for guessing games today.

"No."

"That you misread your parents' attempts to help. This may be the first time you have said—without pre-analyzing your response to give the correct answer—that you misread the intent of your parents' behaviors after you disclosed."

"Uh-huh." I could not care less right now about psychoanalyzing this pain as it rots away the core of my being.

"I know these emotions feel overwhelming, but you are making progress. Your thinking brain is stepping aside to make room for them to surface."

"Okay, I guess, but I don't have the energy to go any deeper. Maybe another day—not today."

"Thank you for telling me that you aren't up for something this difficult. That's also a sign you are taking care of yourself a little more and trying to please me a little less."

"Maybe a little." What I do not say is that I don't have a choice. I am barely managing to stay upright. Sinking into these smushy couch cushions, letting them envelop me, approximates the hug I crave that I will not ask for.

"I also want to say that it was—that it is—okay to feel let down by all the adults at the picnic that day. You should. You were let down—but not intentionally. Children need to believe their caregivers can and will watch out for them. It is the entire basis of their sense of safety. From what you've told me, in other realms, you experienced parenting that, at least from your mother, could be described as overprotective."

"You can say that again. She watched us like a hawk around people she did not know. She stopped every attempt I made to take any sort of risk. Carrie did take dangerous risks. Mom was forced to rein her in. For me, because I feared, well, everything, her protection became an intrusion. I didn't do stupid-dangerous stuff like jump off a boulder into three feet of water."

"Give me an example. How did your mom hold you back?"

"Any time I made a new friend at school and got invited to their house, she had to know everything about them, their parents, siblings, etc. She wasn't that way with church friends."

"Did she know the parents from church?"

"She thought she did."

"How did that make you feel?"

"Confused."

"Yeah." Piper gives me room to sit with this for a bit. How does this woman, so removed from the time and space that causes this much pain, understand it better than anyone I've ever met?

"No one's made that connection before, thank you. I do think both my parents were protective in their own ways. My mother avoided all the dangers she could see or anticipate. My dad's protection was more about security than danger. He worked hard as a provider but also to plan to provide for us long-term. His daughters needed to be able to take care of our adult selves."

"That is admirable, how did he demonstrate that?"

"He made sure we understood our education was a top priority. But, more than writing the checks, he respects my mom's nursing abilities and degree. He never failed to mention that if something happened to him, we would be okay. Mom could support us. Both my mom and dad grew up with enough, but nothing extra. They relished providing some extras, vacations, summer camps."

"That helps me to understand that for your dad, care and love manifested via providing. We're out of time. We can work on this again next week."

What I do not realize is that we are at the beginning of work that will take months of cyclical processing—two steps forward, two steps back, and two steps forward again. Work that Mr. Jay's serpents will erase any retention of from one week to the next.

"Between now and then, think about how your parents responded when you told them as a fifth grader. With that in mind, imagine how they would have responded if they'd had even the slightest suspicion about Mr. Jay."

As I leave, I consider the vast majority of women. How different will their evenings be from mine? After today, mine will consist of nothing but cuddling with the Chili Peppers. What would the aftermath of such a session do to their schedules? Picking up the kids, chatting with other parents at soccer, as though they have not just experienced the emotional equivalent of excising a tumor the size of a baseball from their abdomen. All I have to manage is to walk out and drive home. Dinner will be the half-eaten tub of rice pudding in my fridge.

What did we eat for dinner the night after I told my mother? Let alone dinner, what about breakfast the next morning? We were not a house that began our day with Pop-Tarts or cereal. Pancakes or scrambled eggs were more typical. Had she felt this drained... even worse?

If we treated psychotherapy the way we treat other forms of healthcare, an overnight hospital stay would follow such sessions. Nurses would care for our wounds and incisions. They would attach us to monitors assuring our hearts tolerate the trauma of the extraction. Chest X-rays would determine if pneumonia is likely to settle into our overtaxed lungs. Protocols would mandate that someone volunteers to drive us home. Instead, we expect mothers who unearthed more dark humors from their depths than contained in one thousand boils to return immediately to holding themselves, their families, and our nation together. Even as the anemia of these weekly bloodlettings drains the color from their cheeks, they leave the building wondering—what's next?

CHAPTER 15

Mom

It takes a few days to recover. I throw myself into work, catching up on grading, and clearing a backlog of emails. After that, I focus on recovering any stored away details from the days after I told my mom. I don't have any sense of what to search for. I went to school. Yet, I have no memory of being there, only coming home. In fifth grade, I arrived home well before Carrie. Mom was likely astute enough to put three-ish-year-old Sam down for a nap. I was a tuned-in kid. I read her mood each day much the same way a politician reads a crowd.

A lot was going on back then. Mom was serving as the de facto home health nurse for her aunt with terminal cancer. Even then, I knew it took a heavy toll. Would she welcome me home today or be caught up in how sick Aunt Laura was? Energized from helping her feel a little better or demoralized because no one, not even my mother, could nurse away chemo? Was she busy with housework or expecting a detailed report of my day?

There was an entirely different atmosphere in our house when one of us was sick. My mother's whole being exuded a nurse's care and compassion in the face of illness. However, neither she nor I had a way to equate mental anguish with physical ailment. Emotional suffering is private. Crying and distress were regular states for me, but not for Carrie. Mom often said that she didn't know how to handle me as a tiny kid because I cried whenever I needed scolding. Carrie went right on doing whatever she wanted with defiant determination. Carrie and Mom have a lot in common, which reinforced my belief that my feelings were wrong. According to them, emotions were conditions one must master and contain. I came to expect responses like, "You need to learn to control your emotions; get a hold of yourself; stop crying; you aren't hurt; don't be such a baby; don't be so sensitive." I had no idea what to expect once the reason behind my inexplicable tears was out in the open.

Yes, it is an exaggeration to say I was a modern-era empath raised by Roman-era stoics, but most days it felt that way. On a volume dial for feelings, my family hovered around three to five whereas my insides were set somewhere from seven to nine. This mismatch convinced me that my childish emotions were not acceptable. I did my best to stuff them down with the only brain-altering substances available in our tee-totaling household, food and candy. I learned that feeling overstuffed was better than feeling anything else. Even my parents' projected shame over their chubby daughter was no match for Mom's chocolate chip cookies, Gramma's angel food cake, or the Jell-O pudding pops I snuck out of the garage freezer. Gratefully, there was no alcohol, no unsecured medicine cabinet, no razor blades. Otherwise, Dr. Hettes would not have found her way into the world.

On that particular afternoon, I remember arriving home from school and sensing there was no need to engage my defenses. There would be none of the usual multi-tasking once I was available to keep Sam occupied. She was waiting for *me*. Her mom genes pumped out the molecular equivalents of love and protection as she set aside whatever she was going through to focus on me. Today, I can recognize the terror and confusion she sequestered to do so. There was no telling how much of this mud her spongy girl had absorbed.

She must've spent the day learning about this new ailment—the sexually abused child. She'd contacted a victim's resource center from two cities away that recently began running a low-budget TV commercial. There was a tow-headed girl in a frilly dress as well as a creepy man and a phone number. The first time I saw it, it stopped me in my tracks. Something evil was haunting our television.

As we settled on our couch with the hideous 1970s orange and green floral pattern, she told me about her phone call with a lady named Paula. Mom spoke in the tone she reserved for other kids—like her Sunday school class with whom she interacted more gently. It felt off and foreign, but also kind. She told me that she explained to the lady what I'd told her. Paula said that this happened to *a lot* of kids, and it is never ever the kid's fault. The lady asked her how it ended. There was something like pride in her voice when Mom told me that she told Paula I ended it—I told him no. Moreso, Mom's next report held something that went beyond pride. Paula said that since I stood up to him, even without any adults knowing, I must be a very strong girl.

I would not have known to name the power behind Mom's voice hope at the time, but that is what it was. Hope to absorb some of the overwhelming guilt and shame I later understood she felt. I took full ownership of that guilt and shame that I will spend many more sessions attempting to reconcile. Guilt and shame, which, even in that moment, belonged squarely on one man's shoulders. Yet, that was the day Mom and I began our unconscious battle to carry the burden of his actions for each other.

In that moment, all I felt was confusion and discomfort. As a fifth grader, my heart craved attention. At the same time, my brain was preparing for independence. I found myself keeping my parents at arm's length when all the while, I was weeping for them to hold me and keep me safe from the enormity of what was happening. The normal confusion that makes kids that age relate to books like Judy Blume's *Tales of a Fourth Grade Nothing* multiplied with every mention of Mr. Jay. My fearful disposition did not help. I was the one who was afraid of the roller coasters; my sisters were the ones stretching their necks to make the height limits.

For example, our neighbor's son had a yellow van with small round windows high on the side panels. I hated that van. Surely the only purpose for such a vehicle was to kidnap little girls tasked with weeding the flowerbeds along the front fence. Whenever I saw it coming, I ran back to our entry door. My mother observed this peculiar behavior one day and questioned what I was doing with an accusatory tone. My behavior, if nothing else, made me embarrassingly odd. More likely, it was further evidence of my laziness. Lazy was and is the most despised character trait among both Hetteses and Van Sickles. To avoid accusations, I admitted that I was afraid of being kidnapped. My distress convinced her I was serious but left her dumbfounded. How could a child of this woman—this woman who would not let a mosquito bite her daughters—think that she would ever allow someone to kidnap me? Remember, she had no idea about Mr. Jay at the time.

This revelation led to a serious but reassuring conversation where I asked what she would do if kidnappers took us. I felt more loved and valued by her answer than at any time in my life before or since. She said she would do whatever it took to find us. She would never stop looking. I must have asked her if she would pay a ransom. She told me that she would pay all the dollars we had to get me back. She and Daddy would even sell our house. I believed her. The magic of that moment wrapped in her undivided attention and concern sent every one of Mr. Jay's serpents into hibernation.

If she'd protected me from this unsubstantiated fear of a van, how much more would she want to protect me from Mr. Jay? From the real-life villain who kidnapped my self-worth?

"God fucking dammit, I fucking hate him," I scream into my empty living room as Chili hops up beside me and buries her head in my armpit.

CHAPTER 16

Asking for It

Session 29

Piper does not even wait until we reach her office to ask, "How are you?"

"Better. Last week was a doozy."

"Yeah, wanna talk about what it brought up?"

"A lot. It brought up a lot. But most importantly, there is no way on Earth my parents would have let him touch me for even ten seconds. Thinking back over some of the things my mom said after I told her, I can see how much, how often, she searched her memories for any clues she missed."

"How about you? What do you think you might've misread in their reactions?"

"There were maybe some things Mom tried to explain or talk about that I took as suggestions that I was to blame for being such an easy target."

"Do you think you recreate that dynamic today when you blame yourself for what happened back then?" Well yes, Piper Manna, great insight. How likely is it that Dr. Hettes will ever permit Stacey to admit that?

"There was one thing she told me that I couldn't twist into being my fault. How easy it was to see Mr. Jay's behavior as kindness. That he would say things that sounded benevolent like: Why don't you ladies go shopping and out for lunch? Compared to my dad, who would not have thought to make such an offer if she didn't ask, it must've seemed thoughtful. There was another time when Mr. Jay brought me a puzzle and held me on his lap as we put it together. She remembered thinking it was odd that he brought a gift for me and not something for Carrie too."

"There is a big difference between thinking something is odd and suspecting someone of molesting your child."

"I know that," I respond a little too defensively. "I have no memory of the puzzle. I'm guessing I was super little. Mom said something else I still struggle with." My eyes hit the floor, searching for a gray spot in the carpet. The memories with the most shame have the hardest time finding their way from my brain to my mouth.

"She said I was super affectionate. I liked to crawl onto people's laps." To say this aloud, for me, feels like admitting I spent my preschool years on the streets hustling for ten dollar blowjobs.

"Stacey, I am not connecting what you just said to the shame you feel."

Silence.

"What if I was asking for it?" hurls out of my mouth. I can predict what she will say. Half a dozen therapists have said something similar. Right on cue:

"Asking for what? To be molested?" Unlike other therapists, Piper's tone reveals how invalid this fear is without invalidating my right to be fearful.

"I know. I know it makes no sense to think that Mom was implying it was my fault. But I was in middle school and her favorite way to put down my friends was to call them boy crazy."

Since this secret is out, I decide to drop the big one. I introduce Piper to the viper whose fangs may never let go of my soul. "I still do think I asked for this." It's the deepest wound I carry. I have named it again and again in these rooms. Like a cancer, it keeps growing back. It is the faucet from which the words, "I'm bad, I'm bad, I'm bad," flow out of my mouth.

Piper's words are measured and thoughtful. "First, I am sorry you've carried such thoughts for so long. It is not fair that anyone ever has to feel this way. It is hard to comprehend, but it is such a common experience among victims, with child sexual abuse especially. They take on the responsibility for the abuse. It is why therapists and social workers spend their initial contact reiterating that it is never, ever, ever the victim's fault." When I do not respond, she says, "Stacey, I need to see your eyes. I need to know you are okay."

I look up for as long as I can hold it. I understand shelter dogs. The ones whose videos show up all over social media. The ones who sit facing the corner of their cage blocking out the world. Please, God, let me feel as loved as a newly adopted pound puppy someday. Piper continues, "I do not want this in any way to discount what you are describing, but I need to respond to your interpretation of what your mother said. Stacey, this does not match anything else you have told me about her or how she responded to your disclosure. HOWEVER, and this is the most important thing, if... IF she were saying that, and I am 100 percent *not* saying she was. It would. not. be. your. fault."

How can I get through to her? "It feels like it is. Like this falls into the category of saying I am too sensitive and that is why I let all this affect me. If I were tougher, like my sisters. If I had not been so affectionate and clingy, maybe this would not have happened. I made it easy for him to come after me. I made it easy for other adults to not see what was happening."

She lets us sit for a few beats, which gives my brain a chance to regroup. "It sounds less realistic when I say it out loud than when this tape plays on repeat in my head." That's all the ground I'm able to concede on this particular point, on this particular day. Somewhere, in the back of my mind, it registers that a horrible moment of victim blaming catalyzed my return to therapy. No wonder these wounds ooze blood and puss all over again.

"Can you humor me with a little exercise? Can you imagine, even if you do not believe it's true, any other reason she may have told you that?"

Apparently, Stacey, the A-student, is out sick today. "I can imagine that I might be able to at some point. It's not that I don't want to try. I hear how crazy this sounds, but my soul is convinced." My brain is afloat in shame and self-loathing. What time is it? Will this session never end?

"And that is okay, but we will revisit this. Can we try one more thing?" I nod, knowing she's in the mood to push on regardless. "What if you watched a little girl, three or four years old, approach an adult with a book and crawl in his lap? What would you think she wanted?"

"I'd think she wanted him to read her a story."

"Right, what about a puzzle?"

"I'd think she couldn't put it together by herself and was looking for help."

"Exactly. Why would you think that you, Stacey, engaging in the same behavior, especially when Mr. Jay brought the damn puzzle with him, means you were asking to be molested?"

"I don't know. I don't know. I don't know!" I force myself to stay seated. To let this truth sink in. If I were wearing a lab coat and safety goggles or at a podium participating in an academic debate, Piper's words or any other words would be met by an entirely different person. On Breakdown Saturday, the one sitting on her couch reverted to the child she never wanted to be in the first place. "I am trying, Piper," I say, desperate for her to know I need her to cut me some slack.

"There's never been a time I thought you weren't." She pauses and I manage to look up for a full second. I hope my eyes say the thank you my jaw is too heavy to express. All I want to do is curl under Softee blanket and have my mom tell me she loves me so much she would sell our house to get me back.

CHAPTER 17

How I Ruined Everything

Session 33

Where is this agitation coming from? Hand mixers are stirring the contents of my stomach and brain. My leg muscles randomly twitch. Why the fuck am I even here? If this body could tolerate another thirty pounds, I would just eat my way through this. I'd stuff it away like the boxes hauled from California and stacked in the attic with the packing tape intact. The thing is, my body cannot absorb anything more, even if I'm convinced it deserves it. This is killing me, slowly perhaps, but I know I will die younger than I would otherwise. Some days that frightens me; other days it cannot happen fast enough.

I promised my mother at seventeen that I would not take my life. I had to. She found the journal, which held thoughts similar to the ones that presently fly about my skull. I'd unleashed so much tension—so much sorrow in our shared family space—I silenced my voice and retreated to my room to write. My sister, Sam, recently told me she has almost no memories of me during those years. "You had a pair of polka dot Keds and short hair. That's it."

***

When Piper appears, I smile resignedly. She deserves a warning that an invisible swarm of yellow jackets circles my head. As I settle in, I look at her, but cannot speak. I bite the inside of my lower lip to keep the sewage, which fills me to my neck, from splashing out. She waits as if it is perfectly normal for a person's own filth to choke off their words. I'm even more sorry for her than usual realizing her patients dump such toxic waste here daily. "Can you identify where in your body you feel whatever this is?"

"My jaw."

"What's it like?"

"Pressure." My top and bottom teeth clamp like the tines of a bear trap. I deserve whatever pain this causes. I can't let this bile and sputum pollute the crisp whiteness of her decor.

"Whatever it is, will be okay. It will not frighten me or hurt me. I am here because I want to be."

"I can't."

"That's okay," she says nonchalantly. "I am here if that changes."

"I've ruined enough lives. I don't want to infect anyone else."

"Whose lives have you ruined?"

"My family."

"How?"

"By telling." Duh Piper, Geezus!

"How?"

"My parents got so upset."

"Were you the reason they were upset or was Mr. Jay?"

"No... but if I kept my fucking mouth shut..." My jaw clamps hard again before I can finish.

"What would have happened if you hadn't told?"

"Nothing," I reply. Adding a shrug borrowed from my teenage self's shoulders.

"Really?" She's no longer nonchalant. "You think y'all would have just strolled through life like nothing ever happened?"

"Yes."

"But something did happen." After an interminable pause she continues, "And that something was not your fault."

"I know that," I spit back. I am so fucking sick of people telling me it was not my fault. I know damn well... I know the truth. The truth that no one admits. I know what all the politically correct therapists, the pink-hat-wearing marchers, and #MeToo hash-taggers do not. I broke us. I broke my mother. I broke any chance of my father feeling anything toward me but pity. I was too weak. I did not have what it takes to suck it up and deal.

"Stacey, would you repeat what I said out loud?" I glare at her like a wounded animal that knows it is cornered. One who knows there is no chance for escape but is not ready to surrender.

"I can say it if you want me to." Wow, I even sound like a petulant twelve-year-old to myself.

"Can you mean it?" With that, my defenses crumble. These bones and muscles sit on the cusp of dissolution. Soon I will be a pile of globular flesh spilling off the couch and over the rug. I want to blurt out, "Pick up your feet!" I wouldn't want her to get any of me on her shoes.

"BUT IT IS MY FAULT!" My whole body turns away. I fucking hate this office. There is nowhere to hide my head. I pant from the exertion of holding that back once it's out.

"What is your fault?"

"EVERYTHING! EVERYTHING IS MY FAULT! I LET HIM TRICK ME. I LET HIM KISS ME. I LET HIM PUT HIS HAND INSIDE ME. I LET HIM..."

Rage drops to silence. I will not say aloud what I am still unsure of. Piper takes every blow, every arrow I sling. "I can't explain how this changed everything." At this particular moment, the abuse itself pales in comparison to the shame and guilt. If I could go back in time, I would let him do even worse things if I could tell myself to keep my fucking mouth shut.

"I am not sure how else parents who loved their daughter would react." She pauses. "But Stacey, you were ten or eleven."

"*SO WHAT*? I should have been able to take care of myself." She leaves a space of silence that allows enough self-loathing to clear the room until I can see her through the haze.

"If you went to a park and there were children there, what do you think the six- and seven-year-olds would be up to?" I am in no mood for this today. Ever the dutiful pupil, I answer half-heartedly.

"Playing on the playground?"

"Yeah, they're pumping on the swings and swooshing down the slide. What about the eight- and nine-year-olds?"

"Um, playing tag?"

"Tag sounds good."

"How about the ten- and eleven-year-olds?"

"I don't know, playing a game of kickball? Do kids still play kickball?"

"I'm sure they do. Anyway, that sounds about right. Do you think any of them would be acting like adults? Chatting with the mothers, or laid out on a blanket reading?" Resignation begins to displace the agitation fermenting in my stomach.

"No, but that's not the point."

"Then tell me the point."

"It was awful."

"What was awful?"

"Seeing my parents upset." Her posture shifts, as though we're finally getting somewhere.

"Yes... I imagine for a little girl, who loved her parents deeply, who was tuned in to others' emotions, who was caring and kind, it was awful to experience that confusion, that anger, that sadness along with her parents. But it does not mean she did anything wrong. It does not mean they were upset with her. If she had asked her parents the next day or the next week if they wished she had never told them, how do you think they would have responded?" This jogs my memory.

"That Saturday last fall, Breakdown Saturday, when I called my mom, I said 'I am sorry. I am sorry that I needed to call you. I am sorry I need your help.' She told me she was glad I called and that she already knew I was struggling. She wanted to help. She wants to help. She wants to know."

"Do you believe her?"

"Yes. I could hear it in her voice."

"If she wants to know, to help her independent, capable adult daughter, how much more do you think she wanted to know what was happening to her little girl?"

My agitation is spent. I have the stamina to endure sadness in the same way I have the stamina to swim for hours. Frustration? Frustration instantly consumes me, like attempting to run for even ten seconds. "Thank you for saying that. I just feel bad."

"It is okay to feel bad, to feel sad, to feel grief. But you do not deserve to feel shame."

"I do, though. I am even more ashamed that I can't manage all this because other kids' abusers were in their house. Every kid imagines monsters under the bed. What about the kids who... A REAL MONSTER CRAWLED INTO THEIR OWN BED? Mr. Jay did this to his daughter whenever he wanted!" These thoughts leave me breathless. "I was fucking lucky by comparison, which makes it even worse."

"And that's something we can work on, although I am obligated to remind you that drawing comparisons is not helpful." I want to roll my eyes, but Piper probably thinks they'll revoke her license if she fails to reiterate that. "Remind me, what prompted you to tell your parents about what Mr. Jay did to you?"

"That woman talked to our class."

"What did she tell you?"

"She told us if anyone ever did things to us like she talked about, we needed to tell someone."

"That's right. You told your mother what was going on because an adult—an adult with authority—said to. Stacey, look at me. You were a good kid. You did what adults, including Mr. Jay, told you to. When he escalated, you knew it felt wrong. You found the courage to stop it. When you told your parents, did you anticipate that it would hurt them?"

"I thought I was in trouble."

"Exactly, everything you did was what we'd expect from a child growing up the way you did." My eyes fixate on the bit of gray in the mostly white rug. This shame, locked away for decades, is blending with a new source—the shame of needing something so obvious explained by someone who was not even there. "Why is it that you, as an eleven-year-old, should've carried this burden all by yourself?" I do not answer with words. I hope my body language conveys that I have conceded the debate. It is a step. Time will prove that I have not hung up the lash.

"Thanks, Piper."

"There is one more thing I want you to consider, especially since we know you were not the only one Mr. Jay was doing this to."

"Fifty," slips out.

"What?"

"Fifty, Mom eventually told me that Mr. Jay confessed it was about fifty girls." This must be the first time I've revealed the number. Piper cannot hide her shock or disgust.

"That is appalling."

"Yep."

"It also makes what I am about to say more important. Disclosing to your parents, for sure, *for sure*, protected other girls and likely saved lives. You telling them was the catalyst for the actions they took to be sure he could not harm anyone else."

Those words end our session. They provide me six minutes and twelve seconds of relief before the gremlins who squat in the folds of my brain twist them right back around: *See that, Stacey? If you were brave enough to stand up and tell sooner, fewer little girls would have been hurt.*

CHAPTER 18

A Big Angry Secret

Sessions 34, 35, 36, 37, & 38
"Stacey, look at me please." She waits the eternity it takes to lift my eyes. "It is okay to name these feelings." White-hot tears of rage threaten to flood the room.

***

Dear Piper,
Have you noticed? I kinda suck at anger. There are many things I never learned as a kid, how to tap dance or master a cartwheel. I definitely never learned how to deal with anger, the worst of all emotions—mine or my parents'. I honestly don't remember being angry after I told them about Mr. Jay, only confused and afraid. I did learn, however, that anger is dangerous. After Mom explained to Dad about the scene he walked in on the night I told her, he desperately wanted to shoot Mr. Jay. There is still a whole different kind of fear in her voice when she talks about that.
For me, anger came later, when we met with Jane, the lawyer. She introduced me to three words: statute of limitations. There'd been a lengthy span between my disclosure to my parents and my maturing toward an interest in and understanding of justice and injustice. Jane illuminated what male legislators decided long ago. If you snooze, you lose. You lose out on any chance of standing in a courtroom and

saying, he took my life, or at least the one I hoped for, and he deserves to go to jail for that.

I wish my anger toward society and its systems ended there. It doesn't. Because that's when my ire multiplies by fifty, by fifty girls and their families. It infuriates me that we were discouraged from saying, "Enough is enough; he has to pay" while we still had the chance. To be clear, I do not blame my parents or any other victims' parents that Mr. Jay was never brought up on charges. My mother lay awake at night searching for a way to make him pay without further damaging me. The justice system of the mid-1980s was one that every person whom my parents sought advice from counseled them to keep their little girl far, far away from.

WHY WAS THAT? Why IS that? You've told me yourself that not much has changed. That you often, against your own desire for reprisal, warn women off from seeking the justice that should follow, open and shut, but rarely does. I am dumbfounded by this fact. And yet, we all know that the rules of power are simple. He who holds the power makes the rules… and prints the newspapers. That's the other still-corked source of rage. The secrecy of it all. Remember, he was a church deacon. What he did not only played out under his authority in that capacity but also beneath the smokescreen it provided. A deacon in a church that proclaimed the wages of sin—even the smallest infractions—was not just death, but an eternity on fire. Literally. That is unless the revelation of those sins might singe the church and his fellow leaders by association.

Is that how his sins were successfully concealed? Or, were they in plain sight but ignored? How? How did he do all this? FIFTY GIRLS PIPER. FIFTY! How did he keep us all silent? It's like they have a playbook. Priests, deacons, coaching staffs, dysfunctional families all seem to know how to ensure the sins of their brethren will never be found out.

That my disclosure was met with belief and at least the exploration of legal action makes it rare for the time. Which might be the source of this fumbling courage that finally compels me to write, though it wishes I would shout instead. HOW DO THESE OLIGARCHIES OF MEN MAINTAIN THE SECRET SILENCES? Yes, once in a while high profile stories carry enough weight to garner attention. For the millions of workaday women, like me, the silence surrounding our stories multiplies the burden of our shame.

When I meet women today and they share with me their efforts as young girls to reveal their abuse, they were met with a near-scripted denial. It's as if the shoulder shrugs, rejection and accusations of sluttiness twisted back at them were choreographed by the same director.

We want to be done. Done being helpless to do little more than whisper that it happened to us too. Done pardoning this nation as we avert our eyes while predators ravage our greatest assets. Done standing by as, time and again, the cycle of abuse quashes our hope for something—anything—better. What would happen if someone stood in the town square and shouted MEN STILL REACH INSIDE LITTLE KIDS. WE NEED TO OPEN OUR DAMN EYES AND DO SOMETHING!

I need a minute. Let me get Chili and Pepper their supper.

***

I wish I could be as grateful about anything as Pepper is whenever a meatball makes its way into his bowl. Piper, just because sexual predators leave behind psychic wounds rather than physical ones, these marks are not invisible. Yet scars of any kind cannot be seen or acknowledged when our neighbors' backs are turned. What will it take for us to face this reality at ground level? Where, when, how have advocates of any stripe effectively confronted society's leaders with the truths they'd rather ignore than guide us toward grappling with? We do voice some unspeakable truths, don't we? We deal with the sense of overwhelm some abominations create. Why not this one?

Is it because child victims' experiences are too much? Too much for us to face? Maybe we're not capable. Maybe we have to believe that their malleable bodies will simply grow out of it. For me, this onslaught of flashbacks has reawakened what the world looks like through little-girl eyes. These memories convert the inner surface of my eyelids to their own private theater. Maybe they're little Stacey's way of calling me out. These testaments affirm she did not grow out of it: I buried it.

As I face that fact, I find myself compelled to call for a societal-level reckoning on behalf of all who limped toward safety on still-growing limbs. But I am afraid. How will this anger not consume me? Worse, how will I cope when no one listens? What if I prove as ineffective in the defense of my tribe as I was in defending myself? These questions keep me complicit, keep my truth under seal.

I need to see more. We need to know more. We survivors of atrocities that began before we could tie our shoes need our stories to be heard. We want to start conversations of not only sympathy but also consideration. Conversations that may finally put an end to our concealment and thereby disrupt the ongoing cycles that continue to add members to our ranks.

But how? How do we face a topic that's met with stunned silence? What is the proper balance of immersion in and protection from stories like ours? For me, movies afford, by proxy, private forays into the capital-T Traumas for which I can find no words of response. Yet these scenes evoke intense stirrings of sympathy and empathy. Could they transform into action? If only I could join a gathering band of troops and commit to their efforts toward progress.

Have you noticed that film's most popular offerings fail to deliver a single portrayal of a tiny-girl body as it transforms into her private battlefield? Could such scenes ever be cast upon a silver screen? Impossible. These images would curdle our stomachs. They would do more harm than good. Triggering most of us while titillating those seeking to continue the very cycle of depravity I wish to disrupt. Agreed. But without genuine depictions, how will a critical mass ever peek through the curtains hung to shield us from little girls' nightmares? Would we have the fortitude to face it with open eyes if such a movie were greenlighted?

On occasion, films popular enough to enter the zeitgeist employ allusions to these unshowable acts. One that comes to mind is Hannah Hall's portrayal of darling little Jenny in Forrest Gump. Did anyone else notice that its director, Robert Zemeckis, offered us a hint of the world from Jenny's perspective? I felt such kinship for her suffering as her father's hips ravaged their way through the corn stalks. My spine shivered hearing his lungs bellow for her to deliver her tiny body unto him. Consider for a minute, from that same vantage, a scene where Jenny lay undefended against that bastard's pelvis in their ramshackle Alabama house.

I identify with the urge to shelter the viewer, Piper. For Christ's sake, I want nothing more than to avoid discomforting you, my therapist, with the details of each flashback. I worry each time I manage to speak Mr. Jay's acts into your office: Does your mind unwillingly cast your precious daughter into my scenes? And so, I willfully deny my memories a voice, despite your urging their release.

In my movie, the scene would place the viewer's eye between Mr. Jay's knee and belt, softening the focus on all but his hand as it grasps at the knob of the bedroom door. A haunting musical score would compete with the whirring that arises from somewhere within my temples. The lens, which halted at the doorway, would guide the viewer's focus slowly back. In the blurring distance, he'd lift the towheaded innocent, gently arranging her upon a bed of satiny peach in a *room with velvet wallpaper. You see, my movie's director also absolves viewers from entering the place where, out of sight, off-screen, this child remains, abjectly, alone. As did we, the screens fade to black as the musical scores give way to the deafening roar of silence.*

My argument is not—is not—a call for gratuitous vulgarity. Piper, you know I would never do that. What my mind conjures is that which film does best. How it places us directly within such nightmares that we might comprehend them.

Have you seen Jennifer Fox's film The Tale? *In it, she shares her story with tactful but gut-wrenching depictions of the complexity of sexual abuse and exploitation by her coach as an adolescent. Its success owes much to her expert knowledge of the art and science of filmmaking. Her skill and depth of perception respected and protected Isabelle Nélisse, the actress, who depicts Jennifer's real-life experiences. I have to ask if* The Tale's *teenage Jenny was the more tender age of* Forrest Gump's *little Jenny, would such depictions ever have been greenlighted?*

Of course, wait, that is worth shouting, OF COURSE! I would never suggest the employment of an actor young enough to approximate anything that happened to me. "It is just pretend" is fine for green-screened space monsters. We must never, NEVER chance the ordeal of dramatizing monstrosities of this caliber for any little child. Jennifer Fox proved that, with the magical technologies of today, we would not have to. Let me say again, OF COURSE, we will not engage child actors to portray such scenes. We have limits. The problem: those limits prohibit (perhaps shelter?) artists from reaching into our realities. They prevent even those who are willing from facing this particular version of the un-faceable.

And what about those who would actively ban such dramatic acknowledgment? Do you think the apologists, who throw up their hands and thereby defend the status quo, can imagine it?

What if they did not have to? What impact could it have if they, even once, experienced an Oscar-worthy portrayal of his face through the vantage of naked little-girl legs? Might then the victim blaming cease? I could not see past my girl belly to where his hand penetrated the mystery of my own body. On my worst days, I cannot evade the memory of his eyes, his lips, the corners of both as they raised with delight.

Is that it? Perhaps the vision of our faces in the act will achieve the desired effect.

What did my kindergartener's face, encircled by peach satin, project back to him? What would viewers observe as I strained for control of my eyes? Beyond my body, he demanded mastery of my eyes, ordering them opened or closed as his acts mandated.

A more important question: If violence against children is so grotesque, so heinous, that an industry that thrives on the moment-by-moment portrayal of humanity's worst sins will not—cannot—display it, what does that tell us? Why then, have our leaders not rallied all moral, legal, and medical resources to assist those left to live as refugees from childhood?

It is time to pronounce my reckoning. A reckoning for us—as citizens of a society kept blind by the juxtaposition of our pride and our shame, too proud to admit this continuing failure. Too ashamed to concede that debased, depraved guerrillas walk among us. Beyond walk. They thrive. Thrive in the sanctuary and immunity of institutions whose pride is the predators' secret weapon, whose shame is their golden ticket.

I have something to say to Mr. Jay and his board of deacons. To all the empowered men, who keep the rest of us in blinders, or muzzles, or both. Live from this day forward in full awareness of the curse of your power and your privilege, for you sit in the seat of proclamation. Pronouncing us—women, children, all forms of the other—as worthy or unworthy of respect, or even attention or concern. You define or ill-define us by your declarations or lack thereof. Such power protects your pride and conceals your shame. But you are cursed. Cursed to live with hands cramped as they clasp the mantles of your systems and institutions. Mantles on which you refuse to relax your grip. A grip that extends to the flesh of the little children in your homes, your sanctuaries, your dominion.

Live with this knowledge. Each day you erode the foundation of democracy. Each day you trample the sprouts of hope. And thus, each day it is up to us, whose legs still shake with the terror of memory, to plant hope's seeds again. I ask the powerful a final question. Who, when betrayed in ways which we cannot tolerate to portray, betrayed while saddled with the confusion and fright and curiosity of innocence, is left with the slightest chance for hope to blossom? Our lives are the price this nation pays for the illusion that you've cultivated a world for which you deserve acclaim as well as pride.

Moreover, what of women? Shall we consider our culpability in keeping this particular secret? I want to grant myself a pardon as I grieve. I too have a reckoning to face. What next after healing, Piper? I suspect deep inside there is a whisper of a notion that I will come to the other side of this. If the work we carry out is worth the weekly heartbreak to do it, will I be the same after these efforts to restore me to myself? I must hope not.

In the exceptional film Spotlight, Stanley Tucci plays Mitchell Garabedian, a real-life lawyer fighting for victims of clergy sexual abuse. In conversation with Mark Ruffalo's character, an investigative journalist, he says, "This city, these people, making the rest of us feel like we don't belong. But they're no better than us. Look at how they treat their children. Mark my words, Mr. Rezendes. If it takes a village to raise a child, it takes a village to abuse one." Piper, I want to become the global village that compassionately does the former and *fiercely fights the latter. I'd gladly trade my remaining days in the classroom if I had any idea how to engender such a world.*

Perhaps one day the courage to at least tell my story more frequently—with more honesty—will come. Like the woman who made her life's work speaking to classrooms of fifth graders, maybe I one day will say, there is something dangerous out there, more so than they taught us to believe. It is a malignant danger. It can resurface after remission. Let me tell you my story in the hope that it will never become yours.

Finally, we have no chance of birthing justice if the proclamation of our ire and frustration is not paired with equal acknowledgment of those who wage war on behalf of us all. You battle without ceasing to reclaim us. To you, who sit with our sorrow—who head into the secret darkness of the predators' dens—I require better words than thank you. Something more profound than gratitude.

Many souls have walked with mine, none farther than my own mother and father. I owe you gratitude in equal measure to our rage, in equal measure to our sorrow. To you, Piper, to all the Pipers, to all the good moms and dads, please take care of your own selves too. We need you to steadfastly resist the temptation to hide your eyes, to close off and protect your souls.

I hope there comes a day when I can read this aloud. Just now, I fear these words as much as I fear my fingers for typing them.

Still, thank you,
Stacey

Session 39

"How are you?" It amazes me how many words my mind devotes to abuse—to considering its webs of connection—self, self-image, self-acceptance, self-loathing, social interactions, society, work, work-life balance. I spend entire insomniac nights mapping integrations that would take a forest of trees and gallons of ink to put to paper. In response to Piper's question? A query that requires this ball of neurons to transition from questioning to feeling? Silence.

"It's hard to admit."

"You sent a letter this week. Wanna read it?"

"Not ready." As those syllables span the divide between us, I bite the inside of my lower lip until it bleeds, an old habit. Long ago, it took my therapist, Mary Anne, an entire session to draw out why I'd enacted a similar mutilation. When she suggested there was something I'd wished to restrain myself from saying, we uncorked a memory. It is no wonder we as a society cannot face child abuse. Survivors' own bodies thwart our efforts.

"I want you to tell me the first thought that pops in your head when I ask you this question. What are you feeling?"

I manage to pry open my mouth and allow two words to slip, "I'm pissed."

As punishment, the tears of a child caught misbehaving fall from my ducts. You know the ones, so often met with the retort, "Are you sorry for what you did, or are you sorry that you got caught?" Just because I wrote a call to reckoning does not mean I can accept either the fury or the guilt such an action unleashed. Good girls, especially good girls attempting to fix the family they broke, do not admit to anyone they are angry.

"I can see how hard it is to acknowledge that," Piper responds. "I am curious to understand why, but first, I want to say how glad I am you said so. Since the beginning, you've instantly shut down anything resembling anger, Stacey." For the first time, I recognize that she employs my name to cause me to look up. It works. I am grateful to see in her eyes the authenticity of what she says next. "I am angry too. We certainly have the right to be."

"It never felt like I did."

"Why do you think that was?" I fight tears of a different kind—tears in recognition of the betrayal of Mr. Jay's abuse—as well as the duplicity of a world, which prefers our torments and the shame they manifest remain secret. Rage-filled tears hold more heat as they make their way to your chin.

CHAPTER 19

There Is a Power in This Girl's Bones

Session 40
I grasp for determination. It's been so many weeks, so many tears. They flush out the anger that the words I forbid myself to speak cannot. At least there's that. In college, a professor born in the Soviet Union gave an address about his boyhood. During the Q&A, I asked how he dealt with anger. He looked me square in the face—I was down front as usual—shrugged and said, "Anger is not productive." I adopted his words as a reason to dismiss my own.

Next, I think of a supervisor who regularly frustrated women to the point of speechlessness and strangled outrage, at which point he swiftly admonished and dismissed us with the phrase "Tears are not professional." More prompts internalized without question because an adult, an adult man in power, proclaimed it was so.

As Piper waves me back, I will myself to mentally flex like a prizefighter. The Muzak version of *Eye of the Tiger* plays in my head. It's the best my brain has to offer.

"Have you thought any more about reading the letter?" My diaphragm buckles.

"Can't you read it? Just this once?"

"I can, but you know why it's best to read it yourself. We can wait."

"No. Let's get it over with." The back of my throat fills with cotton. "Can I practice?"

"Sure, I'll wait in our lounge. Text me when you're ready."

"Could you bring me some water when you come back?" She nods as she exits. As I read into the empty room, tears blur the words. You can do this, Hettes. Clamp down your insides and get to it. I apply vice grips to my heart and try again. It is now or never.

"Here you go," she says as she closes the door behind her, "Before you start, I want to tell you this. You are not going to hurt me or frighten me. There is no need to filter yourself." I draw back to the courage that got me through my doctoral defense. If those men did not destroy me, surely my own words will not.

By the final third, righteous indignation is a mile in the rearview. Forty-plus years of rage fill every square inch of her office. The paper shakes as the confession that I feared my own fingers comes over the horizon. When I look up, Piper appears as though she is facing a stranger.

"Stacey... oh my god... I... holy shit."

"That bad?"

"Bad? *Bad*? No... not bad."

"Then what?" I interject, "I'm afraid you think I need to be committed."

"What would make you think that?"

"Good girls don't get this angry. They do not question. They do not argue. They do not draw attention."

"What happens if they do?"

My mouth has no response. My eyes offer a glimpse of the fear that consumes me as the melody to the church song *Trust and Obey* cues in my head—*Trust and obey, for there's no other way, to be happy in Jesus, but to Trust and Obey.*

Session 41

A week later, I better comprehend the origin of my long-held belief that I must live out my life as a penance. Two bodies participated in those sins, even if I was left to deal with their aftermath—including this forbidden anger—on my own. However, I still have no idea how to take Piper's reaction to what I read.

"I wonder if, after the shock wore off, your thoughts about my letter changed."

"That's an interesting way of asking. I wonder what you think my thoughts were, to begin with. In fact, let me do something I rarely do. I want to guess what you think that I thought as you read your letter." That is a bit of a mind-bender, but I get what she means after a beat. "I am guessing you think my stunned response last week was evidence that you are some sort of psychopath." Knowing she'd never call me one if it were true, I relax my shoulders a little as a smile appears, the embarrassed type that forms when Sam calls me out for doing something dumb but harmless.

"The thought crossed my mind a few hundred times this week."

"Stacey, look at me. There is nothing in this letter to suggest you are bad. I wish I could convince you, even for a minute, that your anger is fucking amazing—amazingly powerful. I am not afraid or sickened by it. I am in awe of how you articulated it."

"I don't know what to say."

"Who played a role in making you believe your anger is dangerous?" It takes a beat to muster the courage for this admission.

"My concerns over what you think reminded me of my therapist in high school and college, Mary Anne."

"How so?"

"I was journaling a lot back then. M-F'er had become my favorite word." It is funny that I sanitize the MF-bomb. Neither Piper nor I have any trouble dropping F-bombs with each other. "Mary Anne told me to write a letter to Mr. Jay. When I showed it to her, she said it was vicious."

"Hmm, how did that make you feel?"

"From this distance, I can see that she and I were not the best match. It made me more afraid of myself than I already was. The other thing..." I need a few breaths to prepare to change the subject to something about Mary Anne that's bothered me for a long time. "The other thing that way more messed with my head was asking about Mr. Jay's penis."

"Huh, how did she bring that up?"

"I was struggling with the abuse itself, a lot, back then. Probably because by college, my body manufactured enough estrogen and testosterone to become mildly successful at hooking up."

"What counts as hooking up?"

"Mostly kissing, sometimes more, but not dating—weekend drinking and pairing off kind of stuff. I dated a few guys later in college, but I botched those relationships quickly."

"Sorry, wanted to make sure I was following." Piper looks like she is writing a mental note to return to the idea of dating at some point. I'd gladly ride a tangent about college hookups out to the end of the session. Beats the alternative. "You were saying she asked you about Mr. Jay's penis?" No such luck.

"Yeah, she asked me if I thought he ever made me touch his penis." There is the trigger; I stare at the corner where the two far walls meet, eyes unfocused. "I thought about it and told her that there was one time when he walked me a good distance on the dirt road to the waterfall." I can see the log that he found in the woods and said we would take a rest on. I'd just strolled right into a trap. "If anything happened like that, it was that time." I want to stay focused on the therapy in college. I decide to wait for some other time to tell Piper what happened during grad school when Indira led me through EMDR, which was still new at the time, to reengage this memory.[5]

"Did Mary Anne ever explain why she was asking? Because I must say, in my experience, plus research also suggests, that the details of what happened, genital involvement or not, penetration or not, are not all that important when it comes to how someone is impacted by abuse." I take this in. It once again silences me. If I answer Piper and we are nearly out of time, I will spend the next week in suspended animation.

"How much time do we have left?"

"Plenty, about twenty-five minutes, but it's okay if we run over." This is code for: I have a free appointment block after you, no one is waiting on you to exit. I go to dive in, but I am aware of the chilling effect of these waters. I opt to dip in a toe rather than take a running leap.

"She had a way of minimizing things." My neck stiffens. My gaze locks. Piper must notice the shift. She holds the space, washing it in safety. After a forceful exhale, my voice shifts to a whisper, as if someone might be listening at the door. My eyes close. Maybe if I cannot see, I will disappear.

"She told me she was quite sure he made me touch his penis." This is as far as words can carry me. It was inevitable that therapy with Mary Anne would surface while the topic was anger. My time with her provided a cocktail of doubt, shame, and fury.

Piper asks as gently as she can, "Did she explain why she thought that?" It is as if a tidal wave is heading toward me. My

---

5 EMDR (Eye Movement Desensitization and Reprocessing) therapy is a particular practice of stimulating the brain with patterned bilateral eye or body movements. The goal is to access and process traumatic memories so that they no longer negatively impact the patient. In the decades since Indira and I used it, its effectiveness has been well established by both neuroscientific and clinical researchers. It was developed by Dr. Francine Shapiro in 1987. "What is EMDR Therapy," EMDR Institute, Inc., accessed August 4, 2024, https://www.emdr.com/what-is-emdr/.

frozen body stares from the beach as it crests.

"She said I wouldn't be this upset if all he did was fondle me." I would rather say fuckity-fuck-fuck-fuck to my great-grandma Dee Dee than that particular f-word. It takes everything I have to keep my amygdala from declaring a complete mental lockdown. As Piper takes this in, she lets out a long slow breath. It serves as long-distance resuscitation, reminding me to breathe as well. In an attempt to wall off this tsunami of shame, I slip into an adolescent sarcasm. "So, yeah, further evidence that I'm overly sensitive, overreact, should shut the fuck up and quit my bellyaching." My body pulls at the fictive restraints that hold me in place. I am too exposed front-to-front, but these goddamn smushy couch cushions...

"I will say again, remembering the details of the abuse rarely matters to a person's ability to recover. I work with many women who have no concrete memories of what happened—just a sense that something did." This sounds preferable. At this moment, while my skin reenacts the sensation of his hands pressing my shoulders into him as the inside of my mouth experiences an unfamiliar pressure, I hold deep sympathy for such women. My ridiculous ability to recall details of my early life is a handicap. On the other hand, it drives me insane that I may never know for sure all that happened while he sat on that log. At least her comment brings me back to the room, back to the present.

"Before I let you go, I want to talk a little bit about the other thing I see in your letter. In a letter where you call for a reckoning, I would expect you to call out Mr. Jay for the abuse itself. You didn't. You aim your anger at men in power, including him. Who else in your life do you recognize as holding similar power?"

"Everyone, especially when it comes to anger. If I was angry with my sister, my parents shut it down. If I was angry with them, they got defensive and came back at me twice as hard. If I was angry with my sister and my parents weren't around, she could be brutal. I never learned to release it, only to stuff it down."

"Has there been a time more recently that you felt you had to shut down your anger?"

"Yes."

"Will you tell me about it?" Five seconds of intense eye contact let Piper know I am not at all happy with her question.

"Dean Grant." Piper realizes naming him is threatening to blow the circuit boards inside my brain. As she breathes a sigh of satisfaction that I was at least able to speak his name during a conversation about anger, my brain flashes me back to a Saturday shortly after I told my parents.

***

They'd been to visit some friends. A family my dad knew since he was a kid. I admired their daughter; both she and their son were nice to me. They were smart and good students, but they both seemed comfortable in their own skin. It felt odd that we did not go along with Mom and Dad, but they were eating in a restaurant, which somehow equated to my sisters and me staying home with Gramma and Grampa.

***

My parents are back and they're all chatting. Restaurant meals were out of the ordinary back then, despite the fact that my grandfather's work ethic had found a way to overcome his lack of education and opportunity. Gramma expected a detailed retelling. "I had the salad bar," I can hear Mom's voice saying as though she is next to me on Piper's couch. She sounds like she did when the phone rang while she was yelling at us. I hated how she could go from a red-faced shout to the most pleasant "hello" in the same breath. I can't remember what my dad ordered. My mind imagines him saying, "A hamburg."

***

My grandparents are gone. Carrie's got Sam outside. My dad turns off the TV. They proceed to tell me they, in fact, did not have lunch with their friends. They went to see Mr. Jay and his wife. My dad admitted—for the first time in my life—that he, but somehow more importantly, my mother, lied. My mother just lied a whole story's worth of lies to her mother and father. Because of what I confessed—because of me—my mom would not go to heaven if Jesus came back right now.

Dad says he talked to Mr. Jay. Mom talked to his wife. Mr. Jay admitted touching me, but that's it. After everything else, somehow, I still struggle to believe he lied about the details of what happened during this confession—i.e., that his penis was a co-conspirator. He insisted he never forced me to do anything I didn't want to. My dad spit back that being an adult, with an adult-sized body, was its own kind of force. His wife asked Mom, "When and where?" as if she might be suspicious but wasn't sure.

What happens next confuses me more than the lies. My dad says Mr. Jay feels really bad about it. That he felt so bad he'd thought about committing suicide. That he did this because something bad happened to him when he was a kid. Our particular brand of Christianity placed a heavy emphasis on forgiving others their trespasses—as if the Lord's Prayer is contractual. If we do not dismiss the wrongs against us, God is under no obligation to forgive ours.

***

I manage to share the gist of this with Piper. "I think I

misunderstood what my dad was trying to say. It felt like—before I even had a chance to comprehend anything about what happened to me—that in order to be a good Christian, I was expected to feel sorry for Mr. Jay, to deny any anger, to forgive, to pardon, and to forget. Like I did not even have the right to understand my own feelings. Like it had already been decided—during a conversation I was not privy to."

"God, Stacey, that's awful. It's also pretty sophisticated rhetoric for an eleven-year-old. Is that something you processed later, maybe?" Sometimes it's hard to remember that Piper was not there for the first, second, or even fifth bout of therapy.

"Probably. As a fifth grader, the overwhelming memory is confusion. Confusion I did not have the words or ability to formulate into questions, sophisticated or not. It wasn't until later that I matured enough to consider how much my thirty-something dad must have struggled with both those conversations. Hours before, he'd held it together enough to confront the man who had done unspeakable—more than that, unthinkable— things to his daughter without any support." I let out a little chuckle of disbelief at how complicated this is, even from this distance. "Anyway, thank you for saying that. I'm sure our is time up."

"We can take a couple more minutes. I want to make sure you are okay."

"I am drenched in shame."

"Let's talk about that. What makes this feel shameful?" The sarcastic adolescent takes over once again.

"Yeah, Mr. Jay molested me, so fucking what? Everything after the actual times with him is more my fault than his. So what that he did what he did? I shouldn't let it bother me."

"That is a message I want you to try hard not to send to yourself. You have every right to be angry. Not only about what Mr. Jay did but also how little power you had over the way it was handled. On top of that, how thoughtlessly, even if unintentionally, people like Dean Grant and Vic re-injure victims." I resist the temptation to give her another thank you for saying that. Any form of thank you seems trivial. If these were the only words that Piper ever said, they would be enough.

I check my phone to break the silence. "Shit, I'm sorry, I can pay you cash for an extra session." Piper smiles the way you might at a friend who's being silly.

"You are so funny sometimes, you know that?"

Session 46

"I was looking back this week over the letter you sent. It's interesting that you initially focused your attention on how institutions set the tone for our response to child sexual abuse. I'd like you to tell me why society's silence about abuse was the doorway into this anger for you."

"For months, memories and flashbacks have flooded every neuron in my brain. The fact that this topic remains on the top ten list of subjects thou shalt only speak of in whispers, leaves me more isolated and disconnected from others than ever. When I do manage to share something with a friend, it feels like it's a one-shot deal."

People don't seem to mind when we expose a tragic moment, but then we're expected to buck up and move on. When the PTSD is on the rampage, every thought becomes unacceptable. There's no room for release. Then, when I try to switch topics or return to work, my brain releases an ear-splitting scream inside my skull: How can you think about X when, in some lightless place, a pedophile's abusing a child right this very minute?

"Whose made you feel this way in the past?"

"Don't ask me that." Her waiting game is in top form today.

"Discomfort. Discomfort sent me this message."

"Whose discomfort?"

"Please don't make me say this." Prolonged silence. "Mine, okay? Are you happy?"

"Of course not, but your answer is important, even if it's hard for you to say and hard for me to hear."

"I'm sorry. It's no fun to acknowledge that the thing you needed the most help with was the thing that, when you named it out loud, stunned pretty much everyone into an excruciating silence."

"How did you interpret that silence?" Fucking hell Piper, you are really gonna make me say this, aren't you?

"Knowing that just hearing about it upset others made me think I should never, ever, mention it again. That what seemed to make people happy was to hear that I was doing fine."

"I am sorry to hear that it felt that way. Stacey, if you let the people who really care about you know, they'd care enough to stick with you through this journey." My mouth has no more words, but it knows this conversation could eventually change everything.

PART THREE

Deprimere, Latin: "to press down"

... arriving on the nightmare
Praying for a dream

— *Maya Angelou*

CHAPTER 20

Base Camp

Depression was, indeed, the hand of a friend trying to press me down to ground on which it was safe to stand—the ground of my own truth, my own nature, with its complex mix of limits and gifts, liabilities and assets, darkness and light.
— Parker J. Palmer

Session 52

Piper's running a little late. I am glad she is as generous with her time with other clients as she is with me. However, I fear I will lose my nerve. After this long, one might think the struggle to admit things or to tell her when I want to discuss something in particular would ease up. The past year needed to be about processing memories, considering the complications they add to relationships, the anger about them. In some ways, though, our time thus far is the equivalent of climbing out of a hole I'd stumbled into after I tripped over someone's outstretched foot.

We've arrived back at base camp, a destination I've reached many times before without climbing the mountain. The lump in my throat tells me it's time. Time to tackle the mountain of myself.

A hiking metaphor makes me think of a grad-school friend who was planning a trip to Alaska to study the aurora borealis.

I didn't see her for weeks and bumped into her at the dog park. In between tosses of my beautiful girl, Canyon's, floppy frisbee, I asked how her study went. "Oh, I haven't done the fieldwork yet. This trip was to buy supplies, make contacts, get the lay of the land, and stuff." Wow, all that time, work, and expense and she hasn't even seen the northern lights. All the therapy, past and present, were practice runs for the trek Piper is preparing to help me navigate. I have zero confidence in my ability to reach the summit.

If asked to choose one guiding question to sum up this past year, I'd say that Piper and I have examined many answers to: What happened to you? Despite the fact that there are old memories and buried emotions left to excavate, we are transitioning to a second question: What did it do to you?

"Stacey? You can come back." Piper's voice startles me away from my thoughts.

"Oh, hi," I say as I hurry to get up.

"You seemed extra deep in thought."

"I was."

"About something you'd like to talk about?"

"I don't know." Piper reads my face for clues. Here goes nothing. "I think it's time to talk more about myself." This bursts out as if a meddlesome friend—who actually has my best interests at heart—shoved it from my mouth. I manage to suck any further details back in before this so-called friend exposes more without my consent.

"Thanks for your willingness to tell me that. But, we've been talking about you all along. Why the apprehension?"

"I don't know. Maybe I'm worried about what you will think." I pause, but she offers no affirmation. "It could be because we're approaching the point where I usually bail on therapy. Once I reach the state I'd describe as 'happy enough,' continuing on seems indulgent and attention seeking."

"Okay, but those are two very different things. In terms of bailing on therapy, I won't let that happen. I will fight to keep you."

"Thank you. I hope you won't have to."

"I'm glad you told me. Let's take it as a sign that you want to stick with it. Back to what's making you worry. You can trust me not to judge you."

"I know that. It's still hard. I try my best to trust you—and I do—way more than most people."

"Let's talk about that. Tell me something I've done that's allowed you to trust me."

"The way you handled it when I told you about my conversation with my college counselor, Dr. Fedora. Remember? It was the time I told him about what I did to my pink doll."

"I don't think I remember." It still surprises me that sessions, which tattooed themselves on the surface of my brain failed to register for Piper.

***

If the emotional energy it'll take to crawl out of my dorm room and make the trek across campus to Dr. Fedora's office was channeled into physical exertion, I could win the goddamn Boston Marathon. As I sit on the edge of the bottom bunk, a tiny slip of drool spills from the corner of my mouth, landing on my thermal. Sucking it back in was too much. No time to shower. Lucky for me, girls wearing baseball caps with a ponytail pulled through the back was a staple of '90s college anti-fashion. My feet slip into my Birks as I douse myself with Bath and Body Works Juniper and Aloe and layer on a flannel I stole from my dad. My roommate used to say the scent smelled like me, rather than the other way around. Most friends went for Plumeria or Sun-Ripened Raspberry. I wanted to be original.

"How's it going, kid?" Dr. Fedora asks as I pick which throw pillow to hug for this session. He spends the next twenty minutes prying loose a brick or two from my fortress to gain a peek inside. As his eyes land on a particularly nasty corner of my self-hatred cupboard, he asks, "If a new student transferred in next semester and was assigned as your lab partner, do you think she'd come to the same conclusions about you that you've come to about yourself?"

"No, but she wouldn't know what I know."

"What do you know?"

"Whatever was inside Mr. Jay that made him do what he did? I'm afraid he infected me with it too."

"Explain that to me." I squeeze the pillow so tightly the stuffing might disintegrate.

"After one of the times with him, I did to my doll what he had done to me. At least I tried to. Her pink body had nowhere to put my fingers. I guess that means I better never be around kids. What if I hurt them the way that he hurt me?" His voice takes on the deliberate, measured cadence he reserves for his most important questions.

"How old do you think you were when that happened with your doll?"

"She was my kindergarten doll. I got her for Christmas. Her hair was shiny and smooth, not all ratty like doll hair gets over time. My best guess is that I was five, turning six."

"Can I tell you about something I learned while training as a psychologist?"

"Sure."

"Can you guess what the number one sign to watch for in little ones as an indication of abuse?" He knew not to say sexual or the m-word. Dr. Fedora recites his answer like something he memorized for an exam, "Imitation and recreation of sexual acts with toys or other objects, such as dolls or stuffed animals." I just stare at him, something

I did a lot back then. "I hate to break it to you, kid, but your analysis of these data is completely off. You concluded that what you did to your doll meant you'd become an abuser. In fact, it's completely the opposite. If anyone had seen you do that to your doll, they might have realized what was being done to you."

"I only ever did that under the covers with the lights off."

***

My conversation with Dr. Fedora about my pink doll came up with Piper early on, while I was filling her in on my lengthy therapy history. As part of my answer to today's question about trusting her, I go on to tell her, "Since picturing my little-girl hand between that doll's legs still rattles me—and the fact that I was such a mess when I first met you—the story was coming out all choppy and disjointed. You got confused and thought I was saying that, as a college student, I imitated sexual abuse, as if I'd brought the doll to campus with me."

"Now I remember."

"I could see something shift in your face that day. You calmly said that we would need to talk more about this in the future. Also, you didn't think I would harm a child that way in real life because I would never ever want to hurt someone."

"Yes," she says, adding, "and I know that to be truer now than I did back then."

"I didn't realize that I failed to describe everything clearly until it woke me up later that night. I wanted to call you right away, but I waited for our next session to explain."

"What happened then?"

"I clarified what actually occurred and you let out a great big, 'Oh! I get it.' The important thing is, and to finally answer your question about trusting you, I realized that even within that misunderstanding, you were willing to continue to work with me. For a moment, you thought I was suggesting something very, very bad about me. Even then, you made it clear you wouldn't abandon me."

"Whew, glad I didn't fuck that up." Why does it seem like she is making light of this?

"It was a particularly important step forward for me, but it would have been way too intimate to tell you that at the time."

"How does remembering that exchange between us make you feel today?"

"There are some truths, and untruths, that I have to admit to. Things about myself that I think my heart knows, but that my head, polluted by Mr. Jay's serpents, tries to convince me of."

"You said some things, not thing. What are they?" Silence.

The emotions I've kept on lockdown so that we could make our way through this conversation are pounding on the cell door. I look her in the eye. My lips are trembly. Surely, she can see the quivers from across the rug.

"Can you tell me one?"

"What Mr. Jay did broke any possibility for me to ever love or respect myself."

CHAPTER 21

When New Wounds Traverse Old Scars

Session 53

"Stacey, if you want to give me an update on your week, that's fine. At some point, we need to talk about what you told me last week. It did not surprise me to hear you say you do not love yourself, your whole self, but it concerns me to hear that you are still convinced you never will."

"I know you want that for me. I cannot imagine ever doing that, ever feeling that. I need to tell you something else, though. We had a meeting this week. Vic and Dean Grant were both there. It brought back the sexual violence forum and the part I played in it." Piper knows when my non-answers are meant to signal not to push too hard for more on a particular topic.

"Okay, what about your part specifically?" I don't have a scripted answer worked out. Responses about myself are more difficult to articulate than answers, which focus on the wrongdoings of others. It's still too raw to consider that this midlife unraveling is my own doing. It is important to distinguish between my own doing and my own fault. I did this. I put myself out there when I spoke out against Vic's tirade. I unleashed the "authentic voice" that Dean Grant later attempted to co-opt for his own benefit. Breakdown Saturday began with my amygdala's choice to respond—it chose to fight, rather than flee, freeze, or fawn.

Speaking up was not, was not, me seeking a spotlight. I've

done that—I know what that looks like. This was not that, but I did dive headlong into a murky ugliness. The institution I married my life to was flailing a bit. I mistook that for drowning. My overdeveloped sense of responsibility mandates that I do something. But. Did I have to do this something? Did I have to say—did I have to believe—that betraying my little-girl secret was the only way?

I remember two things. First, I was confident that the compromise I was about to suggest would remedy the situation. Coming to academic administration from science led me to view most situations as problems to solve. Second, this half-cocked plan to grab some power back from Vic by shouting the loudest #MeToo our faculty and staff had yet to hear? There would be no going back from this.

How are the women who shouted louder than me, who shouted on a national platform in front of TV cameras dealing, now that the cameras have moved on? The media has declared us to be post-#MeToo, as in past that snippet of time. For women like me, who shouted our most vulnerable secrets, our most private experiences, will there ever be such a thing as post? There is a before followed by a now. A now whose reality requires me to set foot on campus every day knowing that, for me, it will never be the campus it was before that faculty forum.

The situation is what it is. I did not create the initial controversy, but my hand did rise and my mouth did open. It was my choice to reveal something that personal. The majority of attendees have long since forgotten my confession. Truthfully, I bet most did not give it another thought, the way I forget that a powdery mist of yellow pine pollen blankets South Carolina each spring. I do not have allergies. If I did, I bet I would find a way to blame myself. And why not? My head blames me for many things that my heart knows I had no control over. Yet, if I only look at my life through the lens of what happened to me, rather than what it did to me, I may never fully grasp who I am.

***

"Sorry Piper, can you repeat your question?"

"What about your part in the forum is troubling you?"

"It's hard to explain. I don't want to admit that I exposed myself, outed myself, by responding to Vic. I could have, maybe should have, stayed out of it, just like I wish I never told my parents in the first place. I chose to say in public that I was a victim of sexual violence. I think I said survivor. I feel like a victim again. Anyway, look what happened? Maybe it got the job done, but I threw my little-girl self to the wolves."

"If you had it to do over again, what would you do differently?"

"That's the million-dollar question, isn't it? Could I have made the same motion to resolve the issue without saying that I was a survivor? Was it as necessary a revelation as it felt at the time?"

"Why do you think it felt necessary?"

"It was hard to know what to do and to decide how to respond in the moment. Prior to the forum, I already had been struggling with whether the larger conversation over our assault policies was as black and white as some argued. Those speaking with the most confidence on both sides made it sound clear cut. It certainly was the case that not everyone agreed. In fact, I struggle with the gray areas myself."

"In what way?"

"It's more a hunch than a fully formed idea. God, this sucks. The thing that nags at me is that I feel like I betrayed myself and beyond that, all women, by making this motion that was, in fact, a compromise. I didn't choose a path of compromise for Vic's benefit. I was trying to get us to the other side of a conflict and out of a room where people were hurting."

"I am going to ask you a question. I want you to tell me the first thing that comes to mind. What is it about this moment you find so challenging to reconcile?"

"I betrayed myself for my job. I used a private thing to fix a problem someone else, and I will just say it, a powerful man, created. There was a victim-blaming attack taking place in that room. Instead of defending myself and the other survivors, I helped the attackers out of a jam."

"Okay, we know the issue. There are many times, many places where you have the opportunity to participate in larger conversations, like what does or does not count as betraying the sisterhood. In this room, we will stay focused on you." The cacophony in my head ceases. She has seen right through my attempts to externalize to a broader argument to avoid facing the connection to another memory. Upon this realization, my body, my mind, everything curls inward.

"Stacey, what's happening?"

Sweet Jesus, these words are Velcroed to my vocal cords. "I am making a connection back to Mr. Jay."

"Can you tell me?"

Each word snags the next as they pile up in my throat. "It's the same as when Mr. Jay tried to unbuckle my rainbow belt." Piper does not know about this time but is patient enough to provide the eternity of silence I need to prepare for what comes out next. "He couldn't figure it out." My middle folds over. This shame wants to hide as much of the surface of my person from Piper as possible. "I did it for him. Good Lord, what kind of depraved sicko does that? Now can you see why I don't deserve any self-respect?"

After a pause, Piper pushes out a deep, slow breath. I know her well enough to know what this means. It's also validating.

Validating that I am this upset. That I am this confused. Validated in my own self-loathing. It takes her longer than usual to find a way to approach this one.

"Stacey, if Mr. Jay asked you to get him a glass of water, could you say no?" She gets a shoulder shrug in return. "I know it seems different, but to a child, there is no difference between him asking you to undo your buckle and him asking you to get him a glass of water. As a child, you did not have the agency to say no."

"Thank you for saying that. I wish I could remember how old I was."

"Why does that feel important?"

"Because I suspect I was older. My body seems bigger. My tummy was fatter. I should have known better than to get in the car with him."

"Tell me about the car."

"The door was heavy. I had to yank it. It slammed with a thud. No one else was with us. I got to sit in the front seat. I can see its enormous green hood pulling into our driveway. He drove all the way from my gramma's to pick me up. They came up to get apples from Kern's orchard. His wife and my gramma were putting up apple sauce. He'd take me back up with him, which would help keep the kids out of their way. Funny, they didn't ride down with him. I don't know where Carrie and my mom were. It was me and my dad. Sam wasn't born yet."

"So, you were less than eight?"

"Apples mean fall, probably seven and a half."

"Do you think a seven-year-old might be excited to have kids to play with?" I want to say no. I am afraid to let go of this self-accusatory narrative.

"Yes." Opening my mouth draws bile into my throat. "When he showed up, I gave him a hug and he picked me up. We were not expecting him. I can see the reflection of myself in his arms in the sliding glass door. I was wearing yellow fuzzy socks." Gah! How was I so fucking naive?? "He drove way out of the way back to my gramma's house. He went three or four extra exits on the highway. I don't remember what all happened, but he had at least thirty minutes with me. My pants were corduroy this time." My body tenses against what comes next.

"You are safe, Stacey. Keep going."

"I knew the moment I was in trouble. He reached his huge hand across my body and pulled me by my hips." I demonstrate, reaching my right hand across to the other side of the couch. "It was a bench seat, not buckets, but the armrest was down, and he scrunched my body against it." Was my hair in braids or loose? I picture myself again in the glass door. It was loose. I am wearing a purple sweatshirt.

***

"How does this come apart?" he asked as he flittered the buckle between his middle and index fingers. My body goes gray as nerves retreat into my spinal cord. They want no complicity in what's coming. The muscles have nowhere to hide. As if attached to marionette strings, two arms lift from my sides, fingers repeat the series of motions they'd practiced to release the figure eight clasp. Did he undo the copper rivet or did I? I can only guess that he spent the rest of the drive massaging my little-girl clitoris. Every frame of film after the belt of many colors remains blank.

***

Is it plausible that he reached all the way inside me from that angle? "The next thing I know for sure, he pulled over partway down the exit ramp."

"Why did he do that?"

"So I could fix my pants. I did the zipper, rivet, and belt myself." These words come out of my mouth as matter-of-factly as saying I brushed my teeth before bed. "I saw some Queen Anne's Lace out the car window. Those flowers would make everything okay. I got out to pick some. I could hear the panic in his voice. 'Stacey, get back in the car, get back in the car.' After, Gramma asked me where I picked the flowers. He chimed in before I could. I can't remember what he said, but I knew it was a lie. The times I was aware that he was lying sounded like the teacher in a Charlie Brown cartoon—'Wat wah wat wah wat.' "I remember thinking, that's not true. You pulled over so I could pull my pants up. He spent the afternoon making me a bow and arrow out of a sapling tree."

"There is a lot to process here. First, I want to check in and see how you are."

"Why didn't he kiss me that time? It started with kissing, but after that first time, I don't remember him kissing me like that, only on my neck from behind. Didn't he want to kiss me anymore?"

Piper's face responds with rare confusion and a lengthy lag between my questions and her answer. Maybe to manage her own disgust at the topic. "I don't know, Stacey. He is the only person who could possibly understand his urges or why he chose to do what he did. What makes you curious about that?"

"I don't know what matters and what doesn't. But kissing seems like something you do to show you care about someone. Shoving yourself inside them doesn't."

"And it makes sense to feel that way. It is confusing and it is overwhelming. It is also sad. All of these experiences are tragedies—the victim blaming at work, Dean Grant's insensitivity, as well as Mr. Jay's lies, deception, and abuse. It makes sense that, given the way Mr. Jay manipulated and deceived people to gain access to you, that you would struggle with ambiguity and the motivations behind men's behaviors. Mr. Jay used an act of kindness—driving to your house to pick you up—as a cover to molest you." I cringe at the m-word but try to stay present. "It makes sense that the ambiguity of a situation at work, especially when victim blaming came into play, caused you similar distress."

"I just wish I had not said what I did in the meeting. I wish I had found a different way."

"Tell me how you were feeling by that stage."

"I was flooded. I would not have known to call it that at the time. Once you described it, that's the perfect word." My mind jumps to waiting in the backseat of our 1970s Chrysler after the engine wouldn't start. Dad called what happened to the car engine "flooded" too. This feels like that.

"That's right, and in that moment, instead of fleeing or freezing, you went into fighting mode, which we know is the least comfortable for you. However, since someone was collectively calling out victims, you put your body between Vic and theirs. You said, hey mister, if you're gonna call us out, here I am. I *am* these women you chose to treat as abstractions. Bring it. Oh, and by the way, I will call you out for this shit show we're in. At the same time that you put us in crisis mode, my amazing brain is going to solve this problem since you can't solve it for yourself, dumbass." She's found a way to vent the entirety of both our frustrations.

I squeal with laughter at that—grateful for a break in the tension. Piper has ten thousand times more gumption than I do. It tickles me every time she lets it slip.

Her face says she's relieved to hear me laugh. This was a tough one. "I want to say one more thing then I need to let you go. Not only Dr. Hettes can solve problems. Little Stacey solved them too.

Many times. Your limbic system recognized you were in danger, which let me also say, un-fucking-believable that he did what he did while driving a car. Anyway, you followed orders and did not resist. This was the advice given to women who found themselves in similar danger. Your brain, once again, protected you by blacking out. It kept you from being subject to the memory of that awful experience."

I cannot find any words. I shake my head yes. I am spent. There's no energy for a "thank you for saying that." "One more thing and I really have to let you go. Would you write a letter to little Stacey? How about sharing your thoughts on this with her?"

CHAPTER 22

A Temporary Pardon

Dear Little Stacey,

I wish you had more time to be a kid. You grew up too fast and learned to endure rather than enjoy life. It makes sense that this was the result of the awful, awful things that happened to your body. A grown-up that your family trusted betrayed all of you. Even though he was kind of a jerk, they did not suspect he could do the things he did. Mom and Dad were shocked. The way a whole town is shocked when they discover one of their neighbors is a murderer. I want you to know they did the best they could because I want you to know that I am doing the best I can.

Am I the clueless TV police detective to whom the audience screams about the killer lurking in the shadows? There are answers out there. I promise you I will not stop looking, even if it takes years and years. This is really hard, but you are worth it.

I hope someday I will remember you more as you were, not in the way that you were convinced others saw you. You were a creative, smart little girl who enjoyed thinking as much as moving. I wish you felt like that was valued, even celebrated, from time to time. Maybe it was. I think you would have enjoyed a life filled with art supplies and permission to be messy with them. I am sorry that we did not know to ask for that. I hope we can make lots of pottery again someday soon. I miss that, and I miss feeling closer to you when I am up to being creative.

I also want to tell you that you were brave. You have a barrel of courage inside you. When you tap into it, you are awfully good at protecting yourself and others. It is not fair that Mr. Jay was able to blindside you. It is not fair that he was a bully and all the other things that allow grown-ups to take advantage of kids. It is not fair that he was so sneaky. That he fooled your parents, your sister, and his own son, but he did. It's not their fault either, but it does not make it hurt any less.

I have a lot of work to do. I promise I will keep at it. You are worth it. You and I can figure out how you can make the world a better place because that's the nature of our heart, not because we need to prove something. I've gotten us off track by thinking the only way to be worthy is to work us to death. I will try to give you more time.

Session 57

"I brought the letter."

"Good. I want to check in and ask how you are doing first." When I'm this apprehensive, I would rather get it over with.

"Okay. Writing her a letter was something of a relief. Writing slows my brain a bit and reverses things when my engine is revving too fast. I wrote what I felt, I didn't try to make it erudite or insightful."

"Good, then writing is a good strategy for you. Sometimes it seems like you'd rather process what we are talking about further in your own mind than continue talking."

"Sometimes. More like I wish I had a recording of our conversation that I could replay. It's frustrating when you said something important but I can't recall how you put it. I get stuck on your exact words instead of drawing out their meaning." I have no idea where this moment will eventually lead—that writing with this goal in mind will be the thing that saves me. "I am ready to read my letter."

"Sounds good. Remember, I will respond from a place of conversation, not evaluation."

"Got it." It turns out, I appreciate that Piper overtly removed the pressure to perform. I make it to the end of the first paragraph, but facing the words, "You are worth it," causes my voice to crack. I fight back tears once I realize I have to say them aloud a second time.

"How did that feel?"

"It was harder than I thought it would be. It is easier to hate her, to blame her, to think she is bad."

"Easier than what?"

"Easier than accepting that she was not safe. That I couldn't keep myself safe. Easier than accepting that reliving all this has played out as a re-disassociation of my mind and body. Her body—my body—was an active participant in these crimes against nature. Crimes against the construct of the human condition. Crimes my mind wanted nothing to do with. I think my mind and soul have been plotting ways to escape the confines of this wretched dwelling."

Piper pauses, letting us sit in the depth of this answer. "How do you want that to change?"

"I'd like to be open to a reconciliation, a sense of re-embodiment. That seems overwhelming. But I might be ready to remove the sign tacked to my chest proclaiming this body abandoned and condemned."

"It makes me happy to hear you say that."

"Remember what you told me when I first met you… about child abuse being one of the worst traumas?"

"Uh-huh, but tell me what you remember."

"I think I get it now."

"How so?"

"Well, something must be pretty bad if you come out of it believing it is better to perpetually punish your body—yourself—better to look for anything else to blame for how you turned out than accept that it happened." Piper is quietly supportive. The way she says what she says next leads me to imagine there are celebratory fireworks going off in her mind.

"I think you are exactly right."

CHAPTER 23

Tracker Jackers

Session 64

Maybe I will not tell her. Internalized societal conditioning makes me wonder whether I am just getting my period. As I wait for my turn, I think back to a few weeks ago when I was more optimistic. That optimism seems as naive as the way that hikers, about to embark on a treacherous and potentially deadly expedition, bolster their spirits with a sendoff party the night before.

"Hi, Stacey." I need a deep inhale to respond. I manage a hello on the exhale. "Uh-oh, that was quite a greeting." I flip through a reserve list of benign topics to fill this session with. Why is it that I wait all week for this appointment, hoping to climb another foot or two up this fucking mountain? Once I arrive, I want nothing more than to distract Piper with a story about one of my students or to hear about something funny her daughter did.

"How is your day going?" Piper never fails to laugh at the fact that her day spiraled out of control before it began. She knows that, with me, modeling confessions that her life is not perfect loosens me up to share the shame that presently overrides my every neuronal circuit.

"It just never ends," she says with an eye roll. "As I kissed the boys goodbye, I told my daughter she needed to put her bike in the garage before she and I left." After running back upstairs in the hopes of having three minutes to slap on some makeup, Piper realized it was already time for her partners' morning virtual consultation call.

"None of the other therapists ever put on their makeup as we discuss patients we might need some assistance with. I said, sorry ladies, my husband still hasn't upgraded our Wi-Fi. I'm going to need to keep my camera off. My colleague was just getting us started when I heard a crunch followed twenty seconds later by a scream, 'MY BIKE,' through the open window. With one eye made up and the other naked, the laptop charger yanked out of the socket as I headed for the stairs to console a grieving preschooler while reminding two teenagers to be more careful. So, that was my day so far, how about yours?"

"Oh no! I can't imagine who felt worse, your daughter or her brothers. Glad no one was hurt."

"I had to remind myself of that too, but I need to know how you are doing." She's not gonna fall for any distractions today.

"Umm, you could say I'm struggling a bit." Each time I admit this, I wait for her own exhale of frustration. It never happens. The only time she gives away any hint of the enormity of the task that is me and my nonsense is when we enter a yet undiscovered room in this house of memories. She takes it in, rolls up her sleeves, and says, okay, let's do this. Meanwhile, one of the serpents slithers up from its crevice to roll their eyes and entertain the others. Another responds by pantomiming playing the violin. Our culture subjects women to so much gaslighting that we allow parts of ourselves to fill this role, even when current company refuses. Internalized gaslighting. I bet some psychologist somewhere already wrote a dissertation coining this term. Regardless, this practice becomes innate, becomes impossible to reverse.

"Anything in particular you want to talk about?" She settles in for an hour's vigil as my brain makes every argument for why I am the most despicable human on Earth.

Session 65

We have reached that part of the journey when mountain climbers just put one foot in front of the other. Here at ground level, this equates to dragging myself back to Piper's office each week. I understand why I never stuck around for this part of the work with other therapists. It is harder to talk about and comprehend what sexual abuse does to how we see ourselves than to re-tell and relive the actual events. To realize we have steeped in a tea of self-loathing and shame since it happened. Combined with the exertion it takes to own up to this fact means that during every therapy session, Piper must work me up to a sweat that oozes that shame out of my pores. At this point, the only reason I care about getting out of bed is to buy the Chili Peppers their Milk Bones.

"Are things any better this week?" There's concern in her voice. Normally, she manages to stay neutral so that my feelings, not hers, set the tone. All I manage is a side-to-side head shake. Seeing her face today was painful. Dull jabs of deep pressure, as if someone's squeezing too hard, repeat across my shoulders.

"Stacey, whatever this is—we'll figure it out. I know what it's like to stare into the abyss. I want to help you find your way back." I raise my eyes from the floor but fall short of reaching her face. I cannot define this or reach the source of its blackness. "Do you think you can describe one emotion or even a thought?"

"It's not... that I don't want to... no words."

"Take your time."

"Despicable."

"What is despicable?"

"Me."

"When do you feel most despicable?"

"It's hard to be around children. Even a show with kids—I

can't watch."

"Is this new? Have you felt this way before?"

"Sometimes. I'm not around little kids all that much."

"How about recently?" I give this some thought. I did not get to visit Carrie and her boys during winter break. A memory manages to cut through the fog.

"A few weeks ago, I ran into a friend at school. As we were catching up, she made an innocent comment about her son being lazy, how she's constantly following after him to get him to do anything. It stung." I tap my finger at the base of my neck. The floodgates open. "Now all the negative things anyone said about me, especially from when I was younger, play on a continuous loop. Every rebuke, every hard truth, every mean comment, every dig about my weight, the tangles in my hair, or my skirt hanging longer in the front than in the back is one more piece of evidence that I was—I am—worthless." I proceed to give more examples from elementary school through my teaching evaluations from students.

"Does it feel at all like you are using these to beat yourself up?"

***

Nope. Not ready to hear this.

"*You* think I am doing this on purpose?" My eyes aim right at hers as my words propel like blow darts. "That I am wallowing in self-pity? If I knew how to shut this off, I would."

"Thank you for telling me that." Piper sounds as though I just commented on how lovely her hair looks. "I never want to trigger you or make you feel worse."

I'd like to accept her kindness. The darkness absorbs every photon streaming from her face.

Session 66

We ease in today. Even the most inviting waters sting a bit when your skin is this raw. I give it my level best. Which lasts all of eight minutes before the tears barge in uninvited. Piper sits in supportive silence as I battle myself.

We've arrived at the third consecutive session spent drawing on my every professor skill to argue that my self-perception is indeed reality—the dark side of "being smart." Finally, I go for the nuclear option, "God, Piper, aren't you sick of me? I don't see how you can stand to put up with me!"

"I am going to stop you. That is an intrusive thought. It is in no way true." I have nothing to give back. If that hurt her, I cannot fix it.

"Piper, this is hopeless."

"What feels hopeless?"

"This. Me. Trying to get better. The fact is no one liked me. That's why Mr. Jay could do what he did. No one wanted me around. They were happy to get away from me. I was an annoying little shit. My sister, my parents, his son... the truth is they didn't like me. I was a burden. That's why they didn't notice when I was gone—when he'd siphon me off. I am inherently unlovable. I deserved this."

Piper appears as serious as I have ever seen her. "I know what it is like to stand on the edge of the abyss. It seems impossible to keep it from drawing you in, but I want you to fight. I am here, Stacey. I will fight to keep you."

My muscles relax a bit, but an attempt to take a deep breath backfires. "I need to tell you my neck feels weird." Piper sits up tall.

"Anywhere else?"

"No," I gasp in air as if someone stuck a penknife between my ribs.

"Stacey, let's breathe together, okay? Take a deep inhale and push it out hard. Okay, this time, I want you to hold it in a bit." After several rounds, we manage to stem the tide of the panic. I sit in silence for most of the remainder of the session. Finally, I remember where I am.

"Thanks for your help." My voice sounds weak, even to me.

"You are welcome. You are always welcome." I keep breathing in and out. "Do you have any sense of how much I care about you?"

"I appreciate you saying that. I do. I'm sorry. I am trying."

"What evidence do you have that your sisters and parents didn't like you?"

"I was horrible. My body got fatter and fatter, especially after I told them what happened. They thought I was annoying. My dad yelled at me at a picnic for drinking regular soda instead of diet." Uncharacteristically, I look straight at her. I want to see her reaction. I can anticipate the look others get when I mention anything about my weight. I expect Piper's face will project something like, "Well yeah, you definitely want to stick with the diet there, fatso." Even Indira told me all that weight would just "melt off" once we completed therapy.

Instead, Piper looks as if she witnessed concerned parents being a little too harsh with their daughter. Her face expresses what mine does when I observe someone else's kid in a similar situation. I too would try to project love and support after they were knocked down, intentionally or not, by such words.

"We are about out of time. I want to spend a few minutes cooling down to make sure you are okay."

"I appreciate your help. I am okay. I will be okay. I'm sorry I make this so hard."

"I wish there was a way to convince you that you are not making this hard. It just is."

Session 67

"Hi." A hopeful smile encircles her face. "How are you?"

"A little better." I attempt to force a smile but barely manage the last waning crescent before a new moon.

"How's work been?"

"So far so good. It takes a while to settle in with a new group of students. I am teaching an upper-level class. The material is more interesting. I've taught some of these students before but not others. It's important not to play favorites. By the second or third week, we usually find a good rhythm."

"Which class is it?"

"Systems neurobiology"

"That sounds heavy. What's it about?"

"It's studying particular systems, for instance, the auditory system. First, we identify detectable information, in this case, soundwaves, then move on to how the brain works to process it. The neural circuitry, which combines distinct sounds from both ears into a single experience is tricky. Next, we look at the perception or meaning of the sounds. Finally, we study behavioral responses. For instance, if you heard someone honk their horn as you were crossing the street, you'd run to get across faster. If instead, you were waiting for someone at the airport, a honk could point you in the right direction. It's how your nervous system executes its functions, start to finish."

"That sounds interesting. I sometimes forget how much you know about brains."

"If only it did me any practical good. I have no idea what to do with mine most of the time."

"I hear that." We both flash smiles at the unintentional pun. It feels good to be back to where we begin with conversation. This bout of depression deserves a capital D. We chit-chat a little longer before Piper says, "I thought about you this week." It still makes me uncomfortable when she says things like this. At the same time, it seems caring when she says she's taken the time to think about me. "I wanted to text you and check in but didn't want to intrude."

"It's never a problem if you text me. I try to respect your professionalism and not bother you outside of sessions. It's unlikely I'd text you unless it was an emergency." The truth is, I am afraid that if I opened that door, I would come to depend on it. Better to keep the boundaries where they are than reset them and have her regret it.

"I'm trying to decide whether or not to say what I want to." This sits me up and trains my eyes on her face searching for danger signs. "I do not want to compromise the work we're doing. At the same time, it concerns me how much you are struggling." I have no response. Christ, say what you need to say.

"It seems like you are struggling. Like you are battling some sort of conflict." Okay, that's obvious. This must be a warm-up. Fuck.

"I feel conflicted about all the ways my family did not like me. It's as if all their opinions set me up for feeling like I do. Every negative thing anyone ever said got recorded as a résumé of my self-hatred." She takes this in realizing that, while this emotional storm is winding down, my (mis)perceptions remain the same.

"That is the thing, though. I do not know if this conflict is with other people, especially your family like you think. I think the fight you are trying to pick is with yourself."

The doors of my mind's penitentiary clang shut. Words continue to come out of Piper's mouth. As far as I can tell, corresponding words come out of mine. I have no idea what they are.

CHAPTER 24

Inflection Point

There is something that happens to our brains when we think someone made the choice to kick us when we're down. Does Piper know she tripped the invisible wire that lies just inside my barricades as a last line of defense?

Her accusation, that "the fight you are trying to pick is with yourself," whipped these negative thoughts into a hurricane. After seemingly never-ending weeks dragging my mind and body to therapy, I have nothing left with which to batten myself down against this storm. If I were in a better place mentally, it might not have hit me so hard, but that's beside the point. My limbic system is screaming to cut and run. It cannot take any more suggestions that I am my own worst enemy. No one comprehends what it is like inside my head when one-hundred-mile-per-hour winds whip through my brain.

By midweek, the gusts diminish enough that I can lift my head a bit. Piper and I have done enough work that my frontal lobe knows it's facing a choice. I will not ghost her. I will find a way to convince her that I am cured. There are old scripts I can revive. I've performed this character before, several times. I will give her all the credit, promise to keep in touch, yada yada yada, we are done. The problem: when introducing her to my lengthy history with therapists, I revealed this page from my playbook. As a final attempt at honesty, I try writing her a letter.

***

Dear Piper,

I hope the move to your new house is going well. You work hard. You deserve to enjoy the fruits of your labor. I'm excited you will finally have enough space for your horses. I'm writing as a way to process what you stated in our last session. I need to detangle the thoughts and feelings you left me with. I am trying my damnedest to appreciate that you were honest with me. My goal here is to be honest with myself. That means there's a good chance you will never have access to these words.

So then, to be honest, I recall little of what we discussed after the statement I remember to be this. You said that I stay focused on old negative messages—along with the triggering and flooding they cause—to avoid facing a truth. That the battle I want to (need to?) have is with myself. To that, all I can say is, okay then, now what? What made you decide to dump this shit on me this week? I do not want to tell you, but it felt like a betrayal. A little 'b' betrayal, not a capital 'B' betrayal, similar to how we talk about little 't' versus capital 'T' trauma.

I thought you were on my side. Last week felt like the one person in the world I can accept help from tried to tell me to quit blaming others for my problems—to admit I am my own worst enemy. Admit that I'm an attention-seeking whiner who should be grateful for what she has. This message surfaced a lot as a kid, especially when I was the most desperate for help and could not find a way—the right way—to ask for it. It's like you and my high school counselor, Mary Anne, had a consult or something.

Maybe if I understood what you want to accomplish, your statement would make some sense. After you said what you did, I do remember that you asked if I might be open to writing out more conversations between myself and little Stacey. If I am going to do that, I have to do it honestly. Not as an assignment for which I try to earn a make-up A after receiving a failing grade. You know I have tried to earn metaphorical A's all my life. As such, I rarely engage in any activity or relationship with a decent prospect of earning less than a B+. After last week, I suspect the best I could manage is a B-. I dropped calculus my sophomore year rather than risk a B-.

This applies to more than schoolwork. When I couldn't make things work with Bobby, after thinking for a whole year that I'd finally found my soulmate, it was my worst failure ever. I don't know if I will ever be able to tell you about him in person. He was my "it'll happen when you least expect it" person, or so I thought. He was in the applied genetics graduate program with Leah, one of my housemates. I'd seen him around but never talked with him much. One Friday night, when I was home alone, he called our house looking for her. Somehow, we went from that to him cooking dinner. There was something about his voice. He needed some company. We ate salmon and capers, plus artichokes with a sauce so decadent he must have borrowed the recipe from heaven.

As we loaded the dishwasher, I asked, "Wanna light a fire in the chiminea? I'll grab another bottle. How about a red this time?" There were no expectations, nothing threatening. It was all just spontaneous and... easy. I knew I didn't have to pretend not to be smart. I knew him well enough to know he was way smarter than me but so interesting. And interested. We talked about anything and everything for two more bottles before Leah and her boyfriend came home. Even from that first evening, I could have spent the rest of my life on that little slab of concrete drinking the fruit of California's vines as the incense of the pinon wood consecrated the bond between us.

I believed he could have done the same. He said so on a similar night many evenings later, after a meal we cooked together. I bet it was *fresh mozzarella, grilled eggplant, and red peppers drenched in olive oil with fig balsamic vinegar. We sat at the table Leah scavenged from a thrift shop under the twinkly Christmas lights I'd strung to make the little patio more like a terrace. We talked about housemates—how lucky I felt to have good ones, how his never managed to switch their clothes from the washer to the dryer. We speculated on what it would be like to be share a house, concluding that we were equally messy. Our proclivities matched—I didn't mind cleaning the bathroom, he had no problem scooping the gunk from the kitchen sink.*

He said the words only two other men ever hinted at. On those previous occasions, my whole body responded with a desire to unzip my skin and climb out. Not this time. Hearing Bobby say, "I feel like I could spend the rest of my life with you" caressed me with the sensation that my dusty desert yard was awash in effervescent spring water.

"Really?" He didn't need to answer. He had gently, matter-of-factly, dissolved the walls around my heart with his kindness, with his conversation, with the irises and lilies he'd arrange himself to surprise me. No doubts remained by which I could resist his words. I willfully ignored that he did not look me in the eye as he said them.

After he ended us, there was nothing left. I gave up. What a fucking sucker. Again. Third strike. I wasn't even good enough to be a beard.

I opted for dogs. I can be an A+ dog mom, which is manageable, even on the low days. They allow me complete control. I selected college professor as my singular identity. Teaching is the work of my soul, but also my heart. However, it is not lost on me that in my classroom, I hold the authority. I try to be a benevolent, thoughtful servant leader. Most days, I manage okay.

When you said what you did about beating myself up, it turned the volume all the way up on the old tapes. First, I am telling myself that you are sick of me. You are angling for someone new, someone worthier of your time. I take the fact that you asked months ago if I wanted to take a break or dial back as evidence of this truth. The fact that I wanted to stick with weekly sessions made me feel selfish—like I take more from you than I deserve.

Remember when I told you that I do not deserve to take medicine? This feels like that. At the same time, when we miss a week? The two-week stretches are hard. Another old tape is that you are just like everyone else. That you don't care; that all you want is for me to lose weight—the only evidence the world will accept that I am over all this.

Writing you is tough. I can barely hold my head up. I don't think you, or anyone else, believe how tired I am. Scratch that, one person knows how draining this is the author Parker Palmer. The story he tells of depression is spot on. "People walk around saying, 'I don't understand why so-and-so committed suicide.' Well, I understand perfectly why people take their lives. They need the rest. Depression is absolutely exhausting."[6] Out of context, especially to those who might not know him, this might sound like permission to do that. It was not. He said it as part of a conversation to convince others that depression is incredibly serious. For me, it helps me know I'm not alone. It permits me to stop berating myself as a lazy, self-indulgent attention seeker. What you told me last week made me feel like one.

After our last session, I tried to examine what it left me with, without judging or criticizing you or myself. Eventually, I cried. A wailing, desperate cry. I repeated "I hate you, I hate you, I hate you" over and over again. It took me a while to figure out whom this blubbering basket case was referring to. To be clear, it was not you, Piper. I think it was the girl trapped inside me saying how she feels toward my adult self. About how desperate she is and how unsupported she feels.

---

6 Krista Tippett, *The Soul in Depression: Interview with Parker J. Palmer*, On Being, podcast audio, February 4, 2021, https://onbeing.org/programs/the-soul-in-depression/#transcript

I have no hope that this will change. I left the womb wired to hate myself. This is my lot.

Despite that, I invented a persona, Dr. Hettes. People like her despite her weight. Thank God for Santa Claus. At least society has one example of a fat, jolly, generous person. If people who look like me can find a way to be Santa Claus-like, most people can call upon their memories of how they loved him to tolerate our presence. The problem is sometimes even Santa runs out of gifts. Then, we feel useless. Feel unlovable all over again. I show up with the gifts of compliments, a supportive learning environment, and taking on grunt work. These too leave me weary.

I wish things were different. If I could switch out my operating system, I would be willing to give it a try. I do not have anything more to give our work, or anything else. I cannot rally the energy to fight for anything better than where I am today. It is not a bad life. I believe that my students—when they think of me—experience a few seconds of remembrance of someone who was once valuable to them. That is my legacy. It is more than most get.

Thank you, Piper, thanks for trying. Still, I would hate for you to feel like a failure or that you should not have risked saying what you did. I have Chili and Pepper. They care about me. I should appreciate that I've learned to accept love from dogs. It makes me sad to think some people do not even allow themselves that.

Session 68

Only my first day in this waiting room left me more nervous. I breathe in the familiar scent, attempting to reconnect with the warmth and caring it came to represent.

Piper greets me as if it is any other day. I decide to play along. "How have you been?"

"Good, how are your students this week?" If she is probing, she is hiding it with levity.

"Um, okay, I guess."

"Anything special happening?" Here goes nothing.

"Well, I thought a lot about what you said last week."

"What in particular?"

"About how I distract myself by focusing on other people and all the negative things they might think about me. You said that you think the battle I need to have is with myself."

"Hmm, I am not remembering that."

My jaw drops.

This cannot be true. How? How can these words that hijacked my entire being be so inconsequential to her that she does not remember them? The residual sting of the words themselves, adds cayenne to what I say next. "Maybe I am just insecure and don't want to admit it."

"Do you have an idea what you may be feeling insecure about?"

"Part of me hopes I made this up." I hesitate, now terrified of standing on this precipice. "I don't think you want to work with me anymore." I have zero awareness that I am engaging in an act of self-sabotage. Luckily, it will only be a few more sessions before I realize Piper is well aware.

Her response is measured and serious. "Will you tell me what happened to make you think that?" My mind goes weepy. My chin quivers as I drift back to a time when my parents and I were in a session with my therapist, Mary Anne, during high school.

***

"Stacey, would you tell your parents about a time when you felt they were not supportive?"

"You keep pushing me to look at physician's assistant programs instead of pre-med."

As Dad's shoulders shrug, my mom says, "You were concerned about taking calculus. We thought that would be the better option." The fact that I was in tight competition with two rival students for the top class ranks complicated this fact. Our senior-year grades would decide who came out on top. Calculus held the risk of knocking me out of the top three altogether. My attempts to seek encouragement and support from my parents to suggest that I could manage both came out sideways. At some point, they turned that doubt back around as evidence that physician's assistant was the better career choice.

When Mary Anne prompted, I brought this up. My dad shot back *"You are the one who said you couldn't do calculus, not us."*

***

My chin makes the same quivering trembles as it did then. I could not say much for the rest of that session. Luckily, there were four of us in Mary Anne's office. Today, it is all on me.

"You're tired of listening to me be sad, be full of self-pity, aren't you? It's been a lotta dark sessions in a row. The more hopeless I am, the more I need your support. Right when I am questioning whether I will ever make it through all this, it's like I wore out your welcome. Did you say what you did to tell me to put up or shut up?"

Piper's relaxed, genuine voice is back. "I really appreciate you telling me this." When my head lifts, she is looking straight at me with warmth, as you might toward a confused toddler whose feelings got hurt. "I am not tired of you. What I am is concerned. I want to help you find your way through this." Even if she's faking, I believe she's willing to keep me on as a client.

Then, to get everything out—like ripping the Band-Aid off in one pull—I decide to go for it. "There is something else."

"Okay, you can tell me." I confess my assumption that she was hoping to dump me as a client weeks ago when she asked me if I wanted to cut back to twice a month. I barely finish before she jumps in.

"Thank you, Stacey. I really appreciate you telling me that. I am sorry that my question left you with such doubt. I can and will be more careful to explain such check-ins in the future." Relief immediately transitions to shame—silly girl.

This is far from the first time my imagined reasons behind people's words were this far off. Nor is it the first time I let myself suffer the weight of my expectations rather than risk confirming my fears. The serpent who accuses me of wanting attention fills the space left by my assumptions, leaving no time for relief. "I want to be sure you hear me say this," which is one of her roundabout ways of making me look her in the eye. "We can work together as long as you like, as long as it is helping you. I have clients I have worked with for years, some almost as long as I've been practicing."

"Thank you for saying that. We've already worked together longer than I've worked with anyone."

"You've mentioned that before."

"I want to treat therapy like a college course. With perfect attendance and good note-taking, I should ace the test and be done with it. I'm apprehensive because I find it harder and harder to know what's coming next."

"It is important to keep all this in mind moving forward. I get how difficult today was. You continue to impress me with how hard you work."

"Thank you." This moment is too important to trivialize with "for saying that." Does she notice?

"I want you to know that I will try my absolute hardest to keep you from walking away. I will fight for you." I am reminded of my mother telling me she would sell our house for ransom money if someone took one of us. It's been a long time since I've believed that others' circles are expansive enough to include me. I tattoo the words "I will fight for you" on the surface of my brain, right under my mother's promise to never stop searching for us if we were kidnapped.

Yet, something changes in how I trust Piper. I suspect that she is not above hurting me a little to help me a lot. Even as I accept her explanation about picking a fight with myself, I realize there is a serpent who latched on to this statement. He's been coming for me, fangs at the ready, ever since. He knows facing the truth of what Piper is trying to say will transform my mind into a place where serpents fear to dwell.

Session 69

"How are you?"

"I'm here," is said without sarcasm—not even a little bit. A mix of emotions flavors these words. There is a dollop of triumph; walking in the door today was not any easier than last week. There is a pinch of defeat. I am here, but I do not know what good it will do. I bring my hopelessness here as I have nowhere else to lay it. Truth is, this fucker weighs a ton.

"I'm so glad you are. I have to say, I was a little afraid you might not come." I cringe a bit.

"Sorry, I would never make you worry on purpose."

"Of course you wouldn't. I have thought a lot about whether to bring this up. I care about you too much not to say something." She holds what comes next for a beat. "I am a little concerned you are getting ready to vote me off the island." This causes me to pause. I did not think she knew that I was struggling with this very idea.

"I wouldn't vote you off," I say as if her word choice is what is at issue rather than its underlying accuracy.

"You wouldn't do it like that," she responds. "You would hang around long enough to put some distance between whatever upset you and leaving. You would work hard to try to keep me from thinking that I did something wrong." I do not know what to say. I am scared to screw this up, scared that things will not be the same if I do.

"I am trying super hard not to push you away."

"It makes me glad to hear that. I wish I understood what made you want to push me away." I search every database for the right words.

"There were some things I wasn't ready to hear and I am afraid." She takes a minute. She's letting these words absorb deeper than most.

"I appreciate your willingness to tell me that. I imagine how hard that was for you to say."

I am ashamed—ashamed of my fear. Also, I am ashamed that I am ashamed of my fear. I can't look at her, but I try to stay in the conversation. "Uh-huh."

"Stacey, I do not want to push too hard, but it is my job to push just enough. Sometimes those lines are going to overlap. I can tell how uncomfortable you are, but I am glad we have made it to the point of confronting it. If this is as far as we go, it is okay for now."

"I know you care."

"It makes me happy to hear you say that. Would you be willing to tell me what you weren't ready to hear?" I try to find anything in the room to anchor my gaze. I need something specific. There is a painting that I have loved from the first day. Each of the bold contrasting brushstrokes stands out individually. Combined, they become a thick churning waterscape. I zero in on a particular deep blue daub.

"You said the person I wanted to pick a fight with is myself. You said it in the midst of my being flooded, when I was 100 percent convinced my family did not want me around and that is why

Mr. Jay had access to me. When you said that, I felt like you were telling me to suck it up and stop blaming my parents. Like I am a whiny little brat who needs to appreciate what she has and to stop feeling sorry for herself." I say all this without taking a breath.

I experience physical pain knowing that these words left my mouth and reached her ears. Somehow, I know they must be said. This is why. Why I walk away from people. Why I disappear rather than stay when anyone gets close enough to want to tell me the truth—to avoid this sensation. I choose to deprive myself of the people I love rather than go through this.

Guilt compounds the physical pain. Guilt that my words may hurt Piper. Guilt that similar words have hurt my mom and dad. Guilt that I could not find any other option to solve this problem. Guilt that harkens back to being a child and deciding there was no more room in our house for any more anger, any more sadness, any more grief. I unleashed the motherlode by being molested. Worse, I told them about it. I ruined everything. I cannot be trusted. I am too dangerous for other people to care for, too dangerous to love.

"Thank you, Stacey." Piper's response is measured and thoughtful, but there is a hint of relief in her voice. I hope this means she believes we can work through this. Even if she wants to give up on me, she told me she would fight to keep me. She told me she does not lie. She established these conditions. The parameters within which I will learn to risk the power of my own voice.

She holds whatever she wants to say next to give these words time to relieve the pain emanating from just below my sternum. In that interval, I experience enough hope that I am able to look her in the eye. She is still Piper. The same Piper she was a month ago and a year ago. The dial on my fear that things will never be the same goes from a ten to a seven-point three. "It is not at all surprising that my words were triggers. Many child abuse victims' stories are met with invalidation. My words triggered you. Not a trigger for the abuse itself, but a trigger for the invalidation you experienced. When we began working together, I stayed aware of words that would trigger memories of the abuse and learned to avoid them. I'll watch out for words that trigger invalidation."

"No one invalidated me. Lotsa kids tell and experience invalidation, but not me. Mom and Dad never once questioned that I was telling the truth. They confronted him. For Christ's sake, nothing's more validating than that."

"Yes, but how about during the years the abuse occurred until you told them? Were there ever more subtle ways you felt invalidated?" What I remember causes my heart to ache the way it did when I found out my first dog, my soul-puppy, Canyon, had leukemia.

"One time, before I told them, somehow a plan was hatched for me to go to Mr. Jay's house with their daughter for a few days while his son came to our house. There was snow outside. It must have been around Christmas break. Did I tell you this already?"

"Maybe, but go on."

"I begged and begged and *begged* them not to make me go. We were in the car. I was in the seat behind my mother. There was no argument I could make other than to say I didn't want to play with his daughter. My parents had no reason to suspect anything."

It is too raw. I am too unpracticed at confronting things like this, but I suspect Piper gets the connection. This is a perfect example of why we have to revisit a memory repeatedly. We cannot grasp everything at every level the first, second, or even sixth time.

"If this situation happened to someone else, how would you describe it?"

"Invalidating." More importantly, at least for the rest of the session, I comprehend this memory for what it is, not for what the demons in my head want me to believe it to be. My parents did not send me there because they did not want me around. My sister did not want so much to play alone with his son—to have fun without me—that she was willing to sacrifice me. The likely explanation is that Mr. Jay hatched this plan, that he orchestrated the entire situation. My mom relayed the words: "Our son wants a chance to play alone with Carrie. Let's have them play together at your house. Stacey can come to our house and play with our daughter." Mr. Jay could have easily planted the idea. Did he even bother with the formality of running it through his son's head first?

"Stacey, let's stay aware of possible triggers and how deceitful they are. It does not mean we can avoid them 100 percent."

"I get that. Now that I understand it better, I will try."

"If you notice something, will you tell me?"

"Yes." I mean it. It feels good to feel safe enough to mean it.

CHAPTER 25

Fool Me Twice, Shame on Me

Session 73

"How are you?" "Kinda shaken."

"What happened?"

"Last weekend, my sister's teenage neighbor came over. He innocently, even kindly, began rubbing my shoulders, something his family must accept. I tried to ride it out, but I couldn't. I jumped up and left the room. He was caught off guard. My sister covered for me, but I almost had to leave. I know it wasn't his fault." My shoulders knot as shivers run down the center of my back.

"It may not have been intentional, but he did trigger you. How did that make you feel?"

"Frustrated, embarrassed, I wish I had the wherewithal to explain to him what happened. As I fought to hold myself together, I had nothing left to offer. My head comprehends that my body believes it's protecting me from the danger it erroneously perceives is coming next. I wish I could go back after I regain composure and say, I was not reacting to you, to what you said, to what you did. There is too much shame around overreacting to form words."

"Tell me what it is like in the moment to get derailed by a trigger."

"It's as disorienting as being awakened in the middle of the night by someone turning on the lights and blasting music at eighty decibels. It's as if my adult self bails. Some version of a younger self is left holding the bag."

It is such a relief to say this to Piper. She gets it. She won't undermine my answer or cut me off before I finish.

"What would it be like to tell someone else what you just said?"

"Excruciating. Maybe not. If they genuinely wanted to know, I would try."

"Tell me more about the kinds of attention that trigger you."

"It's a lot of things, lately. Anything that approaches flirting, compliments about me rather than my work, overt kindness, anything that seems like someone is saying something that isn't true to try to cheer me up." As I itemize this list, I realize a few of these may stem from my parents' reactions after I disclosed what Mr. Jay did, while others are because of Mr. Jay himself.

"I would have guessed the flirting answer. Plus, I've watched you react to compliments, but the kindness piece is surprising. What about kindness is triggering?"

"It is hard to explain. It's different things."

"Okay, pick one."

"It's feeling like someone is being overly kind to manipulate or seduce me." Talking about seduction is ridiculous since that's far out of the realm of possibility for this body, at this stage of my life.

"That makes sense because of the grooming we know you experienced."

"You don't know about all the grooming I experienced."

"What don't I know?" Ugh, my stomach feels like it is sliding to my knees.

"I had a coach that I was close to—too close." I wondered when he would come up. "One day, he pulled me aside to tell me how concerned he was about me. He offered to go on a diet with me so that I could get in better shape. After a year and a half of starving myself, I couldn't do it anymore. When I did not stay as skinny as he wanted, he gave me the cold shoulder. It messed me up pretty bad." If I could unzip my skin and crawl out, I would. Most bad feelings reside somewhere in my center—in the space between my breastbone and my spinal column. Feelings about him ripple beneath my skin. When memories about him dial up, I cannot even tolerate wisps of hair touching the back of my neck. My posture shifts as if to curl my body away from this conversation.

"Tell me more about this. How old were you?" I didn't even mention him on my intake form way back when. I guess the alarm in her voice is justified.

"It was my first year in high school, fourteen? He said I wasn't reaching my potential because I wasn't in shape. I had never sat alone and talked with a man, maybe not even my dad, for this long in my life."

***

Mom bought the wrong oat bran muffins again. She got the giant crusty ones that tasted like comfort. I need the mushy fat-free, sugar-free ones that taste like deprivation. Deprivation muffins earn his attention, earn the thrill of undressing myself down to my skivvies as he watched. A thin tank top, rayon skirt, bra, and underwear—no shoes, no jewelry. All that could come off did in this semiweekly ritual before the altar of the weight room scale. It was placed there for wrestlers and football players. Coach secreted us there for a private liturgy each Monday and Thursday.

At first, we practiced the ceremony together. After a while, he went there on his own. That way he could strip all the way out of his blue Puma tracksuit. The record of each week's sacrifices appeared as two columns of weights in a race to the bottom of a length of athletic tape slapped inside a nearby locker. As the numbers dropped, so did my self-worth. But who cares about that? All that mattered was that number. If it ever climbed, this would be over.

Bananas, mushy muffins, and skim milk did the trick for well over a year. Oh, and Breyer's light vanilla ice cream, measured out in a quarter of a cup. My strip of numbers dropped by sixty-five painstaking increments before it wouldn't budge. Laxatives gave it a final short-lived plummet (short-lived thanks to Mom catching on), but I still wasn't skinny skinny. My dad told me that once. He said it a lot later in life when his friend's daughter was losing her own anorexic battle with the number. She had attained the coveted title of skinny skinny. I had not. I knew my dad believed I never would. Regardless, Coach lost interest.

***

"How did dieting with your coach affect your health?" Astutely put Piper! One might expect that such weight loss from a body that looks like mine was a good thing.

"I may not have been *skinny* skinny, but I was not healthy. My hair was falling out. My hands turned deep purplish blue when I was cold, which was most of the time. I came home after practice and rode our exercise bike for another ninety minutes... I guess I fell in love with him."

These words tumble from my mouth in rapid succession. I don't even feel like I'm the one saying them. Then, I run out of words.

Piper lets me sit for a bit as I recover from whatever this is. It is different from a flashback, more like an old veteran sharing the account of a long-ago battle, a battle where there were heavy casualties. "He never touched me; it was never physical... I mean there were hugs. Long hugs. There was one kiss on the lips, but it wasn't what Mr. Jay called special kissing. He'd walk with his arm around me. Following me up from the weight room one day eye level with my ass he said, 'I can see it in your legs. I'm a leg man.'"

"How are you feeling?"

"Awful."

"Awful how? Give me more words."

"You can say what you want to about my culpability with Mr. Jay, but this time, for sure, it was all my fault."

"How?"

"You have to understand. I never got to have those preteen boyfriend/ girlfriend relationships. I was five foot seven inches in sixth grade wearing size sixteen jeans. No boys showed interest. A lot of them were downright mean. Plus, there was the aftermath of all the bullshit from telling my parents about Mr. Jay. Any attractions I did acknowledge to myself, I had to keep secret or my mom would call me boy crazy. The only men who ever called me good-looking were adults. Another time, I bumped into a junior high basketball coach from another school who was refereeing a high school summer league game before I got fat again. He asked if I was the girl he remembered. He said I turned out pretty." Even I am getting confused in my own word salad. "I'm sorry this is so jumbled. I haven't talked about this with anyone in close to twenty-five years."

"It's okay, Stacey, that is trauma."

"How? Coach didn't do anything. I was the one who fell for him."

"I think he did do something, or at least he wanted to. You said a few minutes ago that he was grooming you. Can you recognize that as traumatic? Especially when we consider your experiences with Mr. Jay? Were you and your coach ever alone?"

"Yeah."

"Where?"

"In his office with the blinds closed, in the training room, in his Camry."

"Why were you in his car?"

"I babysat for his kid. I'd stay overnight and he would drive me home the next morning. There was a different girl he went on a diet with before me, maybe two. One of them babysat for him too. I think there were others after me as well. Nothing ever happened. I mean, his wife was in the house."

"Not all abuse is physical. Many instances are emotionally rather than physically exploitive, but they are abusive. It is more like sexual harassment than sexual violation. It is real and has real consequences."

"That makes it harder to comprehend."

"Maybe, but it is more important to consider how it made you feel than to comprehend it."

"How did it make me *feel*?? Like a fucking idiot. I WAS an idiot. I was so desperate for attention. It could be that I made it all up."

"Made what up?"

"That he cared about me, that there was more between us than a normal teacher-student relationship."

"Stacey you were a child. He was—" I cut her off.

"I wasn't FIVE anymore, Piper. I was FOURTEEN. Geezus, how stupid can one person be to let this happen twice?"

"Stacey, lots of girls begin to feel attraction toward older men around that age. If my theater club director had behaved that way with me, I would have totally fallen for him." This breaks me out of my dissociative trance as I look up to see if she is serious.

She is. "This is why we have statutory rape and consent laws to protect minors from adults. He was the adult. You were a child. Think about what you know about brain development. At fourteen, you were not developmentally capable of regulating your feelings or giving consent. He was taking advantage of that." None of this makes a dent in my self-loathing.

"It got worse after he wouldn't talk to me anymore. A long time later, I found out my mother called him and told him to stay away from me. She never told me that."

"What do you think led to her intervening?"

"One morning, I had gained two pounds. I was crying in the shower. She heard me all the way upstairs."

"What did she say?"

"Not to let it take over my whole life."

"Your weight?"

"Uh-huh."

"Did she say anything about your coach?"

"No. This was before she found my journal." I felt so desperate to keep losing. If I didn't, his approval, which warmed me like a June sun, would disappear back behind the clouds of despair I was all too familiar with. "I wrote a lot about hating myself and wanting to die."

"What happened when your mom found your journal?"

"She and my dad did one of their ambush talks where they got me alone and confronted me."

"What did they say?"

"Dad basically said he understood how this could happen. It was hard to read his emotions. I wasn't ever sure if he was more concerned about the situation or concerned about how upset my mother would be. My mom was afraid that I might kill myself because of what she read. If I did that, she told me she would never survive it. If I killed myself, it would kill her too."

"Wow, that's a lot. How did that make you feel?"

"Guilty, but I take the promise I made her seriously." I am spent. "So much for staying parked in neutral this session. I should have known Coach would come up eventually, but I didn't see it happening today. Compared to what happened with Mr. Jay, it's easier to dismiss Coach's antics. There are currently fewer triggers for him because the body memories are different. I can feel his arm around me. I can hear his voice."

"Not all triggers are physical, Stacey."

"Yeah, anything that makes me feel used, manipulated, or dismissed for coming up short reminds me of him, and Mr. Jay too. Any discussion about my weight sends me into tailspins."

"That is understandable, and something we need to address when you are ready."

"By the end, I hated my coach the way anyone who casts themselves as a jilted lover would. I didn't, I don't feel like I was a victim the way I do with Mr. Jay."

***

The lesson from this time with my coach? Further proof that my body—that I—was damaged goods, especially once I gained all the weight back, and then some. Overall, I left this situation feeling like I would either be alone for the rest of my life or take whatever man might accept me as is. Any attempt or expectation to change myself for a man became a huge trigger. When I consider that it took over a year to mention my coach the first time, it is no surprise that I rarely have found the courage to mention him in this office again.

CHAPTER 26

Like Mopping Up the Sea with a Sponge

Sessions 74, 75, 76 & 77
Muddy grief seeps out of every pore. Piper mops it up, wrings it out, and empties the bucket for next week.

CHAPTER 27

Real or Not Real

Session 78

The last few weeks leave me feeling like half the blood's been drained from my body. I am a little disoriented as I breathe in the familiar waiting room scent. Please let me reconnect to the time when coming here felt empowering. When I believed I had a chance to scale this mountain and look out from its summit.

As I take my seat, the couch feels more normal. I am less aware of how it sucks you in.

Piper is looking over her notes. It is rare for her to begin sessions this way. "I want to check and see if you have experienced any suicidal thoughts." We do this from time to time. It does not catch me off guard.

"I'm doing okay. It got more intense for a while, but it's subsiding."

"How are you otherwise?"

"Like maybe I'm through the worst of it."

"Good," she says as I smile sheepishly. No one wants to be her therapist's basket case client. "What's this week been like?"

"I can think clearer, more objectively." She seems pleased, but also that she's been impatient for me to arrive at this point. I care less about how pleased she is than how well my statements represent where I am. Maybe I'll celebrate this one by telling Sam about it. She's the best person to muster some celebratory cheer over wins

I won't let myself get over-the-top excited about.

"What are some things you have been thinking about?"

"I was stuck in a catastrophizing spiral." Even as the rawness of these thoughts lingers, they've lost their power. Like after a wicked storm, something about the air still conveys that it happened. "Everything becomes black or white when I circle the drain. I lose all perspective."

"It is good that you can see that. This happens to all of us sometimes, but child sexual abuse can intensify those feelings a lot. I do not want you to minimize what you went through by my making a comparison, but you are not alone in that."

"The exercise about emotions and surviving through the tough ones helps. I tacked it on my bulletin board." My eyes hit the floor as I continue, "I am sorry that I've overreacted to so many things you've said the last couple of months. My brain might be done trying to convince me that my family didn't like me."

"I did not observe anything I'd describe that way. I do not like that label on principle. Overreacted is a word that gets hurled at sensitive people, wonderfully sensitive," she adds, which causes the corners of my mouth to smile. "I am glad you mentioned your family. Tell me more about being liked as a child."

The fatigue forces a delay between the time my brain tells the muscles of my mouth to move and when they execute the movements. "It might be possible that it wasn't as clear cut as I used to think. They maybe didn't dislike me as much as it seems."

"But it still feels like they disliked you?" There's a danger of the sadness creeping back in if I respond out loud to that.

"I brought something to show you. It was my birthday a few days ago."

"Happy Birthday."

"Thanks, I don't like to make a big deal about it, but we had fun. Sam got a cake and we ate sushi. My mom sent a box of gifts. She still gives us $1 for each year old we are in our birthday card."

"That is getting to be a nice pile of cash for you," Piper jokes.

"She wrote a nice message."

"Yeah? What did it say?"

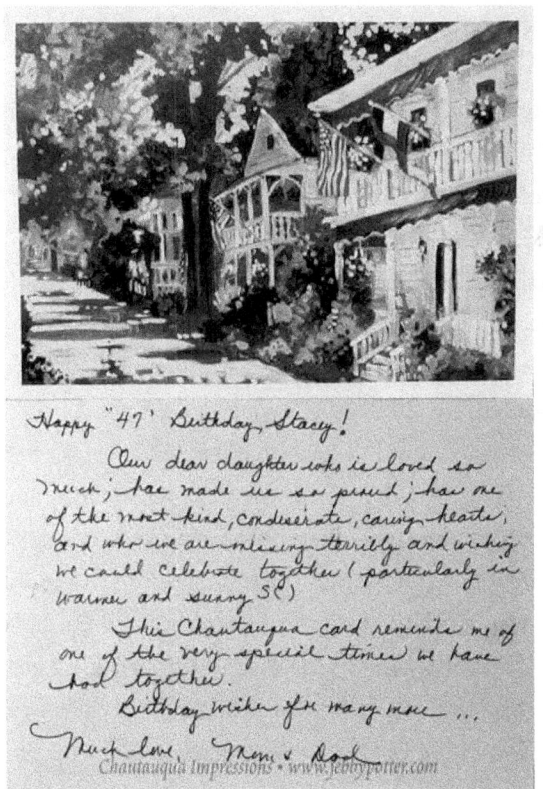

"Happy 47th Birthday to our dear daughter who is loved so much; has made us so proud; has one of the most kind, considerate, caring hearts; and who we are missing terribly and wishing we could celebrate together. This Chautauqua card reminds me of one of the very special times we have had together. Birthday wishes for many more... Much love, Mom & Dad"

"Chautauqua is the lake you go to for vacation with them, right?" I nod, "What a beautiful message." She pauses. "Do you believe she means it?"

"I'm doing better. When I can stay in the present, it's easier."

"How does that make you feel?" She's taking her lines out of the therapist's playbook verbatim today.

"Good, but sad. I don't understand why I felt like they didn't like me."

"Tell me the words your mom wrote to describe you again."

"Kind, considerate, and caring."

"Are kind, considerate, and caring people likable?"

"Yes."

"Do you think she thought you were kind, considerate, and caring as a child?" This one is more challenging.

"One time on a Facebook post, another professor wrote a comment. Something about how caring and compassionate I can be. My mom replied that I've been that way since I was a little girl."

"It is interesting that you chose to say how caring and compassionate you can be rather than how caring and compassionate you are." I hate it when she hangs these suggestions disguised as observations around our conversations. "Can you tell me any memories that you have of feeling liked? Not loved, because I get the sense you believe your parents loved you, but that they liked you?" I have to think for a long time. Any memory that pops up, the serpents swallow whole.

"My dad took me camping, just me. We just went into the state forest behind our house, but I think he had a good time."

"That sounds fun. How old were you?"

"Sixth grade or seventh? I was wearing pink sweatpants and they were filthy by the time we came home." Even as happiness surfaces, a serpent says he did this because he thought he was not spending enough time with me, not because he wanted to. "He took me ice skating once on the pond at our neighbor's farm. Dorothy Hamill was in the Olympics and every little girl in America wanted to be her. My mom let me cut my hair like hers."

"It is interesting that both those memories are of times when you had one-on-one time. Was that rare?"

"With my dad, yes. We mostly did everything together. My parents and my sister always chose to be outside. I didn't love it like they did. I didn't hate it, but Carrie loved it." I stop for a minute. "It was also hard because I could never keep up. No matter what, my dad and sister were way far ahead. My mother was stuck waiting for me."

"What age does it feel like you are when you are thinking about this?"

"All ages. My dad just has long legs. But I was permanently out of breath. I hated it. Every once in a while, my dad would find a place to sit and wait. I would think, just a little farther, when we reach him I can rest. When we'd get there, he'd say 'Oh good, you're here' and take off walking again."

"Did you ever say anything?"

"No, because this was more evidence that I was a fat slowpoke who was too lazy to get in shape. I was too ashamed. There was one time—I don't remember this all that well—but it was a story they loved to tell. We went on a long back road bike ride. It was really far. If you drove that way in a car it would take at least twenty minutes one way."

"Do you remember how old you were?"

"First grade, maybe second? I still had my powder blue bike. It was a kid's bike and had short pedals. Even my dad agreed it was hard to pedal. I was trying so hard to keep up. The gravel road was lined on both sides with hemlock trees. My tears made everything blurry. The story they tell is that I got off my bike in a huff, threw it in the ditch, and said 'I am not going to pedal any farther.'"

"Wow, I would like to have seen that."

"They let me rest, a while. Maybe it was the same time my dad told me he would give me a dollar if I rode the rest of the way without complaining. When they tell this story, my mother talks about how they didn't know what they were going to do if they couldn't convince me to peddle home. After, my dad never offered up the dollar. I asked my mom about it, and she said to ask him. When he pulled out his wallet, he had one dollar in it. They joked that I was taking his last dollar, which made my guilt over the whole situation skyrocket."

"What is coming up for you?"

"I feel ridiculous for telling you this."

"Huh, I'm surprised. I was going to comment on how ridiculous the whole situation seems, but none of that has to do with you."

"*Carrie* would have been able to keep up at my age."

"You think so? If you had an adult bike and were going on a bike ride with a seven-year-old with a little kid's bike, would you expect them to keep up?"

"No."

"Right. I was not there, but don't you think it was unreasonable for them to expect you to bike that far?"

"They wanted to be outside and there was no one they could leave me with."

"That is true, they like being outside and they liked doing things you didn't necessarily like, but that doesn't mean they did not like you." Good try, Piper, the serpents are insisting otherwise. "Were there other activities you all enjoyed?"

"We all liked to swim. If the water was too cold for Mom, she watched."

"When you were swimming, did it ever seem like they wished you were not around?" Something clicks. I tell the snakes to shush; I want to hear this.

"No, in fact, my dad liked to laugh because I could do cannonballs way better than Carrie."

"Have you ever told them what an impact this had on you?"

"No. It doesn't matter. Besides, they have my weight on their side. I am lazy and fat. It's best if I stay out of the way." Piper's face suggests this is sad for her to hear.

"Whether they were trying to help, or ignorant of your struggle, it sounds like they were unaware of their impact."

"They assumed that they knew better what I was feeling than I did. They thought I was making excuses, and they didn't want me to be fat."

"Even if that is true—I am not saying it is—but even if it were, none of that seems like confirmation that they disliked you so much that they did not care if you were molested."

Game, set, match.

CHAPTER 28

Session 115: A Glimpse Into the Future

Last session helped me realize the overlap among times when I sink into the abyss and times when my thinking becomes most black and white. Nuanced discernment, which considers shades of gray, is challenging under the best of circumstances. Finding the subtlety in a data set or the form of a coffee cup fresh from the pottery kiln is easier than recognizing the gradations in the arguments you have with your own mind.

Here's what I am beginning to think: my little-girl amygdala took over the task from my parents of protecting me long before it was capable. Piper describes this as part of my "insecure attachment." Is it once again attempting to shield me with this narrative of a family who loved me but did not like me? What perceived dangers is my limbic system avoiding this time? What possible protection does a narrative that my family did not like me hold? There are the misty beginnings of an answer, but they refuse to come into focus.

Even as I struggle to reason my way through this, these memories seem commonplace. I should not need hours of therapy to rehash them. Younger sisters are younger sisters. They think they're a tag-along; they grow up; they live their lives. Who cares if one Saturday, sometime in the 1980s, a chubby little girl got tired on a bike ride, tossed her bike in the ditch, and refused to pedal any farther?

***

"Piper, do you remember what you said about sexual abuse when we first started working together?"

"I say a lotta things on that subject. Can you help me out a little?"

"Of course," I say with an embarrassed laugh, followed by a lengthy silence. *"I wanted to downplay what happened with Mr. Jay. You responded that childhood sexual abuse is one of the worst capital-T Traumas out there. It was such a relief to hear you say that. At the time, I didn't, maybe couldn't, pay close enough attention to the explanation that followed. You said it's one of the worst because children cannot ensure their own safety. They rely on their caregivers for protection. When their violations are repeated and secret, the child's most basic need for psychological safety goes unmet in the context of having their physiological safety needs fulfilled. This paradox engenders profound confusion. Lacking the maturity to clarify and comprehend what's taking place, they draw conclusions based on complete misperceptions."*

"That sounds like me, filtered through a professor's brain," she adds with an almost imperceptible eye roll, *"but yes, I remember. What's bringing that up for you?"*

"Well, remember a few months back when I was stuck for weeks, convinced that my family didn't like me? That they didn't want me around and that's why Mr. Jay could do the things he did?"

"Uh-huh, it was hard to watch you struggle. I was really worried about you." Even after all this time, I blush.

"I think I understand better the nuance of what was happening."

"Tell me more."

"It was as if my mind was heading toward a reactor-level meltdown. When system failures are physiological rather than psychological, toxins accumulate because organs like your liver no longer

function. By comparison, debilitating depressive episodes allow toxic thoughts to overwhelm our brains' executive functions. Those thoughts forced me to relive how I actually felt during—not just what I remembered from—his invasions. Back then, my child brain could not accept that my mom and dad were not protecting me from this monster. The fact that they treated him like a good Christian—that he was such a big fucking deal at church—no words." My voice trails off for a minute before continuing. "I could not accept that my parents were not able to keep me safe. My little-girl mind manufactured an alternate explanation. They didn't like me and therefore, they didn't care about these desecrations. My brain used normal things, like parents losing their tempers, an older sister's annoyance at a younger sister, as proof. These were the evidence by which it created a story to protect me from an even more frightening reality... It's been at it again for a couple of months now."

***

She sits quietly taking notes. She does not let on that I've scaled another rockface, maybe the most vertical one yet. As a teacher, I recognize this look. It's the look we get after weeks of observing students struggle. Then, one of them suddenly, finally, connects the dots we've drawn the lines among over and over, often bringing the rest of the class along with them. Exasperation, relief, and triumph battle for control of our facial expressions.

These seemingly small but essential victories get lost in the shuffle. I wish we, Piper and I, but also society celebrated them more. However, that would require acknowledging the mental injury, and the mental re-injuries, in the first place, which society does not appear ready to do.

Even when my analytical, thinking neocortex brain areas offer memories as they were, rather than through the survivalist spin my emotional cingulate cortex and amygdala layer on in this present-day attempt to keep me safe, I do not always understand. What in my past—what in my present—is worth our time to consider? What matters? I make a mental note to ask Piper about this next week. I already resign myself to her probable answer: we will not know what matters until my brain dredges up the next memory and commits to the legwork of feeling it out.

CHAPTER 29

Conundrums and Puzzles

Session 79

I arrive at our session late but determined to work. By late, I mean that I arrive on time. I get the sense that I am strong enough to tear off a scab and work toward cleaning out the infection festering underneath. Which scab? I do not know, but the analogy helps. No one wants to go to the dermatologist and have a pus-filled cyst debrided. However, the pressure that builds up, and the hotness around the infected flesh, are also sources of pain.

"Hi, Stacey." Here we go. As I say hi back, I imagine Piper in scrubs, gloves, and a full-face shield with some sort of pimple-popping tool in her hand. It makes me chuckle. For as many proverbial body fluids as this poor woman gets splashed in the face with, even a speck of real-life pimple goo might cause her to pass out.

"What have you been thinking about?" I almost laugh out loud. If she only knew. At the same time, my little internal joke has loosened my defenses a bit, I'm ready to dive in.

"Well, it's hard to explain, but I am trying to figure out how some things are related. It's like I found some puzzle pieces lying around, and I don't know how they fit together or even whether I have enough pieces to know what picture they make."

"Okay, let's start with the pieces."

"I've been thinking a lot about how affectionate I was, how I wanted attention, how..." I stop. Those defenses were not as

239

loosened as I thought. A mushroom grows at super speed in my throat—like how they appear to in a time-lapse nature video. It is pushing on my vocal cords. Then comes the wash of hot, steamy shame. I keep waiting for Piper to step in and run with the attention and affection pieces, but no such luck.

"How it felt good." The scab is off. We hit the motherlode. Piper will need a suction pump to drain this discharge. "It did," I whisper, revealing my deepest secret. Those six words feel like excrement in my mouth, the same way they did when I told Indira. If you tried to hold this volume of shame, it would require an oil tanker. Piper holds the line on her silence. She offers no assistance—no fancy instrument to excise this recurrent boil without spilling its contents. I'm gonna have to pop this sucker myself. "I set myself up for the worst of this. I could have stopped it before it came to that." In my mind, I might as well have arrived at Mr. Jay's house in lingerie and stilettos. Despite her silence, and despite that it's likely the fiftieth time she has listened to me go through variations on this theme—that little Stacey has only herself to blame for everything bad that has ever happened—Piper's empathy and sympathy have not waned.

"Do you remember if you liked getting hugs from your mom and dad when you were young?"

"Yes, I hugged my dad when he came home from work. His clothes sometimes brought home the scent of the machines at the factory. He is an engineer and designed the equipment. If something broke, he was also the one to fix it. My mom used to get upset when he came home with grease on his tie."

"Did you hug your mom?"

"Any chance we got. She hardly ever sat still, but when she did, I wanted to be on the couch with her."

"Describe what it felt like when you got hugs." My body

reflexively softens. "Nice."

"Did you ever give your mom or dad a kiss?"

"Every night at bedtime from at least one of them. We always kissed my grandparents goodbye. We called my grandfather's coarse facial hair his crispy whiskers. Gramma had the softest cheeks of anyone in the whole world. She was a good hugger. Her arms were soft and fleshy. A hug from her was like being wrapped in actual love."

"What about your sisters?"

"I loved holding Samantha when she was a baby. She was a terrific hugger. She would get you right around the neck. She'd make us stand together for group hugs and say 'Happily family.'" I am overwhelmed with instantaneous homesickness.

"What about Carrie?"

"Um, no, she refused hugs unless forced. She was too tough—too tomboy. You know, I never thought about it, but I always tried to follow her lead. Did I deprive myself of the hugs and affection I wanted because I thought I had to be like her? Plus, there was our age difference. She was ready to separate herself as a normal adolescent while I was at an age to happily remain affectionate."

"That is a good insight, but the point I want to make is that there is nothing wrong with giving and receiving affection when it is healthy, respectful of the other person, and mutual. Even with Mr. Jay, any affection he gave you or the fact that it felt nice is nothing for you to be ashamed of. He is the *only* person who needs to be ashamed. He was responsible for controlling his impulses. Your feelings were normal. This is why we have laws to protect children from adults—to protect anyone from unwanted advances or actions. It's why we debate and research ages of consent for purchasing things like alcohol and cigarettes. You could not, nor should you have expected yourself to, decipher his intent or to be aware of when he would cross the line and when he would not. With him, perfectly acceptable exchanges of affection between children and adults, like hugs, were twisted into something that was not okay. Something that became corrupted by behaviors that would terrify and hurt you." She pauses to let this sink in but continues before I can respond. "Once you were aware that it was not okay, you stopped it."

"Thank you for saying that." I need a minute to absorb this. I would have no trouble making this argument to one of my students or on their behalf. I could put fire and fury behind words like these if it were in service of someone else. Instead, I stay mired in my own filthiness.

"What about this statement is hard for you to accept?"

"The struggle of not knowing what happened when. If I knew that once it hurt, if once I was afraid... if from then on, I didn't ever let it happen again... maybe I wouldn't feel culpable... but the time in his bedroom, I was wearing purple pants. I had those purple pants before the rainbow belt. The rainbow belt was in the car, the time I literally helped him into my pants." That last part is accompanied by the loathing I feel. The loathing I feel toward that little girl who was happy to see him that day—fucking disgusting. "But I don't know what happened in the car after I undid the buckle. I blacked out, which also happened the time he walked me to the waterfall, and something—the worst thing—happened in the woods." She stays silent lest this shy, but necessary, confusion wilt.

"The time in his bedroom I was terrified. I can relive every minute of that one. He asked me if it felt good. I said yes. GEEZUS, I TOLD HIM IT FELT GOOD. IT DIDN'T. It hurts all over again. Will this torment never stop? How did I not run away from him and make sure I never ever was anywhere near him again?"

"You tried. Remember telling me about the time you begged

to not have to spend the weekend at his house? Children, including my own, do not always have a say in where they will go, or who will be around when they get there."

"Maybe, it was the time in the woods. Maybe I am confusing the time in his bedroom with the time in the woods. My body seems bigger in the woods. After, when we were walking back to my house, it felt like I'd had a seizure. The woods might have been late spring, early summer. The trees are green. Gypsy moth caterpillars are everywhere. I am almost sure I was in second grade. I completely broke down that year at school. The classroom window was open." I feel the snot dripping from my little-girl nose and the thickness of my saliva. I grab a tissue even though I am not crying in the present.

"We grew bean plants in milk cartons. When we went through the tray, mine was a shriveled yellow stem with one tiny, wilted leaf. It was the last straw. Paul didn't want his. Mrs. Simpkins told him he could give it away. He said, 'Raise your hand if you want this.' I couldn't reign in my ugly cry. She whispered to Paul then gestured toward me. He argued something about me not having my hand up. She got him to give it to me anyway. The lettering on the milk carton was red."

"Is this the puzzle? The pieces you want to fit together are a timeline of when he molested you?"

My head shakes yes in defeat. We have worn out this road. I know what she will say. I have obsessed over this memory off and on for years. I've scoured the internet for everything from what year Fisher Price sold dolls with pink cloth bodies to which years gypsy moth caterpillars were most abundant in the Northeast. Anything that could string together this handful of snapshots into a full documentary.

"What feels significant about this memory?"

I swallow hard and tense my torso. "If anything happened with Mr. Jay's penis, it was in the woods by the waterfall. Whatever happened that time, it was the worst. I can see the log he found for us to sit on." Adult Stacey is in trouble. My stomach contorts and my neck gets creepy. My back arches and my shoulders tense against this memory consuming my body. "Dried leaves crackle under my knees. One flash of white underwear and the fabric of his pants... right in my face." My palm flattens a half inch from my nose. "His pants are a weave of two different thread colors that blend into a pinkish brown. Then, it all goes black until we walked back. He steered my neck with his hand. Did he hold me that way to keep me upright? Was the butterscotch candy he gave me supposed to clean my mouth?"

"Stacey, I am so sorry you had to go through this." It's such an easy thing to say, like the "sorry for your loss" in a condolence card that's somehow supposed to encompass the enormity of grief. She's said it dozens of times. Every time it is genuine and sincere. There are not enough copay dollars in the world to match the worth of feeling understood in my own devastation. "Can you remember anything else?"

"Yes, but I don't know whether it is real or not. I only remembered more pieces when I worked with Indira, and we did EMDR."

"Why would you not believe the memories you recovered with EMDR? You know the science."

"Knowledge is not always power, Piper. The practice was just gaining traction back then. As a grad student, I went into it with a healthy dose of skepticism. Plus, I asked one of our cognitive psychology professors what he thought of it. Without all the data we have now, it was easy for him to dismiss it as hocus pocus. Its validity and utility stand up, but my experiences are more than twenty years old."

"I think Dr. Hettes needs to step aside and let Stacey have a chance to work through this."

"Other than the time at the waterfall, which happens to be the only time I suspect that he took out his penis, I retained enough memories to accept what Indira was able to draw out and clarify during our seven other EMDR sessions. There was also something different about the details EMDR revealed about those other times that felt distinctly more reliable, more believable."

"That's interesting. Let's sit with that and see if anything changes. Is there anything else you remember with more certainty?"

"I used to cry alone in the bathroom with the door locked. This could be around the time my mom reached the top of the stairs as I was coming out of there one day. She asked me what was wrong. I looked straight at her and asked her if she really loved me."

"Tell me what it was like to ask her that."

"I wasn't sure which was worse, living with the question or getting confirmation of the answer that, in my mind, could only be no."

"It took a lot of courage to voice such a scary question." I have no interest in talking about courage.

"If the time in the woods was worse than the time in his bedroom, and I think it was, then maybe the woods happened after the bedroom. Pretty sure the woods were after the time with my rainbow belt. Then... then at least once whatever happened in the woods happened, I might have figured out to say no. If that was in the spring of second grade, then maybe it was later that same summer when we were at his house that I said no."

Piper lets these memories settle a bit. "Tell me again about saying no." She is going to finagle a way for me to own up to my courage—whether I want to or not. This repetition offers me the chance to speak a flashback into existence. "The morning light coming through the door is beautiful. I thought I'd gotten away without him knowing I was awake. When I came out of the bathroom, he was there. His eyes are excited. He said, 'Come watch TV with me.' I said no. I could not look at him and speak at the same time. I turned back toward the basement door, which was a hundred miles away. He asked, 'Why not?' I said the word 'no' one more time."

"My god, I admire that little girl's courage. I am sorry you had to endure such a moment. I get that you want to piece this story together into a complete narrative. Let's talk about what you hope will come from that." I can tell that she wishes she did not have to be the therapist right now, that she did not have to ask me that. Despite my best efforts to shore up a wall of professionalism between us, Piper's voice comes through as the voice of a friend, a best friend. The friend who you know would hold your hair back while you puke, then bring you a pillow and blanket as your cheek rests against cool bathroom floor tiles. Like a best friend, she is also here to point out the hard truths and sit in them with me until I am ready to do something about it.

CHAPTER 30

Forty-Two Reasons

Session 80
"Have you thought more about why it's become important to you to piece together a timeline of the molestations?"

"I don't know for sure. If I can comprehend it, maybe I can accept it. Accept that I am more innocent than I let myself believe. That I am not responsible for what happened back then or for what happened at work. I don't want to admit that I am responsible for bringing this festering mass of my childhood out of remission."

"Having me tell you, again, that you are not responsible for either is unlikely to change things. But, even if what you want to happen was possible, even if we found every puzzle piece, I don't think you would gain satisfaction from that either. I do not want to be the one to dash your hopes that solving this mystery will make everything ok. It's my job to say that it doesn't work that way." She has made similar arguments before. I let them go in one ear and out the other. It has to matter. I need to conquer this narrative.

"Then what am I searching for?"

"That is something we have to figure out." Arggh, what is it like for therapists to watch their patients react to these seven words day in and day out? Some days they land like a punch in the gut. Other days, it is as if I climbed what I believed was the last hill only to see two more once I peer over the horizon. Why can't it be like solving a crime, or at least not make me want to pull my hair out?

"Okay," I say resignedly. "I wish you would tell me when I am wasting your time. I want you to know I am trying, Piper."

"You are not wasting my time. I know. I know how hard you are working—how frustrating this process is—but it is a process. One that we cannot find our way through by understanding it. We have to experience it."

"Oh my god, you have never sounded more like a therapist than you did just now." We stare at each other and laugh, both thankful for a break in the frustration.

"I would like us to do some homework for next week. I want us both to make a list of factors we think led to Mr. Jay molesting you." Again, with the m-word, she will not let up with the m-word today.

"Okay."

"Next week we will compare lists." Will one week be enough time? Better get started.

Session 81

My typed and printed list is in hand, ready to turn in. I almost laminated it as a joke.

It has everything. Style, alliteration, a crescendo toward the most damning evidence that I... sorry, my *inner child*, is as pathetic and culpable as I know her to be. I even throw in some comic relief to keep it light. A+ students need to grab their professor's attention by giving the assignment something that makes it pop. I should know. I've been grading variations on the same damn lab report on metabolic respiration in yeast since 2004. As I stretch to hand the list over, Piper says, "No, I want you to read it out loud." Ugh, every single time. Piper would make such a great teacher. "How many did you come up with?"

"Forty-two," proudly states the overachiever, "how about you?"

"I have two." I have a hunch her two are going to wipe the floor with my forty-two.

"Okay, here goes."

Forty-two Reasons the Snakes in my Brain Want Me to Believe Mr. Jay Did What He Did

(I hope to gain the upper hand by conceding her point while I still make the definitive argument against it.)

1. No one liked me.
2. No one wanted me around.
3. I was a sucker.
4. I wanted attention.
5. I was affectionate.
6. I liked being hugged.
7. I even liked being kissed.
8. I liked feeling special.
9. I liked attention from anyone who was willing to spend one-on-one time with me.
10. I was gullible.
11. I was born on a Saturday (I Googled it).
12. People were relieved to have someone else watch me because I was such a burden.
13. My body betrayed me by responding to his early grooming with pleasure.
14. I was too cowardly to report.
15. I did not understand that I could report.
16. I was so good at hiding my emotions no one knew.
17. I was so bad at hiding my emotions that everyone always thought I was upset. This was no different.
18. I was super sensitive.
19. I cried a lot.
20. I didn't cry when I was frightened.

21. I didn't tell the truth when he asked me if it felt good, so he kept doing it.
22. I blacked out. I didn't learn to be frightened the way I would have/should have.
23. I was unable to read the danger signs.
24. I ignored the danger signs.
25. I was too loud when I snuck out of bed to pee.
26. I was jealous of any other kids when he paid attention to them, so I made myself available.
27. I was too fat.
28. I wasn't fat enough.
29. I was slow.
30. I was ugly with tangled hair and dirty fingernails.
31. I was adorable with blond hair and blue eyes.
32. I was bad.
33. I was dirty.
34. I was a sinner.
35. I was a good girl who did what she was told.
36. I was a good Christian.
37. They said Jesus would keep me safe from all harm. This must not, in fact, be harmful.
38. The devil made him do it.
39. I was mature for my age.
40. I acted like a baby.
41. I liked to play dress up and wear high heels and paint my fingernails.
42. I sucked at Atari. It was never my turn.

Piper's List of Reasons Why I Was Molested:
1. I was female.
2. He was able to gain access to me.

Damn it.

PART FOUR

Better, Not All Better, But Better

Lift up your eyes upon
This day breaking for you.
— *Maya Angelou*

CHAPTER 31

Be Like Iris Dement: Let the Mystery Be

I have no memory of what else we discussed after Piper read her list. I was too busy witnessing her words scald serpentine demons like holy water. While they did not melt into the floorboards of my skull, hissing "What a world, what a world," their tubular bodies sidewinded into oblivion. I am not sure if Piper's airstrike against his serpents is a plot twist of this therapeutic escapade or the plot itself. I do know she is 100 percent right. After so many false starts, I am freaking relieved. Piper somehow located the button for an elevator that brought us fourteen thousand feet straight up.

I am sure I will want to ponder this mysterious turn of events in short order, but not today. Today, I want to ramble along with the Chili Peppers in the late spring sun. I want to rejoice that my body holds an energetic abundance with which I can admire the scent of honeysuckle, the phosphorescent greenness of budding leaves, the gentle delicateness of first of spring grass—to breathe in their newness, to ponder the wonders of their symbiosis with the soil as well as the stinging, biting insects that frighten me and pollinate them.

For days, I've repeated the words *Mr. Jay molested me because he was a child molester* over and over in my head. I even said them aloud a few times. I've gone about this investigation as if studying a serial killer. Mr. Jay was as much a predator as Jack the Ripper, but there is a difference. Serial killers are notorious for having a type, for rituals, for being all the things that make them such compelling characters in crime dramas.

Child predators do not have those things. They are opportunistic hyenas to the serial killer's stealthy cheetah. As I now remember Piper telling me during our last session, child predators have two objectives: to engage in sex acts with children and to not get caught. I was not especially bad, or especially good, or especially wanting attention, or especially blending into the wallpaper. I was just there.

It is fascinating that we, as a culture, gravitate to the stories of serial killers but avoid the stories of the molesters. Maybe this fits under the same umbrella for why the news media obsesses about airplane crashes and seldom considers the number of daily auto accidents. If we considered how dangerous—how more likely we are to sustain injuries in a car crash than a plane crash—we would never take our SUV out of the driveway again. Most people cannot discuss or even face child abuse. It is the pervasive danger. We have lived it. It surrounds us. It has the potential to draw us under its treacherous smothering blanket if we do not keep acknowledgment of it at bay.

Imagine if, instead of disfiguring our insides, once every eight minutes a predator chopped off the limb of a little one? How would society's response be different? I don't know what it's like to live without a limb, but I do know Mr. Jay hacked away part of my soul.

Why this session? Why these words? I make a promise to myself that I will try to answer these questions someday. Today, I want to dance in an orchard of peach blossoms. Thank you, Jesus. Thank you, Buddha. Thank you, Anna O., and your pioneering "talking cure" that inspired Freud and all who followed. Thank you to the women who say "Don't fucking touch me" while they organize opposition to the patriarchal silencing complex.

Thank you, Mom. Thank you, Dad. Thank you to my own heart, which refuses to allow my mind and body to settle for the absence of suffering this time. Thank you, Piper. Thank you for committing to enduring the questions I had to press upon you *ad nauseum* in order to realize that no one can provide the answers, only the space to live them. Today, joy leaves my scientific mind content with observing this euphoric rebirth of hope rather than analyzing it. Today, I am a newborn too busy adjusting to the light—a light that feels like the first true light my retinas have ever known—to wonder where the darkness went. I am consumed with an infant's appetite—to taste, to see, to smell, to grow.

A singular reality occupies my mind. For Mr. Jay and all the Mr. Jays out there, some of us are low-hanging fruit, ripe for the picking, nothing more. He was no more discriminating in his choices than a fox pouncing on the first baby bunny to make its way out of the warren. I am no more to blame than that little rabbit for what happened to me. Predation is an inevitable part of this world—red in tooth and claw. The bunny was unlucky. So was I.

My traits and flaws that I insist on blaming for what happened are not the causes of my experience, tragic though it was. The fact that he was an irrepressible child molester is. And I am the one who brought him down. A willful force inside me tells me to slow my thoughts and write these sentences out by hand as many times as it takes. I manage eight repetitions on a single page before I get a thumb cramp.

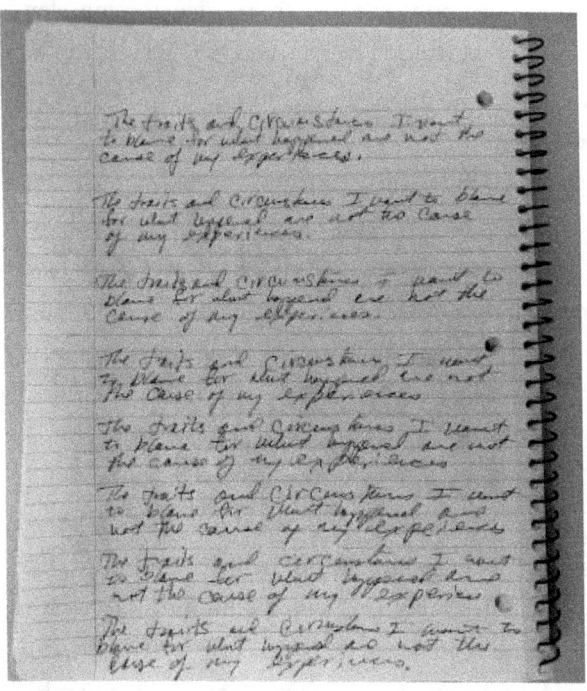

It is true that I did not question the commands of adults. Our culture mandates children obey, especially little girls. I did not want to upset adults. I wanted them to love me. I had zero inclination that defying gender norms was an option. I was one of those little girls told not to be bossy on the occasions I expressed my opinion, even by a grandmother who, in all other ways, supported and accepted me as I was. As a middle child, I was a third wheel in many situations.

None of these, nor the forty-one other reasons on my list, led my body to experience invasion. Mr. Jay made the decision to ignore the consequences both to me as a child as well as to the adult I would become. Society made the decision to turn its back rather than attempt to protect us.

The simple fact is, that without a predator, there is no prey. It's that simple, isn't it? How many more times will Piper and I repeat this exercise before my brain catches up to my heart? Before the serpents shed their skin for the last time and the crevices where they hibernate become their mausoleums.

For the first time since Breakdown Saturday, I have reawakened to the hard-fought realization that my brain's insistence that I am culpable in this capital-T Trauma—and this capital-R Re-trauma—is a bald-faced lie. The re-emergence of these misunderstandings stands in such stark contrast to the life I built as Dr. Hettes. I accepted this life as the best I could make from the scrap heap Mr. Jay left me to work with. This time? This *re*victimization? In some ways it hit harder—hit deeper—because these lies about myself reawakened out of nowhere. In my early years, I knew nothing but this self-loathing. If others were relieved when I was not present, then whatever it was about me that was unlikeable was also the thing that made me culpable. Reexperiencing these memories and feelings after building a life in which I took some measure of satisfaction—and I will go ahead and say it, pride... words don't exist to describe the damage that did.

When Piper and I first met, she recognized that, at face value, my work situation was not my most pressing concern. She could see that these events rekindled those long-dormant flames of self-loathing and self-destruction. She realized this long before we talked at length about either. She hinted as much, but now I understand why it was essential that she patiently inhabited the space where I came to realize this connection. It is easier to look outward and focus on the landmines all around us than to look inward at the areas of ourselves that are the most vulnerable to this shrapnel. Scar tissue appears tough, inflexible, and thick. It also runs deep. If re-injured, it suffers more critical wounds that need specialized attention to heal a second, third, and fourth time.

What now? You cannot rebuild until you have squelched the fires, torn down the remnants, and cleared the debris. Rebuilding on top of a rubble pile will never provide a sturdy foundation. We've made a dent in one of the load-bearing beams of Stacey's House of Trauma. I'd spent months scraping wallpaper off walls that we needed to demolish. Last session was the wrecking ball. Now we have to haul away this rubble.

Is it worth it? In the beginning, it was a matter of survival. I would have killed myself, quickly or slowly, had I not sought help. I have two choices. Live amongst the rubble or construct something new. Rebuilding is the work I never stuck around to do.

I Hope.

Typing those five letters onto this page is a moment of micro-triumph. Last year, last month, last week at this time, I could not have typed them without a limiting qualifier. I could have hoped that it would not rain on Saturday, that Sam would agree to sushi instead of pizza for Friday dinner, that Pepper would let Chili and me sleep late. This capital-H Hope grows somewhere below my xiphoid process, those little nubs of our breastbones that protrude beyond our rib cages. I laugh at the inner nerdiness that makes me want to type that line. God, I needed this reprieve.

CHAPTER 32

Now What?

What a gift this week became. I was able to ask Sam for a hug. I swam four times. I ate healthy food. I even masturbated for the first time in months (three times actually!). I basked in the sunlight finding its way to my insides, but I did not squander it. With the reprieve that Piper's list provided, I am too eager to make more progress to wait for my next session. We have work to do, and I am determined to hold onto this momentum. I decide to fully face the memory that Piper and I have, thus far, peered at through a keyhole. While free from the triggering impact of flashbacks and fragmented thoughts, I set my intention to revisit my EMDR work with Indira. I want to go through the walk to the waterfall. I take note that I am less concerned with reclaiming each detail than diffusing its power. It's clear again. Diffusing a memory's power was the hypothesis with which Indira and I approached those EMDR sessions sometime in 1999.

***

We were coming to the end of our work. I knew I would miss Indira, but she was adamant that once the EMDR sessions were complete, I would not need her anymore. I didn't hold the same faith in this new technique that she did. From the vantage of twenty years later, I can say it worked better than I expected, but even an A+ does not always represent a score of 100 percent. I'd give the EMDR a 96 percent overall in processing what happened, which brings us to the session with Indira when I needed a retest.

EMDR is a technical and prescribed type of therapy. You and your therapist write an outline of the memories in order to work through them point by point. One of Indira's jobs was to keep an account of the scores I assigned to the feelings surrounding a particular event. The goal was to get each down to zero. Some memories started out with scores in the eights, nines, or tens. Once the number reduces to zero, the post-traumatic stress should be gone. I should remember events without reliving them. After we'd worked through all there was to work through, we were coming to a commencement of sorts. Indira asked if any memories held a negative residue. Like a surgical excision, this therapy aimed to leave behind no germs or necrotic tissue from which another infection could resurface.

"*If there is anything, the time on the walk to the waterfall seems like there might be some sort of remainder. Some lingering bits of uneasiness.*" As Indira checked her balance sheet, she found a two sitting beside that memory, not a zero. She chastised herself for being "sloppy." Gorgeous petite women like her—and my mother—do not belong to words like sloppy. I took on her frustration as my fault. "No, no... I should have said something before this." We'd drop that score to zero this time if it killed me.

"Okay, let's go back to the waterfall." I braced myself in the chair as best I could. The concentration these sessions required demanded as little distraction from one's skeleton and postural muscles as possible. Those over-the-shoulder harnesses that lock you into roller coaster seats would have helped. She began the series of sequential hand movements that my eyes had learned to follow. They trigger the bilateral brain stimulation that draws the memories out. "What do you see?"

***

As I join Mr. Jay and my little-girl self walking along the dirt road, I notice my head is the same height as his elbow, crusty with ashy callouses. His belt is dark brown leather. We're approaching the log in the woods. Once he sits, he positions me in front of him. My blue and red shirt has no sleeves, but it isn't a tank top. My shorts feel really short and tight—last summer's clothes pulled out for a warm spring weekend. My hair is in two braids, each on the back of my head, not on the sides. Once he sat, my head stood a tiny bit taller than his. He looks up as he smiles. I didn't know to call his expression desire, but here, watching this memory play out on my mind's silver screen, desire is what it projects. "I want to show you something," he says as his hands wrap around my upper arms, guiding me downward. Dry crackling leaves tickle my winter-white skin as little-girl knees flex so my bottom rests on my feet. My legs experience none of the pain that they would if I tried this pose today.

My body becomes his marionette. My head lifts at the press of his finger and thumb on my chin as he folds down to kiss me. From this angle, his mustache pokes more than tickles. His arms compress me into his soft doughy flesh, pinning mine to my sides.

He's decided it's time. The silver prong at the center of his buckle has stretched the hole of his leather belt from circle into oblong. My eyes widen as his hand undoes his pants to reveal the whiteness of the cotton underneath. Everything remaining of me shrivels. The fabric is so close I can see its vertical weave. The elastic around the top has two stripes, one blue and one yellow. The weight of his belt flops the two halves of his pants to each side.

He draws me toward him. The white cotton comes closer. As he rubs his pelvis against the base of my throat, I strain my neck all the way sideways to keep my airway from being swallowed up by his belly.

He shoves me back. It's out. "Look what happens. I can make it bigger."

I shut my eyes to avoid its ugliness. "Open your mouth." His hands splay across my back, compressing me into him as hard bits of earth press into my knees. I cannot breathe, I cannot breathe. Are you going to let me die for this?

I make a panicked attempt to wriggle free. As he releases me, I begin to sob even before the first deep inhale of the air that he deems less important for me than his pleasure is for him. He pulls me onto his lap and says, "I'm sorry. I'm sorry. I'm sorry I have to do this." His sobs join mine.

***

I hold no conscious memories of this scene, as if a film editor spliced it from the reel of this nightmare. I have vivid memories of the EMDR session with Indira and what it drew forth. There are no words to reconcile the mind fuck of this distinction.

It's probably time to consider how this moment plays into my relationship with snakes. I used to dream that snakes crawled along the paneling of my bedroom walls. In my teens, I told my therapist, Mary Anne, about these nightmares. She commented that Freud concluded that dreaming of snakes was a subconscious representation of a penis. Maybe he was right.

I fucking hate snakes. I have a colleague who studies and loves all things pit viper. More power to him. Snakes are important like penises are important. I happen to have a bad relationship with both. My take is that at least part of my fear of snakes is biological and developed long before what happened at the waterfall. The images of that moment concealed themselves deep in my psyche. I still feel a complete dissociation from this memory. I remember the EMDR experience. How the words I said aloud to Indira reflected the pictures appearing in my mind. But unlike standing on the chair in his garage or unbuckling my rainbow belt, or the caterpillars squishing under his monstrous feet as we walked away from that log, the sound of the waterfall fading, my mind refuses to grant me ownership of the scene my eyes brought forth that day after following the metronome of Indira's hand movements.

***

The shivers that rattle my vertebrae at the sight of an actual snake leave no doubt that I fear them to my core. However, if there is any symbolism associated with this phobia, for me, it is the shame our church sentenced women to carry for Eve's discourse with one over an apple. At least that was the explanation—and shame—church leaders layered onto menstrual cramps and childbirth once they separated us by gender to protect the boys from our "distractions."

The demonic vestiges of Mr. Jay's actions that lurk within me are serpentine as well. They wrap their cylindrical forms around my airways, slither through my mind, constrict my bronchioles. Deep soothing breaths to combat the images they evoke become impossible. Like all reptiles, they sometimes hibernate. I've gone months, even years, without their presence. Once awakened, they resurface by the hundreds the same way some species of snakes work in concert to take down prey. Even here, in the mental safety of writing therapeutically with no pressure to ever share it, my body feels invaded. My muscles twinge and my breaths quicken. Deep inhales of cool calming air slow their advances but never manage their eradication.

This is the life one is left with once another's reptilian desire plays itself out on her tiny frame.

CHAPTER 33

Back to Work

Session 82

As my next session approaches, the euphoria of making more than an inch or two of progress has waned. Yet, it energizes me to think we can begin a new chapter—a new phase—but I have no idea what it should be. If I am not spending our time turning over every stone in my memory to see which holds the hide-a-key to why I was abused, what's next?

Sitting in the waiting room, I take stock and jot a few recurring thoughts into my phone. My joyful mood caused me to sweep these thoughts under the rug until I sat here and readied myself to work.

- I cannot be trusted.
- I cannot be attractive.
- I must stay in control.
- I am afraid.

"Hello, come on back."

Despite my urge to shout, "What's next?" I think it is important to tell Piper how I am doing. So much has happened since my last session. "Before we dive in, I want to say thanks for last week. It was enormously helpful." I refrain from telling her about my trio of orgasms.

"That makes me happy. What in particular was helpful?"

"Your list." She smirks. Piper usually manages to keep them under wraps, but this one sneaks out before a full-on smile follows. She knows I am conceding the point, but she also realizes that I am ecstatic to do so.

"Why do you think it was helpful?"

"I finally heard what you've been saying. I get why therapy feels like walking in circles—why the details of what happened, that I can or cannot remember what happened when, or that the order in which things happened will not be all that helpful."

"Good! What do you think made it land differently this time?"

"I don't know for sure, but for the first time since Breakdown Saturday, the fact that Mr. Jay is the only one to blame for what happened and that no matter the details, it was capital-T Traumatic, sunk in. People have told me this for thirty years. For the last year and a half, it's felt as if I never entertained such a notion. Then, last week, it all made sense again. I could have been all the things I hate about myself, all the things others maybe don't like about me. Without Mr. Jay, the most awful moments of my life would not have happened."

"Does it seem as true today as it did last week?"

"I guess so, why?"

"Well, we've talked about the cyclical nature of therapy—how we need to talk about some things again and again. If we find that we have to revisit this, I do not want you to get frustrated or think that is not a natural part of the process." The molecules of helium in my balloon of happiness commence their inevitable escape.

"So, I cannot expect this to stick?" After Indira's faith in EMDR, this seems defeating.

"Not exactly. More like it is okay if at some point you need a reminder."

"That makes sense. I think too, I understand it, but do not

accept it. I want to distinguish between the euphoria of finally breaking out of this spiraling depression and whatever part of this good feeling might become more permanent. Maybe contentment is the right word?"

"Some euphoria that transitions to contentment sounds like a good outcome. We cannot know for sure whether this will last. Can we agree to stay open to revisiting anything that comes around again?"

Nodding, I say, "I guess it's like cleaning a wound without knowing if you've cleared out every bit of the infection." I pause the conversation.

"What are you thinking?"

"There is something else I am afraid to say."

"I am ready when it feels okay to say it. You can trust me." It's crazy that I need this reminder, but I do. Luckily, Piper offers it as naturally as she asks, "How does that make you feel?"

"Maybe I stay focused on ancillary things, like trying to come up with a timeline, to avoid seeing something else and having to talk about it."

"What is that?" A palpable transition takes place as discomfort displaces the good stuff. I notice that I am less afraid that happiness will never return.

"Mr. Jay molested me and there was nothing I or anyone else could do to stop it. My parents didn't know. I didn't understand."

"That is true. It is awful and I am sad and angry that he did that to you."

"Me too."

"What else do you feel?"

"Afraid."

"Afraid of what?"

"Afraid it might happen again. Not what he did, but what it

did to me. That... I will get hurt like that again."

"People who are hurt the way you were, who were helpless, have every reason to still be afraid. What we can do is gather tools that allow you to feel safer. To better assure your own safety than you could as a child. Can you tell me more about how you might get hurt again or who might hurt you?"

"Anyone who makes me feel betrayed... or used, especially to fulfill their own agenda."

"That makes a lot of sense. Particularly in light of your experience with Dean Grant after the faculty forum. What strategies have you used to protect yourself against those possibilities?"

"I wall myself off from people, keep things superficial, never trust anyone enough that they could have the chance to hurt me." The words I cannot say go unstated but not unnoticed. I cannot draw any kind of attention to myself.

"Has it worked?" I hear metal doors slam shut out of nowhere. I am not forfeiting this point this easily. It is not all going to fall into place lickety-split from here on out. There are still things Dr. Hettes does not want to face.

***

I am back in the sexual violence forum at work. Translucent electric eels swim through the air. Buzzing sounds swirl interrupted with zaps and cracks. I hear myself, my Dr. Hettes-self, in my head say, "You need to fix this." It is, in fact, simple. This moment is nowhere near the worst moment someone might experience. However, it is one of the most horrible moments I have ever felt with this group of people for whom Dr. Hettes decided it was safe to experience a deep affection and sense of responsibility with. This campus is my home; these people are my loving accepting family. What most people reserve for their children and loved ones, I channel to students and colleagues. The professional distance provides me with a dampened-enough level of intimacy to feel comfortable. At least I used to.

So, here we are—me with my overdeveloped sense of responsibility wondering how to fix this. My tribe is under attack and the confusion is palpable. Like we are on a plane that's crashed into the Atlantic and we've forgotten that our seat cushions become flotation devices. No one knows what to do. Maybe it is that no one else is willing to do it. If I am going to suggest a resolution, it has to work. I cannot fail. I cannot fail these people, who trust, respect—and love? —Dr. Hettes. I am guessing every woman and many men in the room has some level of their alarm bells sounding... and then... just like that, my mind flies to that Friday afternoon in my office in time to hear Dean Grant command, "You are the one with the authentic voice."

***

"Stacey? Has your strategy worked?"

"No, no it hasn't always worked. But it does some of the time."

"I can imagine it feels like it does. Can you tell me about a time that it didn't work?"

"When I trust people and care about them as more than a colleague. When I can't control the impact that they have on me because I become responsible for them, or worst of all, believe they care about me."

"That sounds like a lot to manage."

"On top of that, I have to protect others too."

"Protect them from what?"

"From me. I don't want to hurt other people."

"Who have you hurt?"

"I ruined everything when I told my mom about what happened with Mr. Jay." She was right. We are going in circles because this particular nugget is one we have spent months and months trying to process.

"Would you allow me an attempt at modifying that sentence?"

"Sure."

"Everything changed, some things for the worse, but others for the better when you told your parents that Mr. Jay molested you."

"What could you possibly say changed for the better?"

"Well, for one thing, Stacey, you are here. You are alive, and before you suggest otherwise, I'm not exaggerating."

"Thank you." That was too much to hear—too on point—to attempt a rebuttal.

"How old was your sister, Samantha, when you told your parents?"

"Around three or four."

"Mmm hmm," Her eyes hold their stare as mine tear up. We've walked this road before as well. "Do you remember how many kids he molested?"

"Yes."

"How many years since you disclosed to your parents?"

"More than thirty."

"Mmm hmm." She pauses letting the significance of her question settle in.

"I know what you are getting at. It took a long time to get to that place the first time. I am not back there yet."

"What will it take for you to get there again?"

"I don't know, what do you think?"

"I do not know either, but-" I cut her off.

"Let me guess, that is something we can work on?" I say with the tone of a petulant teenager. This time her smile is one of resignation. "I am not getting out of here anytime soon, am I?"

CHAPTER 34

Progress

Session 87

I want to continue riding this wave of contentedness. It is happiness, too, but happiness is fleeting. The fact that I am tapping into contentedness seems more significant. If happiness is the weather, contentedness is the climate. Though we are well into spring—the surrounding farms have already cut and baled their first crop of hay—internally, spring is just beginning to blossom. In the early days of this year's actual springtime, I wished for a longer winter. I was not ready to relinquish its gift of sequestration, which I employ even though our roads are rarely wet, let alone icy. Today, my internal climate matches the external world.

To extend the metaphor, our emotions and mental health, like weather and seasons, play out as cycles. The hope and promise of springtime will give way to summer, a season of buoyancy. A time to float upon the water where my body is most at home. It's interesting that I am drawn to water since in these spaces we have to reveal our physical selves more than anywhere else. The pleasure I gain when its cool refreshment hits my skin far surpasses the shame that I hold toward my body.

Summer too is fleeting. Fall arrives and with it the return to seriousness, to obligation and responsibility. It is also the season of harvest. Here I hold hope that during the coming fall, the labors of the previous year will provide emotional sustenance. I will need it for the inevitable winter. Some winters are severe, some mild, but winter always returns. During its shortened days, I tend to struggle with trusting that, after this dormancy, the world and my part in it will return to a state of flourishing. Many figurative winters of late were harsh and unforgiving. The springs and summers were not as fruitful as they may have been since so much went into repairs after the previous season's storms.

I set my intentions to prepare for the next winter rather than spending it blanketed under three quilts, shivering against the dark and cold that originates from within myself with only Chili and Pepper's radiated body heat to warm me. I imagine a winter where there is plenty of wood for the fireplace, the storm shutters are mended, and the aroma of a hearty nourishing soup and home-baked bread is the story I share of a winter Saturday. Even winter is beautiful. Sometimes beautifully sad, but beautiful nonetheless.

As Piper appears, I consider how many of these internal waiting room missives I would never dare to share with her. If I felt anywhere near as eloquent with spoken words as this little scribe who appears in my head, I might begin our session with this one.

"Before I forget, I'll be on vacation next week." This evokes a slight twinge rather than the full-on panic it did the last time Piper was away.

"Oh good, hope you have some fun planned."

"We are taking the horses on an overnight ride for my birthday."

"Happy Birthday! I am glad you are celebrating."

"Thanks, me too. Tell me some memories from celebrating your birthday."

"It was the most fun in grad school. My birthday is March sixteenth and my old housemate, Leah's, is the seventeenth. We threw a green food potluck each year. They were all fun, but the birthday when Bobby and I were together was the best. He arranged the biggest bouquet of irises and lilies I'd ever seen and baked us a carrot cake with cream cheese frosting." I pause as photos from that night appear in my head. In every single one, my smile looks like a lottery winner's. "His birthday was even better. We drove out to Joshua Tree, climbed up a boulder with a picnic, and watched a meteor shower. I baked an orange poppyseed cake that was way out of my league, but we managed it, thanks to the honeyed crème fraiche icing."

"Sounds fancy."

"Bobby never made me ashamed of decadence. I guess because he wasn't interested in my body." I don't want Piper to take us down a road where she delves into what I just said. I pivot to keep the positive vibe going. Today seems more like friends having coffee than a therapist healing her client. "I would like to try something different today." My better-than-decent mood and willingness to suggest the therapeutic equivalent of an adventure piques her interest. "I'd like to talk about progress today." She gifts me a wide grin in response.

"How do you want to begin?"

"Well, you toss in positive feedback and report signs of progress almost every session. Thanks for that, by the way. There were many days I reacted to it as one would to burn cream after singeing your forearm. Even though it was helpful, even though it eased the sting, I think I was in too much pain to acknowledge that it'd been effective. What if today, instead of treating it like first aid, we treat it like a spa day? A day where one takes care of herself as much to feel good moving forward as to recover."

"I love it. How about you start?" I was hoping she might volunteer. Bashfulness and humbleness will always be parts of me.

"The intrusive thoughts are not as loud as they can be."

"I cannot tell you how happy that makes me. What else?"

"In high school, when things were bad with my coach, I was able to see how frightened it made my mom that I wanted to kill myself. I promised her I would not, and I meant it. As long as she was alive, I would never go through with it. Experiencing this round of re-traumatization at this age, and knowing my mother is aging as well, I have wondered if I could keep that promise if she was no longer here."

"And...?"

"Well, I don't think, whether my mom outlives me or not, I would ever take my own life. Even if things get bad again, I trust that I can ask for help and find a way to walk it back." Piper exhales loudly. "You were holding your breath on that one, weren't you?"

"I wasn't sure where you were going, but I'm happy to hear that."

"Me too." I wonder if anyone, like my dad for instance, who I am sure has never contemplated such an act, could ever appreciate what a win this is. The truth: I wished for my life to end. I thought about ways to do it that would look like an accident so my mother would not know I broke my promise. I convinced myself the world was better off without me in it. To not feel that way—to not plan through such scenarios over and over in my head—I cannot put into words what a sense of freedom that provides.

"Can I take a turn?"

"Of course."

"You can experience emotions and recall memories with less resistance. Many times, I've watched you struggle against feelings as they surface. Even though you understood from your previous therapists what we are here to do, we had to make a great deal of space for that resistance before confronting something uncomfortable. I am glad that is subsiding. I know from personal experience how exhausting it is to have those kinds of battles with yourself."

"Thank you for seeing that. I agree. There are days when I can tell I am holding something in. Those days I get anxious for our session to get here, for the opportunity to get it out, and to get it out safely. I am not as afraid that whatever comes up will be the thing that does me in. I am also no longer afraid that whatever it is will scare you away. Not once have you acted afraid of what I needed to say. That is not entirely true. I think you were afraid that I might walk away, that I might push you away."

"You're right. How did we say it?"

"You said you were afraid I was going to vote you off the island." It's nice to have a shared history with another person again. I have relegated most people to little more than exchanges on social media. This feeling of connection is novel. It makes me all the more grateful for the friends who continue to check in. The friends who respond by saying they've been thinking of me when I manage to reach out.

"I am less concerned at this point that you will disappear." Yet, I have a good bit of work to do on not ghosting people outside of this space. Today is a day for progress, not a day for adding to the list that ensures Piper's job security.

"That makes me happy. I have a sense that even if we tapered off, I will want to check in with you at least once in a while for a long time."

"That sounds like a good plan. What else?"

"It's slow, but I am reaching out to friends more. Mostly texts. When I do make plans to get together, I try to keep them. For a long time, I have employed the vague 'maybe we can get together at some point.' I needed an out in case I was too depressed/ anxious/ overwhelmed to follow through."

"I was not aware of that. I am glad you told me." I drift off into a deeper thought.

After a bit, Piper says, "Where did you go?"

"After almost two years of staying mentally hunkered down,

this feels like progress. Saying them out loud though, they don't seem like much."

"First, I don't think we are done yet. We could point out many more. Second, I disagree. These are big things. Not fairy tale big, but that's why we call such stories fairy tales. 'Happily Ever After' is not what happens. Happiness, along with all the other emotions, is what is real. There will be storms. Some wicked, but we're building a shelter for you to ride them out. You are not being hijacked by or resisting emotions as intensely as you once were. That is its own kind of win."

"Yeah, I'm less compelled to believe the serpents that raise the volume on every negative thing, to turn anything they can into proof that I deserve a life of desolation and despair."

"Great, but those snakes are still there?"

"Yes, but they are sleeping a lot more."

"Okay, let's keep working toward their eviction."

"I like that plan." More importantly, I'm convinced it is possible.

"I want to go back to what you said a minute ago about this progress not seeming like much. How would you describe what things were like when I first met you?"

"I was having a hard time."

"Uh, yeah, you were. More recently you told me that you look forward to our meetings. I do too. Did you look forward to them when we first met?"

"No."

"Uh-huh, you were also in a tremendous amount of pain. As you said, some days it was like you were a burn victim. Almost any words stung you. I had to be extremely careful about the questions I asked. There were all sorts of words, and lots of topics, that were triggers for you. You constantly had to shut down to avoid feeling overwhelmed. Most weeks it was a good session if you relaxed your shoulders a bit. But, you showed up every week. You worked at whatever you were able to work at, at whatever pace you could tolerate. It took you a while to trust me, but it could have taken even longer. You were brave in that way."

"Thanks for reminding me. That is exactly what it felt like."

"What do you think were important moments in making progress?"

"I wish there was more to say. Sticking with it. Giving it time. I suspect, too, that the time I confronted you about how upset it made me when you suggested I was beating myself up, how that triggered me, was important."

"Agreed. Why do you think that was?"

"I was afraid I was wearing out your patience. I tried to use that as evidence that you didn't want to work with me anymore. It was something I was making up—in my own mind—out of fear. But you were patient enough to figure out what was happening and help me get through it."

"Are you still afraid of that?"

"Maybe a tiny bit, but on a scale of one to ten, it went from an eleven to a one or a two."

"That sounds like good progress to me." She smiles. This is good for Piper. We do not verbalize it often, but she told me that her strategy as a therapist relies on the relationships she builds with her clients. It's why she shares more personal things than my other therapists did. Dealing with that misunderstanding was a major step forward. I have a hard time admitting this to myself let alone to her, but the five or so minutes we chat and catch up each week are some of the most important of the session. They remind me that I am likable enough for her to want to know me that way. That I am more than just a job for her.

CHAPTER 35

Checking in with Dr. Hettes

Session 93

There is a boy, elementary school age, and a woman, likely his mother, sitting in my spot as I enter. Not that many sessions ago, this would have thrown me. I cannot help but wonder what caused them to find their way to this waiting room. Would he agree that it smells like mint and warm paper? Do kids even know what paper smells like? As I do my level best to send telepathic waves of support toward his seat, I do the same toward his mom. I take note that I even noticed her. Before, I would have focused on him, praying that he would find his way out of whatever darkness brings him here. I dare to meet his mother's eyes for the briefest second. I hope my expression offers her the strength I've often needed to carry my body from this room to Piper's office.

As I sink into the couch, Piper says, "I have a confession to make."

"What?" My alarm bells sound a warning for my muscles to brace for impact.

"I got your email the other day and had a free appointment block. I read the essay you sent. I know you should read things out loud, and you still can, but I wanted to be upfront about it." I can't help but laugh uncontrollably, both at my assumption that something bad was about to happen as well as her confession.

"Oooooh Piper, you are in trooouuuubbblle... I'm gonna tell

the therapy police."

"Stop! It's not funny. You know how hard I try to be a good therapist."

"I'm sorry. It's funny that you feel you need to make a confession about it. Okay, you are a good therapist, a great therapist. It is fine if you read something ahead. It is quite a compliment that you took the time to do so."

"I've told you this before, but I love your writing. It shows me such a different side of you, one I really admire," adding, "not that I don't admire the person I see when we are together." Piper is never the one turning red first.

"No need to explain," I say, smiling.

"Anyway, I thought what you sent was terrific. Have you ever thought about sharing your writing? I know it is personal, but I think other people might find it relatable." It is my turn to take on a pinkish hue.

"I don't know. I write for myself." I suspect she senses I have no interest in pursuing this idea at present.

"How was your week?"

"Better. I had great conversations with my mom and my sister, Carrie. I took a trip to Trader Joe's. Oh, and my students did well with their lab presentations."

"What do you like at Trader Joe's?"

"Flowers. I love that the flowers are the first thing you see as you enter. If I indulge in the flowers, sometimes my desire to treat myself is satisfied before I reach the chocolate."

"I like that idea. What did you and your mom talk about?"

"Mostly catching up, spring is arriving in the Northeast. I told her to have Dad cut some lilacs at the old farmstead. A few blossoms fill the whole house with springtime. Whenever Dad and I brought her some she mentioned how they grew outside Great-Grandma

Van Sickle's kitchen window, which made it delightful to help with the dishes."

"That sounds lovely."

"I wish they grew this far south." I wish we could discuss flowers for the whole session. It's wonderful to have a mind unencumbered enough to remember the scent of lilacs or how happy my dad was to fetch some with me. How his love and support are there, wordlessly, always.

"Do you ever discuss what we're working on with your parents?" An "ugh" settles at the base of my throat. Break's over, kids, back to work.

"No. They don't need to trudge through all this muck again."

"What about your sister, Sam? You mentioned that therapy has come up. Have you told her things are going better?"

"They might sense that. Mom insists that she can hear it in my voice when I am down. Maybe that means she can hear that I am doing better too."

"What would it be like to tell her?"

"I don't know."

"How would you describe your level of intimacy with your sisters or your mom?"

"I am happy to share the good stuff. The bad stuff, not so much."

"Why? And I want you to consider something besides you do not want to hurt them. That's true but take a step further."

"Part of me wants to cut to the chase and tell you what I think you want to hear—that I have trouble with intimacy of all kinds." Blech, I hate the i-word as much as the m-word.

"How does it play out when you are open to it? What makes an intimate moment of friendship and connection uncomfortable?"

"I am afraid."

"Of what?"

"Of believing someone cares about me. That their kindness and attention is genuine and not a setup for something bad."

"Hmm, for someone who is good at reading others' emotions, what makes it hard for you to believe kindness directed toward you is genuine? You and I have faced this fear to some extent. What is it like to allow yourself a sense of intimacy in our work together?"

"It's contained."

"In what way?"

"It's once a week for one hour." For some reason, she finds this funny.

"So, you are only comfortable with it in discrete, infrequent doses?"

"That would be accurate. Huh, I never realized before why I enjoy committee work so much."

"You are the first person to say that," she replies with a chuckle.

"Working with others in that setting approximates the intimacy of friendship, but it is structured and finite. Other work patterns, working with someone day in and day out, are riskier. There is too much time... too much opportunity to grow too close. Lots of professors are drawn to this life because of the independence it provides. Also, because social interactions are not always our strong suit."

"That's a good insight. Intimacy is also about letting people see you as your whole, imperfect self. I've been wondering how you are doing with the notion of identity. Early on, you mentioned several times that you feel as though your professional life is a masquerade. Other times you described Dr. Hettes as a persona. Does that remain an accurate description for you?" I am relieved for the transition to something I can analyze.

"Off the top of my head, it seems less like masquerade is, or perhaps ever was an accurate description. I don't consider my Dr. Hettes-self as inauthentic or disingenuous. We all have a public presence. Dr. Hettes is certainly mine, but that does not mean she's fraudulent. Not today, at least. There was a time when my impostor syndrome worked overtime to convince me that Dr. Hettes was a sham. Especially when you and I first met. Things were such a mess. I was such a mess." I trail off. Piper leaves me room to mull this over. "I became unsure how to be myself, Dr. Hettes, or even Stacey, in spaces where I no longer felt safe. The shame of being a victim swirled around my head." I pause but keep going. "How do women do it? How do women who experience the actual victimization in a space like work, a space they must continue to inhabit, keep putting one foot in front of the other? All I did was say out loud that I was once a victim. Even that sent me into hiding."

"I am going to interrupt you there. I hear you minimizing that there were other factors, words and acts of others, that played a role in your decision to self-protect."

"Yes, I know, but every attendee of that forum experienced those words. Disclosing that I was a survivor was what made the meeting different for me."

"Except you were the only one in the Friday meeting with Dean Grant."

"Yes, but in the face of Vic's victim blaming, I was the one who said out loud that I'd been violated. It made me afraid I'd changed the way others saw me, which kept me sequestered."

"Tell me what that concern felt like."

"The same way it felt long before I went by Dr. Hettes. The shame in the concealment of it all. Our culture requires secrecy. Add to that, there is shame when it comes to anything to do with mental illness. Announcing I was assaulted ignited that shame. The fire's out, but it's still smoldering."

"Smoldering is better than actual fire."

"Yeah, it is. Things are getting better with colleagues, slowly, but they are. I should say I am getting better at feeling comfortable around them again. The majority of the awkwardness I felt after the faculty forum was coming from me, not them. Luckily, I never lost that sense of easiness with my students. As far as I know, they never heard about what happened. My time in the classroom is a refuge as I sort all this out. I don't know if I ever told you, but the one benefit of my parents keeping what happened with Mr. Jay a secret was with my grandparents. I never had to view their love, affection, or pride as tainted by pity. At least in their eyes, I wasn't damaged goods."

"I am glad for that, both with your students and your grandparents. When we talk about how you see yourself and how others see you, you go back and forth between the words victim and survivor. Do you have a sense of why that is?"

"Because neither suits how I see myself. At least not how I want to. Each suggests a different response to something tragic. At the same time, they both keep us moored to the tragedy. Neither gives us the space, or the hope, to move beyond the abuse. I don't mean forgetting about it, just not letting it define us."

"That makes a lot of sense. If you could pick a different word to describe your relationship to the abuse, what would you choose?"

"I've thought about this quite a bit over the years. I never came up with an alternate. I like the way that Dr. Bruce Perry describes his aspirations for society to work toward becoming trauma-informed. I wonder if identifying as a trauma-informed individual might fit."[7]

"That's interesting. What does that feel like for you?"

---

[7] For more information on Dr. Perry and his work: "About Bruce D. Perry, M.D., Ph.D.," B.D. Perry, M.D., Ph.D., accessed August 4, 2024, https://www.bdperry.com/about.

"Well, as I understand it, his goal is to create trauma-informed workplaces, and such, to better grasp how bad experiences impact the way a person interacts with and responds to situations and circumstances. If I consider myself as trauma-informed rather than trauma-shaped or worse, trauma-damaged, maybe I can separate who I am from the abuse but acknowledge that it impacts my self-awareness. Also, how I react to people and situations. Trauma-shaped might be an accurate match to the term survivor whereas trauma-damaged aligns with victim."

"Wow, why don't you try that out for a while and see how it fits?"

"Yeah, okay, thanks for asking the question."

"I also like the way you phrased 'staying moored to the tragedy.' What do you think that imagery represents in your present life?"

"I am thinking about how we hold on to coping mechanisms, sometimes long after they've outlived their usefulness."

"That's a good insight, can you name one?"

"One thing that comes out big time for Dr. Hettes is perfectionism."

"You don't say." Wow, that didn't even sting. When Piper lets these jibes slip, it lets me know she thinks I am doing well enough to handle them.

"I know. There is a bridge waiting for me. We'll have to cross it sooner or later, but I am not ready."

"I am proud you said the word aloud."

"Thank you. You've cast it out there more than once."

"Uh-huh, and not even a nibble."

"It's interesting the type of trigger that this particular word is for me."

"In what way?"

"Well, most triggers are emotional. Perfectionism is different.

It was, is, a virtue in our house. Cleanliness is next to godliness, after all."

"How do you feel about that?"

"Hmm, more aware that it's a problem rather than the mislabeled superpower I was taught it was. I learned early on that perfection was the only assurance of heaven."

"What did you learn from your church about forgiveness?"

"That was more of a backup plan. Better not do anything that required forgiveness, just to be safe."

"What about forgiving yourself?"

"Please don't ask me that."

"Sorry, no. What about forgiving yourself?"

"The best I could do was try my hardest to trust my mom if she told me she forgave me for something I did wrong. Forgiving myself never happened, I had to just let the bad stuff slowly dissipate."

"How do you feel about that strategy as an adult?"

"I am more concerned about perpetuating that example for my students than anything else. I try to downplay my perfectionist tendencies with them. I want to teach them it is okay to fail, to come up short. I want to teach them to celebrate their Bs or Cs if those grades represent genuine best efforts and progress. I try to convince them of that. All the while I beat myself up when I take longer than I should to return an email or get their papers graded."

"So, there are some things Dr. Hettes is willing to admit she does imperfectly?" I smile and roll my eyes, but I also note that this is one of the truest—not truest. Honest—one of the most honest—conversations we've had in a long time. It is me facing me. Facing a truth about myself, not what the snakes in my brain want me to believe.

Those vipers are asleep, sacked out on the dirty, worn-out couches of the dingy rec room of my mind like teenagers sleeping off a video game binge. "Where did you go?" I tell Piper about the couches, and the snakes, and ask her which gaming console her sons might recommend to keep them occupied. "Instead of making life too comfortable for them, how about we get serious about evicting the little bastards?"

"So, I am guessing we have some work to do."

"Work on what? I am pretty sure I know what you are referring to, but I want to hear you admit it."

"Perfectionism."

"Two times in one session!"

"If we try to tackle that subject, you are going to make enough money to put one of your kids through college."

"Sometimes job security is an added bonus." She is smiling so mischievously, that she barely gets through that sentence. "But seriously, I am thrilled that you are willing to consider that kind of work. It is a good indication of how well you are doing."

"I have not wanted to say these words out loud to you, but I've been thinking them for a few weeks now."

"What's that?"

"Maybe a good way to describe how I am doing is to say, things are better, not all better, but better. I think that matters because it would be easy to convince myself that everything is fine. That I am done."

"I like that. I like it a lot. There is more room for growth in a space described as 'better.' There are times that therapy ends because a client agrees that they are at a good point to pause. Sometimes, there is a single issue that gets resolved. It's finished because we met the goals the client set. But I sometimes worry when someone, someone whose past carries a great deal of complex trauma, tries to convince me that they are all better."

"I've been that person many times. Once the suicidal thoughts get under control, I'm pretty sure I can survive. I used to worry about the cost for my parents or taking more than my fair share in other ways. I talked myself into thinking that not wanting to kill myself was as good as it gets."

"You told me."

"It was the most important conversation we've had. It kept me from running away." Searching for a spot in the carpet to hold my gaze, I say, "It's what allowed you to call me on the fact that I was getting ready to bolt."

"I wouldn't have blamed you if you tried."

"You can thank your couch cushions."

"What?"

"Your couch cushions are squishy. They make it impossible to pop up and run away." This sends her into fits of laughter.

"Oh my gosh. Well, that's good to know. And here I thought I was such a good therapist my clients were sticking around thanks to me."

"You are that good, Piper. I hope you know that."

"Thank you for saying that."

CHAPTER 36

Six Months Later...

Session 127

As I walk in today, I get a sense that I will not like how I feel when I leave. Piper's dialed things up a notch. Our casual volley of probes and thoughtful responses has become more like training for the varsity squad.

About three weeks ago, I stubbornly pushed back as she called out my lingering hesitance to spend time with a wider circle of friends. This led us to a broader conversation about trust and intimacy and how empty my coffers remain of both. At some point, near the end of this session—a session where we might as well have been standing at opposing podiums engaged in formal debate—her frustration leaked through. I did not hold onto her exact words, but they were something like, "Well, if you want to, you can just keep being a professor without ever allowing yourself anything more than that." Can't I be content with where I am? I mean, I am managing to take Chili and Pepper for walks again, not just letting them frolic in the backyard together.

At these moments, there is guilt for my lack of progress. All I have to respond with is my own frustration that I do not even know how to imagine "more than that." I cannot imagine the things she wants me to strive for. I hold vague memories of this type of life—looking forward to parties, conversations over coffee, concerts, etc. These memories seem like recollections from someone else's experiences. I cannot see past this day-to-day existence yet. *(Confession: I have added and removed the "yet" from the end of that sentence at least seven times as I edit).* I cannot imagine a world where I have access to the self-acceptance and vulnerability it requires to sit across from a friend with the expectation to make eye contact. The idea of a conversation that might begin with the words, "How have you been?" seems no more plausible for this tired old body than running a marathon.

***

"Hi Stacey, come on back." Her ever-present smile indicates we will begin today, as always, from a place of hope, at least on her part. "I thought about you this week. I met some students from your college. They're former classmates of my son."

"Oh yeah? I wonder if I know any of them."

"Well, I wasn't sure if I would tell you, but I told them I knew several professors from there and asked which ones they'd taken. One of them mentioned you." Ugh. Whatever is about to happen will land me somewhere on a continuum between blushing and mortified.

"Don't tell me who it was. It'll be weird if it is someone in my current class."

"I think they had you last year, but mentioned that you are one of their favorite professors." My body squirms. "In fact, they said they're not the only one who thinks you are one of the most passionate teachers ever. I think their exact words were, 'Everyone who gets to take her class ends up loving her.'" I will myself not to turn red.

"What makes this hard for you? When you tell me about your week and talk about teaching, your whole being lights up."

"I'm bashful, I guess."

"Come on, you know there is more to it than that." Of course, but I don't want to talk about this today. It appears I just merrily strolled into an ambush. I bet Piper knew exactly how she'd use this information before the student finished their first sentence. Believing compliments for more than six minutes is still way too vulnerable. "Is the fact that I learned something about you in a way that you did not have control over too intimate?" Why does she have to use that word? Gah, I hate that word. She rolls it out every few weeks like she marked it on the calendar.

"Maybe I just don't take compliments well."

"If instead of telling you that I heard what a great teacher you are, I learned something else about you like you are a good dog mom, would that be more comfortable?"

"I don't know, probably."

"Tell me, why was it hard to hear this then?"

"Part of it might be that I struggle whenever you mention thinking about me outside our sessions."

"Why? It makes me laugh how you put it the first time, 'It's one hour, once a week,' like our sessions were piano lessons you dreaded."

"It's not that..." I am afraid if this comes out wrong, I am going to hurt her or undermine her sense of what a capable therapist she is. "It's that I am afraid of ever letting myself forget that you are my therapist and I am your client." Fuck. That is not at all how I wanted that to come out. She gets quiet. I search for that little gray spot in the carpet as regret blooms from just below my diaphragm.

"It's not professional for me to say, but that makes me really sad." Why do people push for truths that I know will hurt them? I imagine other clients might bolt. My amygdala dials straight to "fawn." I want to stay right here and gush words of apology and lament. Instead, my lips freeze and my jaw locks to prevent me from making things worse. This is what makes all forms of intimacy too dangerous to pursue, with anyone, ever. I suspect that for a lot of intimacy-phobes, they don't want to let anyone in so that no one can hurt them. For me, it's the opposite.

It is better to wall myself off and live with the loneliness than risk hurting someone else. I can cope with loneliness. It is a chronic pain like sore joints or an achy back from a mattress that's grown too soft. Damaging others is the worst, soul-bruising form of pain—always has been. I took dig after dig from Carrie. Then, if I managed to pop the cork from my anger and land an emotional blow, it left me devastated. For someone wired like me, the coal fires my little-girl self bore as the penance for disclosing transformed once malleable wiring for intimacy into brittle pig iron.

My mother's voice sounds in my head speaking in the tone she reserved for moments like the one I just inflicted on Piper. Whatever my offense—whatever my grievance—her retort reliably began: "I don't know where I failed as a mother..." Before my brain dives headlong into another flashback, I manage to say, "I'm sorry Piper, I didn't mean to hurt your feelings."

***

Before you and I go any farther, reader, another confession and explanation is in order. You've made it this far, and that deserves a deeper level of trust between you and me. It took months to say out loud to Piper, and it's something we continue to unpack. As loving and caring as my mother was and is, especially in the face of injury, she was also exceptionally demanding—more of herself than anyone else. The impact of her immersion in the world of our church was fathoms deeper on her than on the rest of us. My sisters and I got away easier, in part due to Mom's courage to push back against some of the church's most arbitrary rules, like no going to movie theaters.

What a secret rebellion it was for her to take Carrie and me to see *E.T.* and *Annie* in the summer of 1982. Did she think she'd be risking our souls if those particular hours turned out to be the moment the angels' trumpets sounded, announcing Christ's imminent return?

I try to keep in mind that her entire family, both sides, were deeply embedded in Pentecostal churches. Carrie, Sam, and I at least had the juxtaposition of my dad's side, who were Christians but not fundamentalists. Great-Grandpa Van Sickle, Mom's maternal grandfather, was among our church's founding board members, many of whom mortgaged their farms and businesses to finance the first sanctuary. He and many many others spoke of God's grace, love, and mercy. They also believed fervently that the wages of unrepented sin were eternal suffering beyond a little girl and her mother's wildest fears. It's hard to fathom the weight of the cultural and spiritual pressure Mom carried for us to be deemed worthy by our church's Gotcha-God and his deacon-henchmen. Add to that the immeasurable responsibility she felt to keep her daughters from surrendering to whatever temptations would send us to hell.

Recalling her ire over minor transgressions sends little volts of discomfort up my fingers as I type. Only Sam, with all her pre-teen gumption, dealt with Mom's expectations with a healthy sense of levity. Sometime after I left for college, Sam dropped the nickname "The Warden" on her. When Mom would go over the top, Sam would reply, "Yes ma'am, warden, sir" with such gusto, it usually snapped my mother out of her rage and got a laugh out of the rest of us. What genes were transcribed in Sam to yield such moxie? One thing's for sure, neither the sperm nor egg from which I formed held any copies.

It took a long time to reconcile and forgive, in the truest sense, what comes out in the flashback I am about to relive. However, love is risky. Loving and being loved opens the door to harm as well as healing.

Okay, on to the flashback, which, best as I can guess, falls on a timeline shortly after Mr. Jay first laid me on his bed and broke me open.

***

"Carrie, my stomach hurts." *Whether intestinal or psychosomatic, my insides were a tumult of quease as the other kids gathered their things to head into school.*

"Again? Okay, I will take you to your teacher and tell her you are sick." *The steps off the school bus were made for giants compared to my kindergarten-sized legs. From what I remember, this was the third day in a row that the ride to school had ended as such. Fake white fur surrounds my face from the same winter coat I am wearing in a snapshot with the snowman Grampa and I built on a different day, too snowy for him to drive his 18-wheeler.*

"Mrs. Conway, my sister says she's sick again," *Carrie delivers her proclamation, with all the authority of a fourth-grade big sister.*

"Why does your mother keep sending her to school if she doesn't feel well?" *My little-girl self knows I've done something wrong, but I cannot be here. It's too much to navigate—playing nice with others, running around the gym, getting out of breath, needing help to open my milk carton, wanting three peanut butter cookies but knowing we only get two. Staying in the lines as I color a mimeographed picture of a jack-in-the-box would be impossible. I need everything I have to keep my insides from dissolving and running out of my shoes. Since I am sick, I wait at the table as the others play. The thing is, I loved school. Beyond the chicken pox, I don't think I missed a single day before this week.*

Mommy arrives in full hair and makeup, wearing the new

ski jacket with the dark orange stripe that Daddy bought her for Christmas. She was in her bathrobe when we got on the bus. Her voice is sweet: further evidence I am in deep trouble. This voice is not Mommy's real voice. This voice comes out when my actual mommy needs to disappear. When she needs to deny the reality of whatever monstrously sinful, shameful deeds I committed. This voice will vanish when we are alone. Mrs. Conway repeats her question, but my memory did not store Mom's answer. I imagine it was something like, "She was fine when she woke up; she ate the buttermilk pancakes I made for breakfast." They say their goodbyes as she lovingly ties my hood and zips up the coat Mrs. Miller, the teacher's aide, placed on the hook below my name less than an hour before.

Seeing our Mercury Monarch parked where the buses pull in makes my tummy ache all over again. I feel the hollowness of the space in my throat where the throw-up wants to get to. I climb up to the passenger seat during this time before car seats, airbags, or shoulder harness seat belts.

Here it comes. A videographer could have a field day playing with the angles in this scene. My eyes look up at her fiery face from no higher vantage than her breasts. Her words shower down like the pellets of the acid rain we were convinced would melt all the trees and flowers back then.

"Why do you keep doing this? Who are you lying to, her or me? What kind of mother sends her daughter to school only to have her say she is sick this many days in a row? If you are sick, you need to stay home in the first place. Why ride all that way on the bus if you are going to tell her your stomach hurts as soon as you get here?! Now Mrs. Conway thinks I am a bad mother!!"

My stomach no longer matters.

Here's what does: three lessons sunk all the way into the heart of a little girl whose body cried for help in the only way it knew how. Lesson number one: it is my job to assure my mother never ever comes across, to anyone, as anything less than perfect. The perfect Christian, the perfect nurse, the perfect wife, the perfect mother. She was indeed many of these things. The thing she did not know I needed her to be was the perfect monster slayer. But oh, what a monster slayer she'd have made. Maybe in the 2020s symptoms of post-traumatic stress are considered in five-year-olds. Not in 1979. This is something Mom regrets and laments to this day, even after years engaged in her own reckoning with what Mr. Jay did to us.

Lesson number two: As her frustration towered above my tiny head, my insides' response to what was happening did not matter. Appearances did. The only vocabulary I possessed was "sick." Terrified, depressed, panicked, confused, and overwhelmed had not yet entered my emotional lexicon. Unless I was vomiting or had a verifiable fever, I never asked for a sick day again until high school. By then, the prospect of facing the aftermath of my coach would make these rides on the big yellow bus seem like a trip to an amusement park. There were even times that Mom encouraged me to take a day off to give myself a mental rest.

Lesson number three is the most unfortunate. The combination of my mother's response that day with Mr. Jay's actions was more complex. Further, this lesson entangled itself within the paradoxical teachings of our religious upbringing, the consequences of which would not become clear until Piper and I committed to climbing this mountain of confusion and despair to its summit. This level of clarity can only come from fully living the question, *what did it do to you?* The answer: I was transformed into a child who grew into an adult terrified that being liked and being loved are 1,000 percent conditional. Upsetting or disappointing my mother and committing a mortal sin became one and the same. To my parents' confusion and dismay, I rarely, if ever, could be convinced that anybody would provide the likes of me with love, not even Jesus. Thank the heavenly hosts for dogs.

For all the Sunday school stories of forgiveness and the prompts to memorize 1 Corinthians, 13, the passage on love often recited at weddings, our legalistic church did a better job of convincing this girl—who held the mother of all secret sins in her belly—that when Jesus came back as a thief in the night, there was no chance she'd be swept up to heaven. The rules were absolute. Even a speck of blackness in your heart meant no streets of gold for you. How could I confess these acts that my soul, if not my mind, knew were beyond sinful? My mind didn't even know the names for the body parts that committed them. In fundamentalist circles, Jesus' statement, "better to cut off your hand than allow it to sin and send your whole self to hell"[8] was discussed as if it were a literal instruction. How could I live up to that? These sins happened inside me.

My little-girl self, who missed even fewer days of Sunday school than actual school, steeped in the enormity of these religious miscomprehensions for the remainder of her childhood with little more to engage them than a jar of paste and safety scissors.

***

And so, here I sit. Back on Piper's couch, hoping the apology I issued for my transgression will be enough. It is all I can manage for fear of tumbling into a pile of rags at her feet, begging her to tell me that I did not blow it, that I did not do the thing I dread, the thing that will cause her to never accept me again. She responds with, "Thank you, Stacey, I know you didn't mean to hurt my feelings.

---

[8] *"And if thy right hand offend thee, cut it off, and cast it from thee: for it is profitable for thee that one of thy members should perish, and not that thy whole body should be cast into hell."* Matt. 5:30, (King James Version)

This is not about me. I am sad for you."

She is obligated to say such things, but I don't believe her. The reality that, after all this time, I have done the thing I try so hard not to is evident in the tears she's holding back. Tears that, to me, might as well say, "I don't know where I failed as a therapist."

I have really done it this time. I should come with one of those construction truck warning signs—DANGER: KEEP BACK 50 FEET. Piper goes on to say, "I am sorry, too. I never behave like this with a client. What you said makes me incredibly sad. It makes me think you do not trust me when I tell you things like, 'Knowing there are people like you in the world makes things better when I am having a rough day.' I mean that. It hurts to think that, after all this time, you still will not let yourself be convinced."

"It's not that I don't want to... and, truly, I believe you more than most." Words grind to a halt. The part of me that refuses to lose control has positioned a guard post along my back teeth. All additional words must pass inspection before leaving this mouth. "I never want to say anything that would hurt you. I am sorry that I am not capable of opening up more. It's just not safe."

"I wish I understood why. We've made a lot of progress, but the walls you've built around this part of yourself could reach the sky." She pauses. I can tell she's discussing with the guard at her own post whether to say the words that come next. "At some point, you are going to have to decide to trust us."

"These walls were built so long ago I cannot remember how, or when, or why. Each time someone finds a way in, I wonder if this time will be different. Whether it is a friend, colleague, or back when I was open to dating, I get excited. I'm happy to feel accepted. For a time, I let my guard down and enjoy them. Then something happens and I shut down. Sometimes I walk away and sometimes I try to keep the relationship afloat, but I clamp down and close any doors except one narrow entryway that I can regulate. The thing is, I don't always see it coming. I can be perfectly happy, and then, a trip wire goes off. Once the signal triggers, the gates slam shut. It's hard for people to stick it out until I can manage to crack open a window again."

"Have I ever been close to the line?"

"It's different with you."

"In what way?"

"With you, I am more afraid of the day that you will grow tired of me and my sadness. That you will decide I am not worth the effort. I want to say something else before you respond. You are not doing anything to make me afraid. I carry this fear with me to our appointment each week." I also wish I could say this to friends, but I never find the words when I need them.

"Okay, I appreciate you acknowledging that, but I wish I understood where this fear comes from."

"I wish I did too. It is not a single place. The transactional, legalistic approach our church took didn't help." Words from another therapy session surface. "When I was working with Indira, we spent what seems like months dealing with this issue. I finally, after sitting for nearly the whole session with my eyes shut trying to hold it back, blurted out, 'If my mother doesn't even love me, how can anyone else?'"

"Do you believe your mother loves you today?"

"Yes."

"Do you believe she loved you back then?"

"Yes, today as an adult, I recognize that she loved me back then. The signs became clearer after she knew what happened. Before that, I think my little-girl self was afraid that her love, any love, required goodness, required cleanliness, required godliness. Mr. Jay might as well have mopped the grease stains in his garage with my hair for how dirty it made me feel." I pause to settle my insides. "There is something else I need to tell you." My neck muscles spasm pulling my head and shoulders together.

"Take your time..."

"I asked my mom once who would take care of us if something happened to her and my dad." Fucking hell, this is the first minute I recognize how afraid her answer made me of abandonment, by their deaths or some other way. Saying the words, even now, is terrifying.

"She said Gramma and Grampa would take us. I responded they were old. What if they were gone too?"

"Oh no... did she say it would be Mr. Jay and his wife?"

My throat is paralyzed but my little-girl eyes tell her what she needs to know. Piper gets out her blanket of soothing silence, letting me recover as long as I need. "So, I'm guessing that impacted my efforts to be loveable. Maybe that's what I've been trying to do—without recognizing love in return—ever since."

"That must be exhausting."

"Uh-huh."

"I hope we can find a way for you to see what I see. You are loveable, but so much more so when you relax and be yourself."

"Thank you for saying that."

"Tell me a time when you tried the hardest to be loveable."

"With Bobby, the last man I ever dated."

"What made you try so hard with him?"

"We haven't talked about him much. I still think about him almost every day. He was the only man I ever wanted to hear say the words 'I think I could spend the rest of my life with you.' I was stupid enough to believe him when he did. Then, a couple of months later, it was over, and a few weeks after that, a friend informed me that he had come out. That was it. For me, there was no coming back from that. I walled myself off from any chance of that kind of relationship ever again."

"I am sorry that hurt you. In some ways, things were much more complicated around sexuality back then. I do think he loved you as much as he could love a woman. The fact that he was gay did not mean he didn't love you, just not in the same way that he could love a man."

"I understand that better now. Honestly, it doesn't matter all that much how he felt or didn't feel. What mattered was, for once, someone I felt safe loving said he loved me back. More, I was stupid enough to believe him. For the first time, the only time, I was convinced I could have what I felt everyone but me had a right to. Then it was over."

"So that's the tough part? That you believed you were worthy of love that was reciprocated and it ended?"

"That sounds accurate."

"Then it's something we can work on. I want to know if you are okay. Are you worried because you hurt me?"

"I'll be okay. See you next week."

CHAPTER 37

The First Circle of Hell Is Still Hell...

It's funny, or maybe not, that those kindergarten sick days surfaced and now I'm calling in sick. My stomach rumbles with the same low-grade queasiness from those bus rides. It is Friday. Surrendering the battle to appear normal this close to the weekend somehow seems more defeating. As I lay here, I tap out the obligatory apology email with one finger. If I was honest, it would read, "Sorry for canceling class dear students, but I am a weak-willed fraud." Instead, I make a vague reference to vague symptoms. To be sure, about once a year, I manage to feed myself something I shouldn't have. There is no such thing as teaching class while one waits for the Imodium to kick in.

Today is not a day that requires loperamide hydrochloride. Today is a day that I woke up knowing there is no way to push through. There is nothing to push with. It will be a day of limbo—no anger, no tears—just nothingness. Any stimulus beyond soft sheets or soft fur will become a cheese grater gouging at my retinas, eardrums, nostrils, fingertips. Here I lay, waiting for nightfall. Hoping that, after a day as a nonentity, sleep takes pity on me.

Thank the sweet baby Jesus for my Chili and my Pepper. These munchkins, I tell ya. I've fiercely loved all the pups God gifted me. Canyon, my high-strung shepherd mix, was my lifeline after Bobby ended things between us. She taught me I am a dog person. Russet, the most regal of mutts, held paws with our neighbor's black Lab,

Daisy, under the back fence. My sweet retired racing greyhound, Max, whom my friend Tammie loved to call a "special boy"—in all the ways that description might be interpreted. None of them suffered the foolishness of a day in bed. If I slept later than Max deemed necessary, he'd rub his bony ribs along the spoked baseboard of my mission-style bed to vibrate me awake. With the Chili Peppers, all that's necessary is a quick perimeter check along the back fence and two bowls of breakfast. After that, they're happy as can be to tumble into the unmade covers and cuddle the day away.

When I work through a Saturday or Sunday, Chili won't have it. By afternoon, her relentless toenails tap across the floorboards. When I give in, expecting she needs a trip outside, her paws dash to the bedroom, catapulting into the blankets. The recompense for my extended time upright is a lengthy snuggle, which I happily oblige.

***

After a better night's sleep than I deserve, I wake up, aware that yesterday's stasis provided my mind and body the sensory deprivation they required. I wouldn't call my current state energized, but my emotional fuel gauge no longer points to "E." As I did not bring any student papers home Thursday night, the weekend is mine. My rested brain fills these grading-free hours with an attempt to reflect on yesterday and the peculiar phase of depression it manifested—waiting for a windless, rainless storm to pass.

Session 130

"I couldn't get out of bed last Friday. I canceled class."
"I am sorry to hear that."
"It was one of those nothing sorts of days."
"How do you cope when you feel like that?"

"My body parks in numb. At least it was only one day. On Saturday, I started what could—maybe, eventually—become something of an essay."

"Did you send it? I don't think I saw an email from you."

"Not yet. It's still a collection of disjointed paragraphs, but I like the title."

"Oh yeah? What'd you come up with?"

"*The first circle of hell is still hell.*" Piper responds with a chuckle and an eye roll. "I am not sure anything will come of it. Hitting a numb day, in the midst of doing better, got me questioning where days like this come from—what they are for."

"First, can we acknowledge that mental health days are important? We don't have to vomit up our insides to need or take a sick day. Also, while I am sorry Friday was what it was, what you described is a better outcome than you would have had a few months ago. I remember descriptions of similar states when we first met. You reported more than once that it took a whole weekend in bed to face showing up to work on Monday." I respond with a head nod and a sheepish smile.

"Tell me what thoughts came up as you wrote."

"How all this re-shattered my self-worth."

"All this, as in, life since Breakdown Saturday?"

"Yep."

"Good. I mean, not good that you felt shattered, but good that you're thinking about it."

"I do feel like I have vague memories of having self-confidence, once upon a time." The fleshy bit at the base of each thumb finds its way to each eye socket, resting there as counter-pressure for the lament that pulses outward.

"Tell me more about that."

"It was just a thought. I don't know that it's anything significant.

I had it; now I don't." Talking about this feels like wading through goopy mud. After a prolonged pause, Piper again tosses the idea across the rug that I read the essay. It is my turn to note that, not all that long ago, I never would have considered reading something that's so ongoing... so unresolved. Certainly not something that holds numerous literary shortcomings.

Today, reading seems less like the avoidance of more challenging topics—or hoping for a gold star—and more like a desire to share my thoughts and discuss them. I'm glad therapists are paid professionals. With students, providing feedback on a first draft—especially for something personal like a medical school application essay—is hard work. We have to dig around the half-formed thoughts and stream of consciousness for the kernels of truth from which good communication germinates. For anyone other than Piper, I'd start by saying, let me know when I lose you and I'll skip to the end.

***

The First Circle of Hell is Still Hell

Dante called it Limbo. It is the destination of those judged as innocents, for the most part, but not quite fit for heaven. We who dwell here are in good company—Homer, Hippocrates, and Galen are a few names I recognize, among those whom Dante identifies in Canto IV of The Divine Comedy. He describes Limbo as a verdant landscape, where light and honor abide. Not altogether unpleasant, except for the fact that we who inhabit this margin of the deeper abyss exist with the understanding that we will never reach paradise.

I was not raised knowing about Limbo. Our church's binary included pearly gates or lakes of fire—nothing in between. We congregants didn't need any gray areas considering the Sunday school lessons that proclaimed that every one of us could live our corporeal lives *amid God's celestial realm.⁹ Good news! The kingdom of heaven is in us and among us—right here, right now, if only we'd accept Jesus, for he holds the keys to the kingdom. That is, accept not only Jesus but also his surrogate, the church, whose board of deacons was hellbent on proclaiming more and more contradictory rules to keep us confused and controlled. These men judged every action as one more step upward toward heaven or downward to hell.*

Unfortunately, my insides never felt heavenly, more often infernal. As such, the account of an internalized glory from Luke's gospel confused this girl whose viscera were shredded by one of those very same deacons.

In an attempt to reconcile this mismatch between a loving and a vengeful God, keys serve as an ample metaphor for what I consider the truest and purest gifts of Jesus of Nazareth. Specifically, the gift of access to a sense of personal wholeness that an itinerant rabbi, speaking in parables, attempted to provide us. A gift that was given absent the trappings, power structures, and secrets of the church.

As I linger here in limbo, the most essential teaching to ponder may be one retold in the Gospel of Mark. Namely, that the kingdom of God is the birthright of little children.¹⁰ The first point to glean is that this personalized heaven belonged to us even before we had words to describe it. Second, this sense of wholeness may be lost as readily as a toddler misplaces a toy or book. For survivors like me, this precious bequest was plucked right out of our tiny hands by pedophilic charlatans, who know nothing of a God who aligns with agape (love) rather than exousia (authority).

A question I cannot reconcile: Is it ever possible for heaven to

---

9 *"Neither shall they say, lo here! or, lo there! for, behold, the kingdom of God is within you."* Luke 17:21, (King James Version)

10 *"But when Jesus saw it, he was much displeased, and said unto them, Suffer the little children to come unto me, and forbid them not: for of such is the kingdom of God."* Mark, 10:14, (King James Version)

reside in and among those of us whose earthly corpus is filled from floor to ceiling with such memories? Surely these vestiges of torment leave both mind and body as dwelling places fit only for serpents and demons.

It is funny how the term "keys to the kingdom" lands in my modern ears tuned to a touch screen world. It conjures moats, drawbridges, and multi-layered entries to castles, piled high with padlocked treasure chests. Like much that we value, the map to the kingdom of a self-hood worthy of the label heaven can be mislaid, sometimes for generations. For me, singing the confessional line of Amazing Grace, "I once was lost," as its composer, John Newton, understood us wretches to be, evokes a lengthy and hopeless meandering in darkness. What if it could be more like searching each morning for the keys we absent-mindedly tossed aside the night before? Frustrating? Time consuming? Yes, and yes, but at least the searcher is certain they own a set and they know what they're looking for.

In the grips of our despair, we feel a different depth of loss—not a misplacement but a robbery. Something of the greatest value was taken from us. Worse, we hold no memory of what this lost "something" is or why its theft seems so tragic.

We just ache.

So then, what are we left with, we fledglings from whom the truly wretched absconded with our keys at a time when we knew them as little more than dangly noisemakers? What's more, to hide their misdeeds, these tormentors snuffed out our "little lights of mine." As a result, we wander an internal murky blackness. We hold no flame to shine upon the keyholes by which we might access the portal that separates Limbo from Heaven. We linger here, robbed of ever fully seeing ourselves, of ever fully trusting others' intentions, of ever believing we are worthy of love and belonging.

We long ago committed ourselves to this agony. Sentenced with *the crime of juvenile vulnerability. What's more, we reconvict ourselves daily for failing to safeguard our keys before we possibly could have comprehended their utility. Without the slightest resistance, those seducers—every last one of whom shall one day take their rightful place in Dante's eighth circle—defrauded us of entry to our own castle's storehouses, where caches of all manner of the spirit's fruits—love, joy, peace and the like, await us. If only we could gather the courage to make our way to the locksmith and requisition a duplicate set.*

***

"That's all I have."

"Wow, Stacey, that's some heavy stuff. There's a lot to unpack. And yeah, it may jump around a bit, but I'm guessing that's because you have a lot to say. If you had to summarize your main point, what would it be?"

"Um, like I still have the potential to become, to be, the person I always wanted to be. That what I need to regain that sense of wholeness feels locked away. Mr. Jay added my set of keys to his vast collection before I even understood what they were for. What's worse is how enmeshed the sins he committed on my body became with church, with religion, and with my understanding of both love and authority. This monster was put on a pedestal by men in charge of judging every move a little girl made. Consequently, I've lived my life in a body, with a mind, mired in confusion and doubt."

"That's an important connection."

"I think so."

"It is interesting. You said your body and mind hold confusion and doubt, but you left out your heart. I don't think you mentioned your heart in the essay either. Why do you think that is?"

A clunky "I don't know" tumbles out of my mouth. "I don't

know if I left it out on purpose." Did I mention my heart in what I wrote? I didn't. Gah, how is it that I can spill hundreds and hundreds of words trying to get to the point, and Piper hits the bullseye with no more than a dozen?

"Tell me what you're thinking." A quick glance upward signals a request for some silent support. These words need more time to incubate.

"I still like my heart." She inhales in that way which offers an almost imperceptible hope. "I think my heart still knows how to love other people." Piper repositions, inching forward. These words are huge, but she knows a jubilant response might send them back into hiding.

"I like your heart too... I don't usually say things like this, but I am going to do it anyway. It is one of the most beautiful hearts I have ever known. It's a heart filled with honor and integrity. Despite what you've been through, your light still shines. That says a lot about its inherent brightness."

"Thank you, friend. I like your heart too."

"Stacey, your heart is you. Your body? Even your gifted mind? They are great parts of you. But you are definitely one of those people for whom your heart is you," she says again to emphasize the point. "It's also what makes me infuriated for all the confusion and pain."

"That pain? Those people who hurt me? They left my heart... lonely." My bottom lip folds inward. It's the first time I've allowed it to form the word lonely in two and a half years.

My mind clicks on and begins to flip through its files on both Coach and Bobby. I exposed my heart more to them than any other man. In different ways, each left it worse for wear. But that's the funny thing about Mr. Jay. He never, even for a minute, had my heart. It had yet to learn to associate the things he did with any kind of intimacy, any kind of love.

"It's okay. You are okay. Keep going." My brain digs further and happens upon the memory of a black-and-white photo of my tiny-girl self so ancient it's faded to sepia. The story goes that my dad had a roll of film from work that he needed to finish up. He snapped half a dozen shots of Carrie and me. Even in the technicolor 1970s, these were some of my favorites to pore over in the album that recorded a time before my own memories.

"My heart is the part Mr. Jay didn't succeed in damaging. My heart survived him as the same heart as my toddler self."

"Yes." It's Piper's turn to be at a loss for words.

"Thank you for helping me realize this. It's taken a long time."

"I would work through this with you for the rest of my career."

We let our porous hearts absorb this moment. "There is so much I want you to take in and so much I want to say... Yes, your heart is you. So is your mind... and your body. You're realizing, on some level, that you are a whole person and that none of you is this person whom you insist on calling broken. Were you damaged by what happened to you? Yes, but you are repairing that damage."

She pauses to give me space, but my emotions, like my memories, are with that preverbal eighteen-month-old. "The thing I love about what you wrote, and what comes across in the end, is that there is room for hope—maybe more than hope. You acknowledge that this limbo need not be your permanent residence." She pauses a second time, but again, I have no words as I watch her through tiny-girl eyes. "You and I are on a journey to something better. I wanted to leap out of my chair when you said you like your heart." Her admission breaks the hold this moment has over me releasing a laugh.

"I could see your shoulders squirming," I say with a smirk. "Your best smiles are the ones you try to contain."

CHAPTER 38

Detached Retinas

Session 134

When I ask Piper how her weekend went, she surprises me by saying that she attended a bachelorette party. She's younger than me, but not by that much. My bachelorette party days go back to grad school. It was exactly four hours from our driveway to the Luxor parking garage in Las Vegas. One time, I even let myself imagine I might one day wear the sash with glittery "Bride to Be" letters and the tacky veil. Piper goes on to say this party was for a friend whose getting remarried after a heinous divorce and ten years of struggling to raise her three boys on her own. When I jokingly suggest, "Yeah, but the essential detail is whether y'all hired a stripper," her smile dials up to a ten as her cheeks transition to the color of clown noses. Looks like the "What happens in Vegas" rule applies even in South Carolina.

"How about your week?"

"I bumped into a work friend I haven't seen in a while."

"Oh yeah? What was that like?"

"Hard."

"In what way?"

"She seemed happy to see me but asked where I'd disappeared to. I couldn't read her tone, but my first reaction was guilt. I admitted things got pretty bad for a while. She's always caring enough to listen. I trusted she would accept the truth. I confessed that, at one point, I was too overwhelmed to take care of Chili and Pepper. It was better for them to stay at their doggie bed and breakfast where I knew they'd be taken care of until I could get my shit together."

"Wow, what made you decide to be that honest?" Christ, I thought she was going to say that intimate.

"It was the only way I knew to convey how serious things had gotten. She's a dog person. She gets it."

"Think for a minute what that conveyed to your friend."

"You wouldn't point it out if you thought it was the admission of failure it felt like."

"Right again, but tell me what it does say about you." I am glad we are talking about this now and not back then.

"That I cared enough about my puppers to make sure they were taken care of when I was pretty sure I couldn't."

"May I add that you sacrificed the comfort they'd provide so they had the best care? I bet your friend wasn't a bit surprised you made that choice."

"She said, 'Oh my goodness, why didn't you call me?' Then, she asked me if I realized she could name dozens of people who, without a doubt, would want to help with Chili and Pepper or whatever else I might need. What she said next opened the shutters and let in some light." A lump of sentimentality lands on my voice box, the kind of lump that drops in during moments that force us to acknowledge the love and esteem others hold for us.

"Take your time."

"The thing you need to know about this particular friend is that she's British. Her abundant kindness arrives in the most matter-of-fact packaging, which makes it hard to deny. She said, 'You have no idea you can call any of us when you need help, do you?'"

"Let's skip for a minute your inherent assumption that your friend said all that to be polite. Just for fun, let's accept that she is correct. Why do you think people love you so much?"

"I have no idea." The words leave my mouth enveloped in honest frustration. "I am not just saying that. I honestly don't know. I adore her. She is one of my favorite people. Like we've been saying, my heart's output didn't suffer the damage. I readily connect to the love I feel toward others. But…"

It seems like it's been a long time since this sort of grief has silenced the words coming from this couch. "Tell me what you are feeling."

"I fucking hate him."

"Yeah, I hate him too."

"It's like he detached my retinas. Like I have no sensory organ that recognizes that people care about me. My friend said the words, 'People just love you, Stacey.' She might as well have been telling a blind person that someone painted a beautiful pastoral landscape especially for them to see."

"The comparison helps me understand, but I want you to say it plainly, not as a metaphor."

"Do you remember me telling you about working with Indira, and we struggled and struggled to get me to verbalize the question: If my mother doesn't even love me how can anyone else?"

"Yes, how does that relate to this idea of detached retinas?"

"I had no choice but to conclude my mother didn't love me because my ability to sense love was obliterated."

"That is about as straightforward as it gets, Stacey. Could we reconsider the permanence of the word obliterated? Going back to your metaphor, what if, instead of detached retinas, it was more like cataracts? They can result from injury, too, right professor?" She's enjoying the fact that she found a way to spin this. We both grin.

"Yes, cataracts will develop over time from old injuries. Unlike detached retinas, cataracts scatter and obscure the light that enters our eyes, rather than leaving us completely blind to sensing it."

"Exactly, and—" she pauses, but I get the sense that she wants to drive this one home herself "and there is an effective treatment. Cataract patients will see clearly again once they heal."

"You know, there was a time when you saying something like that would have left me hopelessly frustrated."

"Let me guess, you are thinking of all the times your response was 'I can't even imagine how to begin to work toward what you are suggesting.' Gosh, Stacey, how many times did you begin a rebuttal with the words, I cannot even imagine?"

"I know."

"And now?"

"I cannot imagine how effortless acceptance of others' kindness, or love, might ever grow back. But we've managed to rewire my brain when it comes to other things. Things I convinced myself we would never find a way to fix."

"I don't know that effortless is a goal we should set for you, for anyone really. Effortless sounds a little too much like happily ever after."

"Yeah." My eyes fix on the far corner of the room.

"Where did you go? Seems like my 'happily ever after' comment didn't sit well with you."

"No, I get that. I was thinking about *The Divine Comedy* again and my assumption that I've been confined to Limbo. Maybe there's another option."

"Tell me more."

"Beyond the heaven/hell binary I was raised with, Dante wrote another book, *Purgatorio*. Unlike Limbo, which comes with an eternal perpetuity for the unrepentant, Purgatory is where seekers go to work through things that separate us from Paradise. The length of one's stay there depends on how much they have to work on."

"Sounds like therapy."

"Yep."

CHAPTER 39

No Pieces Big Enough to Mend

Session 136

As I make my way to my spot, I tell Piper, "All this talk of recognizing love forced me to consider the night Bobby ended things between us. I had to gear myself up to acknowledge that there are parts of that night I haven't faced. I've been working on a sort of letter to you about it."

"Are you ready to read it?"

"Ready as I'll ever be. I was living in the desert at the time. Some references might not make sense if I never told you that I went to graduate school in Southern California."

"Got it."

***

My last sense of confidence that I could be loveable ended somewhere in the midst of the following:

I should have seen this coming from the way our friend, Kyle, told me he'd be around later this evening if I wanted to get together. His ever-present cigarette and the perfect warmth of this late-winter midday gave little hint of the storm front that was moving in. Taking it one step further... I dismissed him with an unintentional smugness saying Bobby and I were planning some "much-needed time alone" (wink wink), with a date night at Mario's. I didn't know that Bobby's and my plans for the evening were worlds apart. Kyle did.

As Bobby slipped into the driver's seat of my car, I could tell he was struggling more than usual to relax into an evening together. Before we even arrived at the café, I made the dreadful connection, remembering that Kyle tossed up a second offer to grab a drink later as he snuffed out his cigarette. It landed with a thud right after Bobby declared, "There are some things we need to talk about."

***

The night air was crisp and dry. As expected once the sun departed this landscape that held on to so little. Neither water, nor greenery, nor happiness lingered. It was too chilly for most to venture out to the café's patio—even Eastern transplants like us—but the tension of the car ride foretold what we both knew. We needed the distraction of frigid night air.

The food was expertly prepared. It had been every time we'd lingered over our plates. Sadly, its comfort was lost to me this particular night. The softness of the pasta as it enrobed the butternut squash with its delicate bouquet of spice barely registered with the pressure sensors on my tongue. The viscous butter and olive oil that bathed each ravioli slipped unnoticed past my teeth. Dread that a date night at Mario's would never happen again consumed me. The act of Bobby chewing his brick-oven pizza crust looked as tiresome as I now feared I'd become.

To the other regulars who passed our table on their way inside, we were as we had been—that crazy couple that sat under the stars, no matter the weather. I suspect our usual server, Doug, had a sense that something was off. Our voices were a decibel quieter than he had come to expect. The calls for more wine were two paces slower than he'd learned to anticipate. Tonight, that expertise brought him to the table at a frequency that felt interruptive and awkward.

A misty grief surrounded this final supper. Why did Bobby agree to join me in the first place? My guess? He acquiesced in the hope that dinner and several glasses would ease us toward what he knew would—but maybe held out hope would not—leave a lingering bitterness on my tongue as well as in my heart. He did not want to hurt me. Sadly, he had no other choice.

But not yet. He shouldn't—wouldn't—end things here in the possibility of public spectacle—in the presence of fine china and fancy napkins, along with the bottles of decent reds to which Californians have easy access. Never mind that he was one hundred percent opposed to any form of public anything—affection, conflict, or even the slightest indication that I meant something, anything to him. I had learned to take what I could get. Arriving at a party or a restaurant together came to mean as much in this emotionally paltry affiliation as holding hands or a public peck on the cheek. That, in and of itself, was part of the problem. I wanted the world to know what he meant to me even as I understood he was not willing to acknowledge it himself.

The interior on the car ride home was even more tense—more stifled—as though my shock deployed the airbags and kept them inflated. After a year, his house was still off limits—too private—too necessary a fortress from everything, including me. That was okay. I'd committed to offering up an endless supply of patience. After all, I thought we had our whole lives ahead of us.

As we turned onto my street, I questioned whether he would expect continued access to my Mazda in lieu of his non-existent mode of transportation. Will a facade of lingering friendship become part of the negotiations I sense are minutes away?

I never understood how anyone was supposed to remain friends after such an evening. Why is it always nighttime when a person dashes the hopes of another against a granite edifice of endings? How is there room for friendship after someone provides proof positive that *you are too damaged to love, too damaged to waste any more time pretending, too damaged not to terminate the only experience that ever managed to convince you that life might prove otherwise? "I can't do this anymore."* Those were the clichéd words I knew were coming. They cut my breath to pieces. How had I been so foolish to trust any of his other words, including ones he spoke mere weeks ago... *"I feel like I could spend the rest of my life with you."* I still sense the memory of my cheeks' fatigue that next morning. The joyous muscle aches from holding a smile through an entire night's sleep.

Next, I weep. Even as I hold my head in my hands, I sense his distress at all this emotion. I will myself to stop. Will myself to assure him I won't need anything more than he's willing to give. Much as I had attempted to on all the other nights we shared. His first compliment all those months ago—was to proclaim me *"not needy."* I did my level best to exceed expectations, an effort that remains as the final remnant of this too brief... last... encounter with this kind of love.

After what felt like an hour's worth of silence, I did ask for something. What point was there in trying not to? It must have been trivial enough that, despite my best efforts, I cannot remember my request.

His response? That I remember: *"What is this—a civil divorce?"* What else could it be? He had no idea how much this smidgeon of the intimacy I longed for had meant to me. How rarely I opened my heart, how singularly I believed that just this once, just this time... How foolish I was to consider that this girl with the damaged retinas might've stumbled into the kaleidoscope of images she understood every other person on the planet lives surrounded by.

"I don't want to lose you." Those words left me amnesiac for the proper process of inhaling oxygen. I could not comprehend a morsel of what he might be holding onto between us. He may as well have said, *"I hate you. Every word I told you this past year was a lie. But... but... why let that change anything?"*

From this distance, I imagine he may have gone on to say "You were the one who stupidly allowed yourself to feel... to hope this would become something more." That? The one thing I asked of him—for hope in equal measure to my patience? *"Sorry, but that is way too needy on your part."*

For twelve months, I had lived on hope and little else beyond the greatest conversations, his fabulous cooking, and my elation to have someone with whom to invoke the word *"we."* In reality, our year lacked anything akin to emotional nourishment. How could it? We were wired to feed on different diets. Though it was rare to catch even a glimpse of love or joy or peace in what he brought to the table, like any delicacy, it made the moments when he did offer them up that much sweeter.

Sadly, there was an impassable barrier between us that we both willfully ignored. He wanted a different kind of love altogether. I will always wonder how soon he knew that for himself. One day, unlike me, he found it in the man who stands beside him near their Christmas tree in his profile picture. It is the only glimpse I have of what I hope is indeed his happily ever after. Maybe he didn't know for sure, or maybe he wasn't ready to admit it to himself, but he never, not even in the few hours that followed when we played at something akin to friendship, stated that he was meant for other men. Even now, it feels selfish of me to expect that he might, one day at least, have offered me that.

***

We did have one last moment of actual friendship months later. I ran out of gas one night in the time before cell phones. His was the only number I'd dialed enough to know by heart. As the good person I knew him to be, he borrowed his housemate's car and came to my rescue. I offered to repay his kindness with dinner—not at Mario's, of course. I think we both enjoyed the chance, over tacos and a pitcher of beer, to remember how we had once delighted in the comfort of lingering together. But then, it was fully done. That was likely the last time we ever saw each other.

That last moment also came before confirmation of what I'd heard friends whispering since early on. The revelation arrived in the most humiliating way. At a girls' night, an ancillary friend launched into a story about "this gay guy in the Harrison lab." Of course, I knew she was speaking about Bobby. I held firmly to my position that she, like others, was mistaken. People only thought that because he was slight, well-kempt, and a decent human being. Plus, it was the '90s. One only needs to watch a rerun of Friends to remember that speculation about others' sexuality was practically a national pastime.

I saw it on my roommate's face. That look when they know they hold some news that will not sit well when placed across your overly sensitive shoulders. Mere moments after I said with brazen assurance, "He's not gay-ay," Leah confirmed what I could never admit that I suspected, but which our social circle apparently knew all too well. Indeed, I was the thing I most feared being: the pathetic chubby girl, so desperate she'd settled for playing the part of beard.

I did what I knew best how to do. Walked away. Removed myself from any space or people or memories that revealed the facts of yet another humiliating failure—this one the last. Not even a single vein into this heart was left open for other humans to access.

A few weeks later, on a Sunday, a round little cherub of a boy knocked on my door with a sleeping angel in his arms. "This puppy needs someone to love it. Would you please?" That was the divine gesture by which this fractured human discovered that my sweet girl Canyon, with her jubilant eyes and beautiful unguarded heart, would teach me how dogs could become more than enough.

***

As I finish reading, I wonder what Piper will think. Writing each word offered a deep immersion in this night that I'd kept walled off for far too long. I did not want to finish writing in the same way I had not wanted the actual night to end. Even though Bobby and I were ending, we held some connection until the night became the next day. The next day, we would be broken, but that night, we were still breaking.

Piper's praise offers me a sense that my efforts provide her a breather from the volumes of heartbreak my voice places clumsily at her feet. I owe her that. The need to subject her to such melancholy makes me try my damnedest to write it well. So too, this effort has become a means to honor the fact that, bidden or unbidden, these are the scenes that matter to the course of my life.

Sharing this story immersed me once again in grief deep enough that I do not register Piper's ongoing commendation. What a mistake it was, it is, to allow myself the audacity of wanting. I loved him. I did. I do. It is crazy to feel this intensely for someone I have not laid eyes on in more than twenty years. Someone who may have loved me in his own way, but not at all in the way that I wanted. I foolishly, ignorantly, let myself believe back then that he might if I tried hard enough. The way we ended ultimately convinced me that I would never be good enough to earn the right to know what well-matched love is.

***

Christ almighty, it is going to take the rest of my life to sort this mess out.

Session 156

"Hi Stacey."

"Hi," I say.

"Come on back."

EPILOGUE

Maybe the Final Chapter

Here, on the pulse of this fine day
You may have the courage
To look up and out
...
And say simply
Very simply
With hope—
Good morning.

-Maya Angelou

Session??

I cannot write this session as if it were a lived dialogue, because I have not lived it yet. I can, thankfully, imagine it. I can hope for a day that, years from now, Piper and I will bump into each other at a magical time when we both have nowhere else to be. We might decide to have coffee and chat for an entire hour the way we did during the first ten minutes of our sessions. I would be able to say things like, "You will not believe what I said to my students last week. I've definitely graduated to the batty-old-professor stage in their minds." As I attempt to do for my students, she taught me so much. I remind her of that. Her honesty about the ways she struggled is such a different thing than complaining about struggling. It is the difference between sharing and venting. I hope that, if this collection of words ever makes its way into the world, it is accepted as the former.

I imagine that during our final session, she will check in and see how I am if she senses there is something uncomfortable stuck in my throat. In the way that friends do, when you let them. By then, I will discover a way to be genuine about the ugly parts. I will admit that while I love all my students, there are some I may not like as much as others *(of course that does not apply to any of you, former students, who might stumble upon this book)*. I will say things like "I blew it today." I left them more confused than curious. I pushed too far or too hard and discouragement was the result. But, I will try again tomorrow.

Dis-courage. What a sad word. *Dis*, as a prefix, changes the root word with notions of apart or away. To *dis*courage, then, is to take away someone's courage. That makes it quite the opposite of what a liberal arts education, even in the college's science building, perhaps especially so, hopes to achieve. A *liber*al arts education provides a *liber*ating education. An education that frees us to be courageous.

Liberation—this is what I too seek. It is what I claim again for myself, knowing it is not a one-off—not a one-and-done. This liberation will need regular tending. The seeds, bulbs, and cuttings of self-hatred, fear, and doubt that others planted in the soil of my brain and body will sprout with the changing seasons. However, I recognize that some of this vegetation, which I spent my life to this point cultivating, is not a source of nourishment, but the very definition of weeds—misplaced, unwanted, in need of frequent plucking.

It occurs to me that I am this landscape. I hold both the possibility and privilege of reseeding, of replanting with healthy, delicious fruit. An image of myself as a pineapple plant absorbing sunshine and a salty Hawaiian breeze fills me with a moment of joy. This was—is—the goal of our work, Piper's and mine. She's teaching me to cultivate this landscape that I inhabit rather than to seek to purchase an entirely different parcel.

We have overturned much of the desiccated soil and sod that became hard pack from years of pressing myself down. Piper's watchful hand guided me as I stepped off the emotional steamroller and learned to drive the tractor, the plow, and whichever farm equipment casts the seeds. Plenty of acres remain that need tending. I am learning that I can be trusted in the driver's seat. Today, I can step back and survey the ground we have recovered. I no longer lament that it takes weeks and weeks to bust through a new patch of long unplowed sod.

Moreover, it no longer surprises me that it requires season after season to till in the complexity and fertility that renders fields of moist loam from which the delicate blades of joy, peace, awareness, and contentment sprout. The homesteads of America's great prairies were not claimed in a day or even a season, but built over lifetimes and generations.

On this future day, I will acknowledge that, in my own way, despite the overwhelm that kept me closed off from the prospect of birthing children, my lifetime has and will continue to contribute to a generational shift in the world we inhabit.

As Carrie and I pointed a moving van toward a small liberal arts college from the great behemoth of a university that boasted to itself of its own enlightenment, my friends' questions regarding this choice swirled. I stubbornly left them unanswered. I had a sense that, for me, this was the proper direction. I'd happened upon a place familiar enough that I could make it a home. At the same time, I recognized that it had its own progress to make, progress to which I am well suited to contribute. I am not a person who could live in a place that believed itself at its pinnacle, any more than I am convinced I have reached my own.

In fact, on a trip back West, I had the great joy of visiting a wonderful friend. This friend's own life was among the first to show me the way a woman could strive to uplift all women by first uplifting herself. Where I saw in her a courageous warrior, I came to realize she saw me as my own type of voyager. I had set out for a place that, for her, was exotic and foreign, but also a little archaic—a small college rather than the type of preeminent university where she landed.

After we greeted each other and spent as long as we needed beginning sentences with "Remember when," she asked with a hint of hesitation and a full scoop of curiosity, "So what is it like there?" I told her, with a flare of sensationalism but not without truth, that I felt like a missionary sent from feminism. I told her of the beauty, strength, and promise of my students. I revealed how open and ready they were to receive me, my life, and my influence on their own. Our conversation made me feel brave. It made me feel important. It made me feel, for maybe the first time, that the journey of my life is indeed about speaking up and speaking out, to small classrooms if not cavernous lecture halls.

However, the place I had arrived at that time was not an endpoint, but its own beginning and becoming. Over two decades, I became Dr. Hettes to the beautiful students with whom I share in the blessings of an intimate education. Yes, that's right. Dr. Hettes has discovered the type of intimacy—guiding young people's journeys toward their own becoming—that all parts of myself happily embrace. Dr. Hettes is, I am, a woman whose life is worthy of admiration by a younger generation seeking to discover where and how they too will make their mark upon this world.

I knew how to be Dr. Hettes to them. I have become Dr. Hettes to myself. *"What a long time it can take to become the person one has always been."*[11] A person who, in a singular way, inhabits every portion of her body, even the shadowy, arid acres where the soil still needs tilling. A woman who can accept a compliment from both the giver's mouth and their eyes, and accept it with a simple "thank you," without adding, "for saying that."

As I take the first hesitant steps toward sharing these words, words that I hope offer a useful window onto one laborious journey, there is more work to do. There are areas of damage and regret Piper and I have not yet tackled. Despite this, I hold a great deal of hope. Hope that, whenever we hold our last session, an exit form will not govern it, as though our time merely served to bookend that pristinely typed intake sheet. Work that began with the misunderstanding that my battles were external. Not a goodbye, but a hello and welcome. Welcome to the ranks of individuals who have stared into the abyss not once, but many times, and who commit to as many more times as it takes. We are rare, those who can stare long enough and with enough attention to wait on the darkness as it reveals our truest reflection. To grasp the trifling photons, present in the murky blackness, and in so doing, gain an acuity unavailable to those who live their lives only in brightness.

The hiatus I spent denying that darkness no longer feels like wasted years. Those decades were their own life and were lived as well as they could be. When this protective post-traumatic amnesia fully abates, I look forward to remembering the joy and satisfaction of the work and relationships of those years.

So too, I hope to finally unseal the packing tape from the boxes where more of my past dormantly awaits. Diving into those photo

---

11 Parker J. Palmer, *Let your Life Speak: Listening for the Voice of Vocation*, read by Stefan Rudnicki (Ashland, OR: Blackstone Audio, Inc., 2009), Audile audio ed., 0:14:11.

albums will finally be safe. They will conjure the many, many happy memories of my younger years. How Mom and Dad managed to make a day special by doing simple out-of-the-ordinary things like a trip to the playground that was a little too far away or a canoe ride during a full moon. Dad would position the two of us on the moon's reflection so we floated down the moonbeam. For a long time, this journey required that I focus on the task of plowing under the fields of sadness. Tilling in memories of happy little Stacey would have been too perplexing under the strain of surviving.

What's next? Such a common question when you live your life as a cycle of school years and classes of graduates, each essential, but also fleeting. What is next for me, I think, is to simply live the life I have known I wanted since that day when an undergraduate's Birkenstocks and nubby socks walked me on my first steps to where I am right now. A life of making a difference one classroom, one student, one colleague seeking a receptive ear at a time. A life where I no longer have to punish myself with work that is not mine to do. To know that even if I can be a person who successfully occupies leadership positions the world deems more valuable, more prestigious, more worthy, I do not have to, want to, or need to do that work as a substitute for my absent self-worth. If I let myself enjoy my work for a while, I might again be ready to set goals based on what further contributions I am called to make rather than as compensation for the damage I thought my existence had done.

Sometime in this last session, Piper might say: "Stacey, I want you to look at me when I say this so I know that you hear me. It is okay to do the work you enjoy for as long as your career lasts. You have the right to say no to the work others may want for you that you do not want for yourself. More importantly, it is okay to build yourself a life made of more than work and resting long enough to do more work. No matter how you spend your time, you are worthy... worthy of love, worthy of respect, worthy of admiration. You are worthy."

"Thanks, Piper." I will be sure to look her straight in the eye when I say, "I believe you." When I finally say, "Thanks for all the times you said it before my ears were ready to hear it. Thanks for knocking down these walls with me brick by brick by goddamned brick."

"You are welcome," she will say. "I handed you the sledgehammer and pointed out a good spot in the wall to aim for, but you were the one swinging that fucker. Remember that."

As I walk through the waiting room for the last time, I recognize a familiar feeling that in my life is usually accompanied by a cap and gown. In the movie version of this hopeful fantasy, Piper might gift me a new graduation cap complete with gold tassel to add to my collection, for I will have graduated with another degree. This one in self-studies. I will be ready to join the legion of boat-rockers who do so without nearly drowning.

As with all graduates, there are lessons I have already forgotten and others I will soon forget. Even more, some lessons I may never comprehend, including the distinction between harm done with malicious intent and harm done by ignorance. As a lifelong seeker, I will not give up wrestling with this distinction.

As with all professors, I will realize it is less about the individual lessons and more about the sum total that leads to transformation. As in any course of study, this will have occurred gradually, punctuated by fits and spurts. There were classes and teachers I adored and others whose methods were negligent and downright criminal. Some gave freely of themselves and others confined me to a desk for their own edification. The courage I stockpiled in the presence of my gifted teachers far outweighs the portions, still substantial, stolen by those whose mission, or ignorance, was to discourage.

As I exit this future, final therapy session, I have the urge to shake hands with the clients sitting in this liminal space, filled with that familiar scent of mint, and ink, and warm paper. I want to tell them not to worry about the messiness of their intake forms or the messiness of their lives. They are right where they need to be. They are right where I am.

Source Notes

Alighieri, Dante. *The Divine Comedy of Dante Alighieri. Volume 1, Inferno.* Translated by Robert M. Durling, Ronald L. Martinez, and Robert Turner. USA-OSO: Oxford University Press, 1996.

Alighieri, Dante. *The Divine Comedy of Dante Alighieri: Purgatorio.* Translated by Allen Mandelbaum. New York: Bantam Classics, 1983.

Bass, Ellen, and Laura Davis. *The Courage to Heal: A Guide for Women Survivors of Child Sexual Abuse.* New York: HarperCollins, 1988.

Perry, Bruce D., and Oprah Winfrey. *What Happened to You?: Conversations on Trauma, Resilience, and Healing.* New York: Flatiron Books: An Oprah Book, 2021.

Rilke, Rainer Maria. *Letters to a Young Poet: With the Letters to Rilke from the "Young Poet."* Translated by Damion Searls and Franz X. Kappus. New York: Liveright, 2020.

van der Kolk, Bessel. *The Body Keeps the Score: Brain, Mind, and Body in the Healing of Trauma.* New York: Penguin Books, 2015.

Acknowledgments

It is an audacious thing to decide to write a memoir just shy of fifty—too young to believe you've reached your pinnacle, too old to find any lingering scraps of youthful optimism hiding in the couch cushions. This book would never have made it beyond my computer screen if Dr. Amy Sweitzer had not responded to its earliest pages with the comment I remember to be this: "If I came across this in a bookshop, I would sit down on the floor to keep reading." I have borrowed her statement's audacity every time my courage waned. To Tracie, Trina, Tracy, Jeremy, G.R., Cecile, Kaye, Jewels, Erin, Catherine, Charlotte, Heidi, John, Perry, Jim, Julie, Sally, AK, Micki, Betsy, Anna, Tessa, Mike, Matt, Mara, Sheri, Steph, and Mom, thanks for continuing what Amy started. Your DMs, emails, and conversations are tucked away in a file labeled "people whose opinions I need to believe." So too are the supportive faces of the forty-or-so colleagues, friends, and students who showed up in a downpour to my faculty talk where I read pages aloud for the first time.

Whenever I wondered if a publisher might ever take notice of these words, I returned to the email Dr. G.R. Davis, Jr. wrote upon reading an early draft, "You've got work to do. You need to get this published. People like me need to read this." I am beyond grateful for Apprentice House Press, Kevin Atticks, and my editor, Rebecca Cruciani.

Often the only thing that can undergird one's audacious dreams is education. To writers who make time to offer insights into their practice and craft to those of us who find ourselves in over our heads, thank you. The faculty of The Flatiron Writers Room including Tessa Fontaine, Paul Zimmerman, and Katey Schultz, along with Anna Sutton and Halle Hill from the Hub City Writer's Project were terrific guides and role models. Katey, as I've told you, your Deep Revision course was a game changer. I hope you find a sentence or two that makes you proud. Tessa, I sometimes balk at the audacity it took to show up on your virtual doorstep with my book in the state it was. Your thoughtful sensitivity and honest but optimistic developmental edits combined the grace of a kindergarten teacher with the discipline of a drill sergeant. Thank you.

I've been blessed with wonderful teachers and mentors throughout my life. Dr. Joan Coffin made me want to be a neuroscience professor. Dr. B. Glenn Stanley made me one. Professor emeritus, Dr. Melissa Walker of HeyDay Coaching, you made me want to be a writer who was good enough to write this book, and you got me there, chapter by chapter. Emily Witsell our intent was for you to correct all my mistakes, but you too, taught me a great deal. John Sibley Williams, thank you for your assistance with my book proposal and biography. As many friends have said, "Self-promotion is not your strong suit, Stacey. Maybe that's something to get some help with."

To every trauma-informed person who has spoken, written, crocheted, knitted, marched, and voted, thank you.

They say the last paragraph should include the most important people in your life. I need more words than contained in this book to convey my feelings of love and appreciation for Mom, Dad, Christel, Stephanie, Dave, Wyatt, Aidan, Chili, Pepper, and Marian *Pooh* Peeler, LMFT.

About the Author

Professor Stacey Hettes teaches biology and neuroscience to undergraduates eager to enter the worlds of science and medicine at Wofford College in Spartanburg, SC. She holds a PhD from the University of California, Riverside, and is the youngest winner to date of the Milliken Award for Excellence in the Teaching of Science. Her classes are difficult because life is difficult. They are also full of wonder, joy, and triumph because, like her students, she is a hard-working seeker. She relishes in shared struggle and shared discovery, even when the topic is long-buried child sexual abuse. Reemerging from the shadows of her past was only possible once she resolved to carry the story found in this debut memoir into the light.

Apprentice
House Press
Loyola University Maryland

Apprentice House is the country's only campus-based, student-staffed book publishing company. Directed by professors and industry professionals, it is a nonprofit activity of the Communication Department at Loyola University Maryland.

Using state-of-the-art technology and an experiential learning model of education, Apprentice House publishes books in untraditional ways. This dual responsibility as publishers and educators creates an unprecedented collaborative environment among faculty and students, while teaching tomorrow's editors, designers, and marketers.

Eclectic and provocative, Apprentice House titles intend to entertain as well as spark dialogue on a variety of topics. Financial contributions to sustain the press's work are welcomed. Contributions are tax deductible to the fullest extent allowed by the IRS.

To learn more about Apprentice House books or to obtain submission guidelines, please visit www.apprenticehouse.com.

Apprentice House Press
Communication Department
Loyola University Maryland
4501 N. Charles Street
Baltimore, MD 21210
Ph: 410-617-5265
info@apprenticehouse.com • www.apprenticehouse.com

www.ingramcontent.com/pod-product-compliance
Lightning Source LLC
Chambersburg PA
CBHW050851160426
43194CB00011B/2107